Mirage III/5

Dassault-Breguet

OSPREY AIR COMBAT

Dassault-Breguet
Mirage III/5

Salvador Mafé Huertas

Published in 1990 by Osprey Publishing Limited
59 Grosvenor Street, London W1X 9DA

British Library Cataloguing in Publication Data

Huertas, Salvador Mafé
Dassault-Breguet Mirage III/5
1. Fighter aeroplanes, to 1987
I. title
623.74′64′09

ISBN 0-85045-933-8

Edited by Peter Gilchrist and Cathy Lowne
Printed and bound in Great Britain

FRONT COVER
*This Pakistan AF Mirage 5PA carries two 375 gal
(1700 lt) drop tanks, two Matra R550 Magic missiles, and
one AM.39 Exocet anti-shipping missile on its centreline
pylon* (PAF)

TITLE PAGES
*The Mirage IIIO No 1 prototype was first flown in this
configuration on 13 February 1961 and was named* City of
Hobart (AMD/BA)

Contents

Introduction 7

1 'Raton' flight—a mission of no return 9

2 Birth of a thoroughbred 15

3 Service at home 42

4 Aussie Mirages 52

5 The Israeli connection 62

6 Neshers and Mirage IIIs in combat 72

7 Alpine Mirages 93

8 Iberian Mirages 106

9 Mirage exports 121

10 Falklands combat—the Dagger 140

11 Falklands combat—the Mirage III 164

Appendices 180

Glossary 192

Index 193

Dedicated to Jesùs Romero Briasco
and *Ala No 11*

Introduction

Rio Gallegos Air Base, Argentina.
14 October 1982

Four months had passed since the end of the Argentinian conflict with Great Britain over control of the Falkland Islands, and I disembarked from a Fokker F27 of *Grupo 9 de Transporte*. It was springtime in the southern hemisphere, but despite this a chilly wind welcomed me as I set foot on the airfield. I was a guest of the *Fuerza Aérea Argentina* (FAA), and the commanding officer of the base was on the ramp to greet me. After a welcome late lunch of those big, juicy Argentinian steaks, we crossed to the operational side of the airfield to meet some of the squadron personnel.

Rio Gallegos is a big and desolate air base, sharing its facilities with a civilian air terminal that has little to recommend it to anyone from the outside world. In common with the rest of the Patagonia region, there is a definite 'frontier' spirit about the place. A Ford pick-up truck, driven by an ever-smiling FAA NCO, wheeled over muddy perimeter roads until it arrived at the HAS (hardened aircraft shelter) complex, where I saw several Israeli-made Daggers and even a pair of ex Peruvian AF Mirage 5s. I heard a far-off thunder, and then the familiar whistle of throttled-down Atar turbojets, as two *Grupo 6* Daggers ran in and broke left to initiate their downwind leg.

I was introduced to Major Carlos Napolean 'Napo' Martinez, the *Grupo 6* detachment commander, and like pilots everywhere, we soon began to swap flying stories. He introduced me to several of the other pilots, and while talking to them I could detect in their voices some bitterness and frustration at the recent surrender and heavy loss of comrades. I went inside one of the hardened shelters where a single Dagger was parked, with live ordnance on the centreline MER (multiple ejector rack), and a trolley partially supporting the weight of the bombs. The squadron's aircraft were still being held at a high state of readiness, just in case the conflict flared up again.

I looked in detail at the Dagger, and noticed a white 'score' marking over the port intake, clearly representing a British ship. In some places the paint was peeling off the aircraft, revealing the lighter shades of its earlier Israeli camouflage. It suddenly struck me that this one aircraft was a real war veteran, with a record of service in both the Middle East and South Atlantic conflicts. She had probably avoided MiGs, SAMs, anti-aircraft artillery (AAA) and Sea Harriers to be here, and may even have killed one or more Soviet-built interceptors as well as planting her bombs in the hull of a Royal Navy warship. And yet she had survived, and was now ready for even more combat missions if her services were needed. I touched the cold aluminium skin, and noticed a strange feeling of companionship, almost as though the Dagger was a living thing, wanting to tell me about her war adventures under two flags and half a world apart. Those few seconds made me sure that some aircraft did have a soul deep within them.

This vivid description of his visit to the Argentine AF came from a very good friend and former Spanish AF Mirage III pilot, Capt Jesús Romero Briasco, who now flies commercial jets for Spanair. We were sitting near the fireplace in the Officers' Mess at Manises AB, near Valencia, and our conversation finally convinced me that I should write a book dealing with the development and operations of the first-generation Mirages. I had wanted to do something along these lines since my first flight in a Mirage III in 1979. Since that time I have participated in four other Mirage sorties, and each one has reinforced my original opinion that the aircraft is one of the world's classic fighters—just as appealing in the air as it is on the ground.

Within these pages I have tried to gather in the most complete form possible, the development history and operational career of the Mirage III/5 series, including the Israeli *Nesher* (Dagger) variant, principally with the *Heyl Ha'Avir* and the *Fueza Aérea Argentina*. As the result of the co-operation I have received from many very kind people, a considerable amount of information is published here for the first time.

I have reported in some detail on the aircraft's service with *L'Armée de l'Air*, the Royal Australian

AF, Swiss AF and Spanish AF, and included information on all the other air arms that have operated these magnificent aircraft. I have also recalled some of the more interesting details of my own flights in the Mirage III, which I remember so clearly because I used to carry a small tape recorder on each trip.

In preparing this volume, many people from all over the world helped me, especially the following: AMD/BA Press Office; Jean Cuny; Christian Boisselon; *L'Armée de l'Air* PRO; RAAF Williamtown PRO; RAAF Public Relations, Sydney; IDFAF Magazine; IDF 'Spokesman'; IAI Press Manager; David Eshel; Meir Kedmi; Ezer Weizman; Aharon Lapidot; Shlomo Kleszcesky; Heyl Ha'Avir; Rafael; Swiss AF Information Service; Spanish AF Press Office; *Ala No 11* PRO; Jesús Romero Briasco; Jesús Pinillos; Javier Muñoz; Francisco Carretero; Cesar Sevillano; Miguel Bestard; Agustin Galocha; Jesús Quilis; Rafa Nuñez; José Terol; José Luis Gonzalez; Inter-Service Public Relations (Pakistan); Col Weyer, Directorate of Public Relations-SAAF; Historical Branch of the *Fuerza Aérea Argentina*; Maj Puga; Maj Sanchez; Capts Guillermo Donadille, Guillermo Posadas, Maffeis, José Luis Gabari, Cesar Roman, Gonzalez; 1st Lt Horacio Bosich; the Air Attaché's Office of the Argentine Embassy; Helena de Imaz.

I am also very grateful to Royal Navy Sea Harrier pilots, Cdr Nigel Ward and Lt Cdr Steve Thomas, who kindly replied to my request for their recollections of Dagger encounters during the Falklands Campaign. Last but not least, my thanks to Dennis Baldry, Aerospace Editor of Osprey, for his help and encouragement.

Quite apart from these professional aviation people, I wish to express my deepest thanks to my dear daughters Mercedes and Cristina, my wife Mercedes, and my friend Pitu II, for their selfless support during the preparation of this book.

Salvador Mafé Huertas
Valencia, Spain, May 1989

Chapter 1
'Raton' flight – a mission of no return

The dawn of 21 May 1982 was very cold but clear at San Julian, a civilian airfield located close to the town of the same name on the Patagonian coast, between Comodoro Rivadavia in the north and Rio Gallegos in the south. This small provincial airport had been converted into a rudimentary air base as the British Task Force approached the Falkland Islands. Pierced steel planking had been laid to enlarge the apron, providing a minimum dispersal area for the two combat squadrons deployed there since the end of April. The new base was playing host to an A-4C Skyhawk unit, and to *Escuadrón Aeromovil No II* (2nd Airmobile Squadron), which was equipped with the IAI Dagger (formerly *Nesher*) and formed part of *Grupo 6 de Caza. Aeromovil No I*—also equipped with Daggers—had been deployed to Rio Grande Naval Air Station.

Capt Guillermo Donadille had arrived at San Julian with the rest of his squadron on 25 April, after a non-stop flight from the *Grupo 6* home base at Tandil, in Buenos Aires province. He was then a flight commander, with nearly 3000 flying hours to his credit, half of them in fast jets. He had flown the A-4B, A-4C and Dagger, and was a good and competent 'stick and rudder' pilot.

On 1 May Donadille flew a top-cover mission for a flight of strike-configured Daggers, during which

As the British Task Force approached the Falkland Islands, all the Grupo 6 de Caza *Daggers were moved to airfields in the far south of Argentina. One of the single-seat Dagger-As is seen here at Tandil AB before departure to San Julian (FAA)*

some British warships were slightly damaged. Over the next 20 days he logged many hours on cockpit alert, and even a few scrambles, but all of them were non-productive and terribly boring. The events of 21 May however, were to prove dramatic in the extreme, as the following first-hand account will testify:

I remember receiving a parcel from home on 20 May, containing letters, a scarf and some chocolate bars. The letters were written mostly by my children, and in the circumstances of our enforced separation I found them deeply moving. On 21 May I woke before dawn and went outside to watch the sun rise over the eastern horizon. It was very cold and windy, but the clear skies promised good flying weather as I started my alert duty as Section Leader, ready to provide escort sorties for the strike aircraft. Our Daggers were routinely configured for this role, with three 1300 litre drop tanks, two Shafrir 2 air-to-air missiles and 250 rounds of HEI ammunition for the 30 mm Defa cannons. Shortly after arriving at the makeshift crewroom in the airport passenger hall, we were informed that the British were conducting an amphibious landing operation at Isla Soledad (East Falkland), close to the northern entrance to Estrecho San Carlos (Falkland Sound).

We had to quickly change the weapons configuration of our Daggers, loading all of them with bombs. Initially there was a great deal of confusion, and orders were being followed by counter orders in the tension and nervousness of the situation. I was scheduled to participate in the second wave attack, and as the take-off time for the initial six-aircraft strike approached, I occupied my time by helping the crews as much as possible. The 6500 foot runway at San

Julian was a little on the short side with the Daggers at maximum take-off weight, and I prayed that nothing would go wrong, and everyone could return in one piece.

After their successful departure, we could do nothing but wait in nervous expectation. Then, almost two hours later, the aircraft appeared over the eastern horizon—all six of them! After landing and the agonizing delay of shut-down checks on live-weapons aircraft, the six pilots climbed out of their cockpits and gathered together. With the adrenalin of combat still flowing, they all wanted to talk at the same time, telling us about their experiences of British air defences. One confirmed that 'San Carlos was full of ships!'—certainly it was a full-scale amphibious invasion and not a feint as we first thought. The defensive fire was described as 'very thick', and 'terrific', and when the aircraft were examined, two of them were confirmed as being damaged by rifle-calibre bullet or shrapnel holes.

I began to get ready for my mission. I was assigned as leader of the three-aircraft 'Raton' Flight, in Dagger C-403. My No 2 was Major Gustavo Piuma in C-404, and 1st Lt Jorge Senn was to fly as No 3 in C-407. Senn had been my pupil at the Aviation School several years ago, and I taught him to fly while I was an instructor there. During an exhaustive briefing we were given all the necessary information about the radio frequencies we would be using, the type of formation, our armament load, the *en route* and over target weather forecasts, and the probability of meeting Sea Harrier combat air patrols (CAPs).

After the briefing we donned the heavy and cumbersome personal equipment. This consisted of woollen under-clothing, pullover, anti-exposure rubberized flying suit, survival and life vest, bone dome, oxygen mask, flight jacket and our flying gloves. On top of all this I added a small

OPPOSITE
Ten pilots of Escuadrón Aeromovil No 2, *seen here at San Julian on 2 May 1982. Capt Guillermo Donadille is fifth from the left, immediately under the aircraft's serial number. Dagger C-412 was involved in a raid on RN warships the previous day, and a half-painted 'kill' marking—denoting a damage claim—can be seen beneath the leading edge of the canopy* (Grupo 6 de Caza)

ABOVE
For every mission over the Falklands the Daggers were forced to carry three 285 gal (1300 lt) external tanks. All this extra weight severely limited the warload, and reduced their operational effectiveness over the target area (Posadas)

RIGHT
NCO Paredes from the technical section of Grupo 6 *shows a rifle-calibre bullet hole in the starboard intake cone of a Dagger. These were rarely life-threatening, but they could put an aircraft out of action for several days if any of the systems were damaged* (Grupo 6 de Caza)

individual touch of my own—a thick scarf in the *Grupo 6* colours of blue and dark red.

Following the external walkaround—paying particular attention to the installation of the two bombs and three drop tanks—I climbed into the tight-fitting cockpit and

Dagger pilots 1st Lt Roman, Capt Dimeglio and Lt Aguirre Faget wearing their rubberized anti-exposure flying suits (Roman)

attended to the harness and personal equipment connections with the help of my crew chief. After wishing me luck with a slightly worried expression on his face, he removed the ladder and I closed the canopy. I was then isolated from the external noises and chilly wind, and immersed in my own world of instruments, switches and dials, which all started to come to life as I went through the familiar pre-start routine. Through the headphones I heard 'Raton-3, ready to start'. The voice was slightly distorted because Jorge Senn's mask was not properly strapped. I did not hear No 2 checking in, and the time for our scheduled take-off was approaching fast. I thought 'to hell with it, if he's not ready I'll leave him behind,' and gave the order to start engines. Muted by the noise of the Atars, I could faintly hear No 2 reporting a small technical problem, and asking us to wait for him because he did not want to abort the mission.

The other flight ('Lauchas'—also with three Daggers) was obviously ready, and I called its leader, Capt Cesar Roman, to tell him about our problem and suggest that 'Lauchas' should take off first. The mission plan had scheduled us to leave slightly ahead of him, but if we were going to accomplish the overall six-aircraft take-off time, the change was now essential. It was a change that could easily have proved fatal to all three of us in 'Raton'.

After a brief delay, we taxied out and finally got airborne from the last few metres of San Julian's short runway. The take-off run was an agonizing experience, because our aircraft were carrying very heavy loads of fuel and ordnance. The coast and its attendant flocks of seagulls were quickly left far behind us, and we were surrounded by the cold and unforgiving ocean. The emotionless voice of the controller confirmed that I was on the right course, and we began to lose the good weather as the expected heavy cloud built up ahead of us.

As we approached the islands we descended to about 10 metres over the sea, and increased speed to about 800 km/h. Lt Senn spotted the Sebaldes Islands (Jason Is) to our left. This little group was to serve as a navigational fix, and although I turned my head towards them, I could

barely see the outline through the mist and rain showers. We were about 20 seconds ahead of our estimated time, and slightly off course.

A few minutes later we crossed the north-west coast of Gran Malvina (West Falkland) Island. The weather was getting worse, with heavy rain showers, and I began to fear the mountains ahead because we were very low and the visibility was diminishing alarmingly. Glancing to both sides I could see my wingmen at the same level, bouncing up and down in the turbulent air. 'Three minutes from the target', I called, 'accelerate now!' as I shoved the throttle lever forward to maximum dry thrust. We were going very fast over a yellowish-green undulating landscape, with inhospitable hills rising on each side into a cloudy sky that bathed the area in grey light. 'One and a half minutes from target.' My muscles tensed instinctively, and my mouth got drier by the moment. Almost as a reflex action I leant forward into the Dagger's cramped cockpit, focusing my attention on the gunsight. Through its illuminated symbols I could see the ground below—far too close for comfort. Following that course would have taken us directly into the Sound, without any need for corrective manoeuvres.

'Sea Harrier at three o'clock!' The urgent voice of Jorge Senn almost made my heart stop. I swivelled my head round, and to our right I could see the unmistakable silhouette of a Sea Harrier about 300 metres above me. I had a strange feeling that his wingman was behind us, and at the same time the British pilot saw our three Daggers and started a diving turn to initiate his attack. 'Eject bombs and tanks, break right, go!' I yelled, while dumping my own stores and turning to engage the Sea Harrier head-on. One of my wingmen hesitated, and I repeated the order. Then I saw the underwing stores separate from his aircraft, which leapt like a frightened rabbit in the absence of all that drag, and crossed directly in front of me.

The British pilot maintained a convergent heading towards my aircraft, in a shallow dive. I pressed the gun trigger from a distance of about 700 metres, and I think the flashes from the guns surprised him, because he steepened the dive angle and my burst went high over his cockpit without doing any harm. I went into a 90 degree bank and initiated a rudder dive, lowering the nose to avoid losing sight of the Sea Harrier. I fired again, hoping the Harrier might catch a round or two of my 30 mm ammunition. By then the ground was approaching very fast indeed, and my windscreen was suddenly filled by a dark grey fuselage flanked by two big intakes and a short, swept wing [of a Sea Harrier]. With the stick in my stomach, and watching the yaw, I could feel the G forces pressing me into the seat as the anti G suit inflated to save me from blacking out. I saw one of my wingmen passing over my left-hand side in a hard, level turn, and as I half rolled my aircraft I watched him going away from me with a bright afterburner flame pouring from the tailpipe.

Then I heard a small explosion. It was not very loud, almost as though somebody had burst a paper bag close to my ear, but my aircraft lurched out of control immediately

Royal Navy Sea Harriers were a constant menace to Argentinian aircraft over the islands. 'Raton' flight was not the only one to be completely wiped out by British CAPs (Peter Gilchrist)

afterwards. First it pointed into the grey clouds above, and then it started a frightening pitching motion that violently flattened me against the seat or threw me into weightless confusion along with all the dust rising from the cockpit floor. Suddenly the Dagger started a series of rapid rolls parallel to the ground, and the stick felt completely soft, lacking all control authority. My speed and proximity to the ground made me sure that my life was about to end, and a strange kind of fatigue invaded my body. But then the survival instinct—which is so deeply rooted in all combat aviators—took control, and made me pull the lower ejection handle with both hands. Somehow God protected me, because I was ejected when the aircraft was almost upside down. The parachute opened virtually instantly, and only seconds later I made a very hard landing.

The shock of leaving the aircraft was remarkable. When I recovered my senses I found that my eyes had been affected by the wind blast and I could not see properly for a while, but thank God I had no other apparent injuries. I concealed the parachute and started to move away from the area as quickly as possible. The aircraft had crashed only about 300 metres away, and I could hear the spattering detonations of 30 mm rounds being cooked off by the fire. I walked for about 75 minutes, following a line of telegraph posts until I found an old plough and a ruined wooden hut. I broke up a door and used some of the longer boards to make a rough shelter, and then filled a nearby sack with grass as a makeshift pillow. Settling down for what must have been the longest night of my life, I thought of little but my family and my *Grupo 6* comrades back at San Julian and Rio Grande. They all seemed so very far away in the bitter cold of that bleak and lonely landscape. The cold really was incredible, and it seemed to come in waves, preventing me from sleeping throughout the seemingly endless hours of darkness.

With the dawn the sky began to clear, and my worries about the possibility of an ejection-related back injury waned. This kind of problem commonly appears several hours after an ejection, but fortunately I had no trouble getting to my feet, and it seemed that I had escaped. During that day (22 May) I walked about 25 km, following the directions of a small magnetic compass carried as part of my survival gear. It was fortunate that I had carefully studied the maps of the islands, and therefore knew something

about the geography of the area. There was an Argentine Army Infantry Regiment quartered at Port Howard, and I made my way there without any difficulty.

I arrived at the Army encampment at about 15.00 hrs, feeling more dead than alive with tiredness and dehydration, but I was pleased to be able to send messages at last, first to my family and then to my colleagues at San Julian. I stayed with the Army for about a week, first at Port Howard and then at Port Stanley, and met up with several other ejected pilots, including both of my wingmen from 'Raton' Flight. We were all returned to the mainland towards the end of May, aboard an Argentine C-130.

This first-hand account from Capt Donadille gives an insight into the drama which surrounded most of the *Fuerza Aérea* combat sorties from the mainland. They were difficult missions, often flown at the very limit of the aircraft's range. All the pilots involved gave ample proof of their courage, but the odds were always stacked against them because they lacked the tactical sophistication of the British Forces in the closely related disciplines of air-to-air and air-to-ground combat.

Capt Donadille was shot down by an AIM-9L Sidewinder fired by Lt Steve Thomas, RN, from No 801 Sqn. He has kindly provided this brief account of the incident.

On the third sortie of the day (21 May) I was flying Sea Harrier 009/ZA190, and was wingman to Lt Cdr Ward, patrolling at 1000 ft over the valleys 15 miles north-west of Port Howard. I saw two Daggers together, flying east at high speed and low level. I manoeuvred in behind them, locked, and fired a missile at the nearer aircraft, which blew up and crashed. The leader of the element pulled up and right (presumably going home fast!), and I locked onto him and fired my second and last AIM-9L. The missile was guided well, and went over his port wingroot causing a bright orange flash against the aircraft. We could not see what happened to him, because Ward and I had seen a third Dagger crossing ahead of us, which Ward destroyed with a Sidewinder. The total combat time was about one minute. It was subsequently confirmed that my second Dagger had also been lost, but fortunately all three pilots had ejected safely.

Four Argentinian pilots who had been shot down over the Falklands are seen here at Comodoro Rivadavia on 28 May, immediately after returning to the mainland aboard an FAA C-130. Seated left to right are: 1st Lt Luna ('Cueca' flight), Maj Piuma and 1st Lt Senn ('Raton' flight), and Lt Arca, a Navy A-4Q Skyhawk pilot. The wartime setting is obvious, with taped windows and ship recognition pictures (Gabari)

Chapter 2
Birth of a thoroughbred

After the liberation of France at the end of World War 2, Monsieur Marcel Bloch (the founder of Avions Marcel Bloch in 1929) emerged from Buchenwald concentration camp and changed his surname to Dassault. In 1946 he formed a new aircraft manufacturing company under the name Avions Marcel Dassault S.A. The company was renamed Generale Aeronautique Marcel Dassault in the mid 1950s, and eventually, after amalgamation with Breguet Aviation in December 1971, it became Avions Marcel Dassault/Breguet Aviation (AMD/BA). The French Government acquired 21 per cent of the stock in 1979, and increased this holding to 46 per cent in late 1981. Despite long periods of illness, Dassault himself presided over the company until his death in the mid 1980s, when he was succeeded by his son, Serge Dassault.

Bloch was predominantly a builder of fighters, and the post-war Dassault organization was set to continue that tradition, enthusiastically embracing the (then) new technology of turbojet powerplants in the race to equip the reformed Armée de l'Air. Initially the company designed and built a number of light twin-engined transport aircraft—notably the MD.315 Flamant, over 300 of which were eventually supplied to the French armed forces. While the Flamant was providing day-to-day cashflow to keep the company going, the design team at St Cloud began work on the MD.450 Ouragan jet fighter.

The Ouragan was built to the simplest possible formula, with a virtually straight wing, a single 5070 lb (2300 kg) thrust Hispano-produced Rolls-Royce Nene engine, and four 20 mm Hispano 404 cannon. The aircraft could carry 16 small air-to-ground rockets or two 1000 lb (450 kg) bombs under the wings, and the tip-mounted supplementary fuel tanks could be jettisoned to improve agility during combat. The first Ouragan flew in February 1948, and the aircraft was an immediate success. The Armée

de l'Air ordered 350 production examples in three separate batches, and these were interspersed with orders from India (104) and Israel (75).

The Ouragan was followed into production in 1954 by the MD.452 Mystère IIC. This was virtually a swept wing development of the MD.450, but it was powered by a 6175 lb (2800 kg) thrust SNECMA Atar 101D, and could reach supersonic speed in a dive. The Mystère IIC offered a considerable performance advantage over the Ouragan, but only 150 were ordered because Dassault was already working on the Mystère IV, an aircraft with thinner, even more sharply swept wings, and the increased power of a 7700 lb (3492 kg) thrust Hispano Verdon 350 engine. Well over 400 Mystère IVAs were eventually produced between 1954 and 1958, including substantial additional orders from the existing Ouragan customers, India and Israel.

In 1957 Dassault started production of 180 Super Mystère B2s (SMB2s) for the Armée de l'Air. This was the first European production fighter capable of supersonic speeds in level flight. It was developed from the Mystère IVA, but powered by a 9800 lb (4445 kg) thrust afterburning SNECMA Atar 101G engine, which provided enough thrust to push the aircraft along at Mach 1.12 at high altitude. The French Government originally planned to buy at least 220 SMB2s, but the Dassault design team had already demonstrated the enormous potential of a delta wing planform, and the B2 order was cut to 180.

Mirage III Genesis

The Mirage III was developed in the wake of the 1950–53 Korean War, during which western observers—particularly the NATO Air Staffs—had been surprised and impressed by the excellent flying qualities of the Soviet MiG-15 fighter. In 1953 the

Armée de l'Air announced a requirement for a lightweight point defence interceptor, capable of climbing to 50,000 feet (15.240 m) in six minutes. Radar was not considered necessary, because the new fighter would be guided to within visual range of its target by ground-based radar systems.

A request for proposals was issued, and Dassault responded with the MD.550, an innovative 'baby' delta powered by two licence-produced Armstrong Siddeley Viper turbojets (MD.30s), each delivering 1640 lb (744 kg) of thrust. A number of other contenders were put forward, including the Nord 1500 Griffon, the Ouest-Aviation SO.9050 Trident II, and the Sud-Est Aviation SE.212 Durandel. All of the proposals were designed with the possibility of some kind of mixed turbojet/rocket/ramjet power in mind, and *Société d'Etude de la Propulsion par Réaction* (SEPR) was asked to supply a family of small rocket motors for the purpose.

The Dassault design team was led by Henri Deplante, and the MD.550—which was initially called the Mystère Delta—made its first flight on 25 June 1955 in the hands of Roland Glavany. With just its turbojet power the little aircraft was the fastest in France at that time, but its performance against the specification was disappointing. It managed Mach 1.15 in a shallow dive, but more power and some aerodynamic changes were necessary before it came anywhere near to meeting the requirements.

ABOVE
The diminutive MD.550 01 was originally called the Mystère Delta, but after considerable modification it was renamed Mirage 1. In itself, it was too small to become a practical fighter, but its aerodynamic finesse provided the basis for the whole Mirage programme (AMD/BA)

RIGHT
The Mystère Delta was flown for the first time on 25 July 1955. Powered by two licence-built Viper (MD.30) turbojets, it reached Mach 1.15 in a shallow dive, but after its modification programme the aircraft achieved Mach 1.3 in level flight—making it one of the fastest machines in Europe at the time (AMD/BA)

After the initial series of flight tests the aircraft was extensively modified, with a considerable structural and aerodynamic input from Fairey Aviation in the UK. The British company—which was already flying the Fairey Delta 2 with spectacular results—provided much of the data to redesign the fin and dorsal spine of the MD.550. The fuselage length and wingspan were also reduced slightly, and Dassault designed a small afterburner for the Viper engines. To provide even more power, a 3300 lb (1496 kg) thrust SEPR.66 rocket pack, burning a self-igniting mixture of nitric acid and furaline, was installed under the rear fuselage. In this new form the aircraft was much more successful. The added boost of the rocket motor allowed it to surpass the time-to-height requirement, and on 17 December 1956 it reached Mach 1.3 in level flight—making it one of the fastest aircraft in Europe.

By this time the MD.550 had been renamed Mirage I, and although the prototype continued its test programme, the *Armée de l'Air* had already been convinced by Dassault that the aircraft was too small to form the basis of a realistic production fighter. There was also some doubt about the wisdom of limiting its role to the single point defence interceptor mission. The Mirage I concept was therefore abandoned as a production programme, but the tiny delta had provided much valuable research data, and unwittingly laid the foundations for Dassault's legendary love affair with this distinctive wing planform.

The next project for the design team was the Mirage II. This was originally planned as a growth version of the Mirage I, but with more power and much more internal space for fuel. The aircraft incorporated two afterburning Turbomeca Gabizo engines, each rated at 3395 lb (1540 kg) for take-off, and a larger wing that was clearly influenced by the company's co-operation with Fairey Aviation. Provision was also made for a small booster rocket. The Mirage II design was never completed, but its take-off weight in combat trim would have been about 17,000 lb (7710 kg), compared with just over 11,000 lb (4990 kg) for the Mirage I.

It seems certain that the *Armée de l'Air* would have been happy with a production version of the Mirage II, but Dassault was not satisfied, and pressed on with designs for the Mirage III. This was radically different from the two earlier Mirages, because it was a single-engined machine. The wing was almost identical to that designed for the Mirage II, but the fuselage incorporated the principles of NACA-developed area ruling, which reduced form-drag and gave the aircraft its distinctive 'pinched in' look. The internal structure of the fuselage was specifically engineered to accommodate the SNECMA Atar 101G.2 turbojet, which at 9920 lb (4500 kg) thrust with afterburner was the most powerful engine then available in France. The increased thrust greatly improved the aircraft's sustained-turn performance, and provided a more manageable throttle response during the 'difficult' landing approach phase of the delta planform. The Mirage III was also designed to accommodate an interception radar—although this was not fitted in the prototype—and to operate from dispersed, semi-prepared airstrips as an insurance against the massive airfield damage that could be expected in a nuclear war.

The decision to cancel the Mirage II had been taken at the end of January 1956, and the first prototype Mirage III (001) was flown for the first time on 18 November of the same year—just nine

months after the project was launched. This was a remarkable achievement in view of the complexity of the design, but it was clear from Roland Glavany's reactions after the first flight that the decision had been worthwhile. Only nine weeks later, Glavany took the aircraft up to 39,000 feet (11,890 m) for a calibrated run of Mach 1.52 in level flight, and then proceeded to reach Mach 1.6 in a 30 degree dive. The only major modification necessary during the initial period of testing was the installation of manually operated 'shock cones' in both inlets. These increased the available thrust by a considerable margin—particularly when a more powerful Atar engine was fitted—and pushed the level speed up to Mach 1.6 without rocket power, and Mach 1.9 with the extra boost.

The *Armée de l'Air* showed enormous interest in the future of the new fighter, and ten development variants were ordered under the designation Mirage IIIA. These were all powered by a new Atar 09B engine, rated at 13,255 lb (6012 kg) thrust with afterburner, and a SEPR.841 auxiliary rocket motor developing a thrust of 3700 lb (1675 kg). To take advantage of all this additional power, the wing was redesigned to improve lift and reduce drag. Its area was increased to 366 square feet (34.03 m), and the conical leading edge camber—now so familiar on all Mirage III series aircraft—was also introduced. The thickness/chord ratio of the wing was reduced, and

provision was made for small, flow-straightening fences to be installed at roughly half span (these were later replaced by 'saw cut' notches, which have a similar aerodynamic effect).

The Development Batch

All ten pre-series development aircraft flew between 12 May 1958 and 15 December 1959. Each one was allocated particular tasks within the overall test programme, and brief summaries of the known details are shown below.

BELOW
The prototype Mirage III (001) is seen here during a test flight near Istres. The underbelly rocket pack, and the sharply swept tail which was set well forward on the fuselage can be seen. Also just visible are the manually operated shock cones in the intakes. Using its rocket booster, this aircraft managed to achieve Mach 1.9 in level flight (AMD/BA)

RIGHT
The first genuine Mach 2.0 aircraft in the series was the pre-production Mirage IIIA (01), which flew for the first time on 12 May 1958. It achieved its level-flight Mach 2.0 status on 24 October 1959—making it the first European fighter to do so (AMD/BA)

Mirage IIIA01

The prototype was flown for the first time at Melun-Villaroche on 12 May 1958, with Roland Glavany at the controls. The aircraft conducted all the initial handling and flight envelope trials, and on 24 October 1959 it attained Mach 2.00 in level flight—the first European fighter to do so. It was later used to test the aerodynamic and separation qualities of various fixed and expendable external fuel tanks. 01 flew for the last time on 11 May 1966, after which it was relegated to ground trials until May 1972. It was then retired to the *Musée de l'Air* at Le Bourget.

Mirage IIIA02

Flown from Melun-Villaroche on 17 February 1959 by Glavany. Predominantly used for engine development. Tested both the SNECMA Atar 09B turbojet and the SEPR.841 rocket pack, debugging them and their associate systems, and clearing them for operational use throughout the aerodynamic limits being established by 01. After retirement 02 was donated to the *Armée de l'Air* Public Relations Office as a recruiting aid.

Mirage III03

Flown for the first time on 28 March 1959, again by Roland Glavany. Used for general development trials in support of the first two aircraft. Later, in the hands of test pilot Gerard Muselli, 03 captured the world speed record for a 100 km closed circuit at 1106 mph

(1780 km/h). This was also the aircraft evaluated by IDFAF chief test pilot, Danny Shappira, prior to Israel's purchase of the Mirage in 1961. After its development flying, 03 was transferred to the French Test Pilots School (EPNER) at Istres. On 24 October 1968 the aircraft crashed on approach to Istres, but the test pilot, Alain Brossier, ejected safely.

Mirage III04

Flown on 7 May 1959 by Jean-Marie Saget. The aircraft spent most of its life engaged on equipment and individual systems trials. It was last flown on 28 February 1975, piloted by A Histler, and eventually scrapped.

Mirage IIIA05

Glavany conducted the first flight of 05 on 10 May 1959. During its short career the aircraft performed aerodynamic and operational tests on several different radome shapes. It crashed on landing at Bretigny, after a demonstration flight for the Swiss AF. Test pilot J Blankaert was killed.

Mirage IIIA06

This was the first production standard aircraft, flown for the first time by Glavany on 11 July 1959. It conducted most of the system development trials on the CSF Cyrano *1bis* fire-control radar, and later went on to test some of the equipment destined for use on the Mirage IIIE. Last flight on 11 January 1974 from Bretigny, piloted by Boitier, after which the aircraft was sent to the Dassault works at Biarritz Anglet for permanent preservation.

Mirage IIIA07

The second production standard aircraft, first flown by René Bigand on 10 October 1959. Conducted operational trials on the braking-chute system. After evaluation at the *Centre d'Expérimentations Aériennes Militaires* (CEAM) and the *Centre d'Expérimentations en Vol* (CEV), it was exhaustively tested by the Swiss AF, resulting in an order for Mirage IIIS and RS variants. 07 was finally sent to EPNER, where it continued flying until the late 1970s.

Mirage IIIA08

Production standard. First flown by Saget on 22 September 1959. Used as a weapons system development aircraft, carrying out trials with guns and missiles throughout most of its operational career. Last flown 28 February 1975.

Mirage IIIA09

Production standard. First flown by Bigand on 19 September 1959, and then involved almost exclusively in landing trials, approach profiles, incidence angles etc. Damaged by a Swiss AF pilot and subsequently repaired. Crash-landed for the second time at Cazaux, home of the *Armée de l'Air* Fighter

Pilots School, on 20 June 1961. Damaged airframe was then used for ground tests.

Mirage IIIA 010

This was the last of the preproduction development aircraft, making its first flight on 15 December 1959 in the hands of Elie Buge. After evaluation by CEAM, it was transferred to SNECMA for Atar 09C and 09K-50 development trials.

BELOW
Seen here just after take-off from the Istres test centre, Mirage IIIA 07 was the second true production-standard aircraft. During its development flying it was exhaustively tested by the Swiss AF, which eventually resulted in a big production order (AMD/BA)

RIGHT
The last pre-production aircraft (010) in its original natural-metal finish. The lighter coloured bands on the rear fuselage are big forged and machined mainframes that carry all the primary flight loads circumferentially around the engine. The frame at the rear is attached to the main spar of the fin and the rear spar of the wing, while the forward frame carries the main spar. The Atar engine and afterburner assembly fits neatly between the two frames (AMD/BA)

In addition to the ten single-seat aircraft, a two-seat version of the Mirage IIIA was designed and flown during the development period. This was the prototype Mirage IIIB (01), which formed the basis of all subsequent Mirage trainers. It flew for the first time on 20 October 1959, but the type was not put into production until 1962.

Early Production Aircraft

The first version of the Mirage to reach full production was the IIIC, 95 of which were ordered for the *Armée de l'Air* in August 1958. The aircraft was equipped with a CSF Cyrano I*bis* air-to-air fire-control radar, and its primary function was that of an all-weather interceptor—although its daytime ground-attack capability provided a useful secondary role. The IIIC was powered by a SNECMA Atar 09B-3 engine, rated at 9460 lb (4300 kg) thrust dry, and 13,200 lb (6000 kg) in afterburner. Provision was also made for a single-chamber SEPR.841 rocket motor, which burned nitric acid and Tx11 to deliver an additional thrust (at altitude) of 3700 lb (1680 kg) for one minute and 20 seconds.

The usual armament of the Mirage IIIC consisted of two internally mounted DEFA 552 30 mm cannon, with 125 rounds of ammunition for each. In addition, the aircraft could carry a single MATRA R511 semi-active radar-homing air-to-air missile, mounted on the centreline pylon. The R511 was later replaced in service by the R530, which had an improved control system, and was available with either semi-active radar or infra-red (IR) seeker heads. Whichever primary missile was being carried, the Mirage would normally be fitted with two AIM-9B Sidewinders on the outer wing stations. For ground-attack missions, Aérospatiale AS.20 (and later AS.30) command-guidance air-to-surface missiles were normally carried, but the aircraft could also operate with conventional bombs and rockets.

The first Mirage IIIC was flown at Merignac, near Bordeaux, on 9 October 1960, and by July 1961 the first operational aircraft had been delivered to EC 1/2 'Cicognes' at Dijon-Longvic AB. Production gathered pace very rapidly, and by the end of 1961 nine aircraft were being delivered every month, and four squadrons were either fully converted or approaching conversion to the new type. On 22 July 1962, Mme Jacqueline Auriol brought instant world recognition to the Mirage IIIC by using one of the standard production aircraft (No 65) to break the 100 km closed-circuit world speed record for women. She averaged 1150 mph (1852 km/h) over the distance, and became the first woman to break officially the 1000 mph barrier.

Tail-less deltas have certain flying characteristics that are quite unlike any other aircraft—and this is

The first variant to reach full production was the Mirage IIIC, 95 of which were ordered by the Armée de l'Air. *The 1950s style, tight-fitting pilot's suit is typical* (AMD/BA)

particularly so in the landing approach phase. To prepare for the special training needs of the Mirage squadrons, Dassault developed the Mirage IIIB. The basic fighter fuselage was lengthened by about two feet (60 cm) to accommodate a second seat, and the fire-control radar was omitted from the nose section. This made it possible to transfer all the electronics and radio equipment into the nose of the trainer, leaving the vacated space in the centre section for the rear seat. A similar conversion was later done on the Mirage IIIE, and the resulting aircraft went into French service as the Mirage IIIBE, and was marketed for export as the IIID (dual).

The second fighter version to go into production was the Mirage IIIE, which was a much more capable aircraft in every respect. The first development protype flew on 5 April 1961, and this was followed by two additional trials aircraft. The IIIE had the same wing area as the IIIC, but the fuselage was lengthened and modified to receive a slightly higher-powered and more fuel-efficient SNECMA Atar 09C engine. The major difference between the two aircraft was the installation of a new and very advanced (at that time) nav/attack system, conferring true multi-role capabilities on the IIIE, and giving it a high probability of success in both air-to-air and low-level air-to-ground engagements.

The Mirage IIIE described

The Mirage IIIE was perhaps the most important single step in the evolution of the whole Mirage III/5 family. It represented the transition between an adventurous new fighter, and a fully matured multi-role combat aircraft. In the process, it also provided the foundation for Dassault's incredible export success over the last 25 years.

General description
At 49 feet 3 inches (15.02 m) the fuselage of the IIIE is just under 12 inches (30 cm) longer than the IIIC.

The extra length comes from a 'plug' inserted behind the cockpit, moving the pilot forward in relation to the intakes. The extreme nose section houses the Thomson-CSF Cyrano II*bis* multi-function radar, which has a variety of operational modes, including air-to-air, air-to-ground, fire-control and terrain avoidance. Behind the primary radar is a Marconi-Elliot Doppler-navigation radar; its downward-looking antenna in a radome protruding from under the fuselage.

The cockpit of the Mirage has always been somewhat cramped for tall pilots (the South African AF is known to call it the 'Ace-cage'), but nonetheless it appears to be relatively comfortable, and access is made easy by the rearward-hingeing clamshell canopy. The pilot sits in a Martin-Baker HRM4 automatic ejection seat, built under licence by Hispano Suiza and rated for zero height and 90 knots forward speed. Just below the windshield is a Thomson-CSF 97 gyro-stabilized gunsight, with a fixed cross and moving reticle. This has a semi-transparent glass display—not a true HUD—which shows the aircraft's position in roll, a distance to target in metres, and the heading in degrees, all reflected back to the pilot in a yellowish-orange colour that helps to protect his night vision. To the right of the gunsight is the radar warning receiver (RWR) indicator, which displays a plan-view silhouette of the aircraft, surrounded by lights to show

BELOW
Close-up of Mirage IIIEE (11-24) showing the Cyrano IIbis radome, the doppler antenna radome, and the nosewheel leg with its twin landing lights. The intake has a boundary layer bleed-off plate and half-cone centrebody (S Mafé)

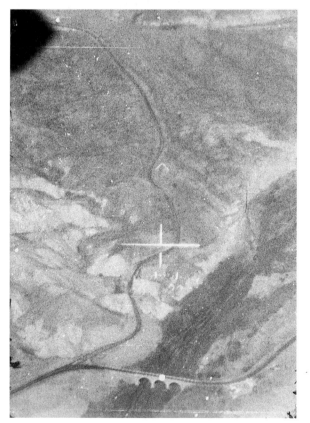

ABOVE
The big electronic equipment bay is located immediately behind the cockpit (S Mafé)

LEFT
A pilot's eye view through the gunsight display, showing the aircraft's position in roll, its heading, and the sighting dot, or pipper, surrounded by a circle of ranging dots. In this case, the pipper is on the central span of the railway bridge (Ala 11 via Roca)

RIGHT
The instrument panel of a Mirage IIIEE. The glass screen of the gunsight can be seen on the coaming, and below it the panel is dominated by the circular radar display. Primary flight instruments are on the left of the radar, with the nav-computer (Doppler) display at top right (S Mafé)

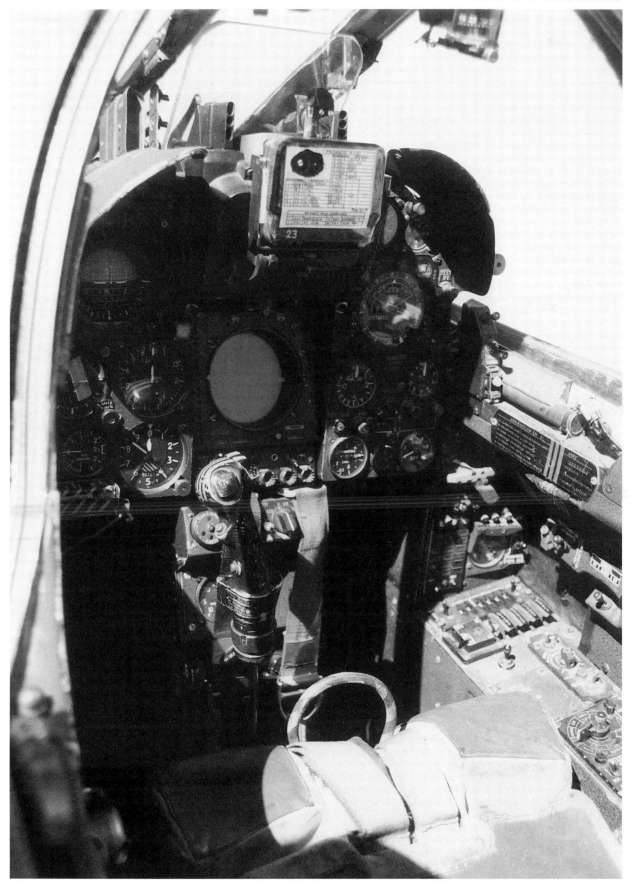

LEFT
The RWR antennas of the Mirage III are located in the tail. The 'bullet' on the leading edge protects the forward sector, while the rear is covered by the more rounded device immediately above the Spanish insignia. The light coloured areas are fibreglass mouldings to protect the VHF fin tip and leading edge comms antennas. The tail navigation light is near the trailing edge; immediately below the fibreglass panel, and the central fairing houses the rudder actuator (S Mafé)

BELOW
The right-hand cockpit console is occupied mainly by the armament selection and control box (the guarded switches prevent inadvertent operation), and the doppler management panel (S Mafé)

the direction of the incoming radar signals. Opposite the RWR, high on the coaming to be within the pilot's line of sight, is the ADHEMAR system, which indicates the aircraft's angle-of-attack (AoA) situation with blue, amber and red lights: this is particularly important information in a delta winged aircraft, especially during the landing phase or in high G combat turns. The instrument panel is well equipped for all-weather navigation, and is dominated by the central radar display screen. On the left-hand console, behind the throttle lever, is a small joystick device for controlling radar antenna movements and selecting the different modes of operation. The right-hand panel includes the radio-altimeter and a navigation display linked to the Doppler system. On the right-hand console, behind the armament selection/control panel, is a small box for the perforated plastic punchcards used by the navigation computer: each of these cards (up to 12 can be carried) represents a different destination, and is used to 'fix' the appropriate map co-ordinates in the computer.

The electronic equipment bay is immediately behind the cockpit, and this houses two UHF radios, the navigation computer, air data computer, TACAN (TACtical Air Navigation) processor and the IFF (Identification Friend or Foe). The removable gun-pack slots into the lower fuselage, directly beneath the electronic equipment bay. This holds the two DEFA 552A cannon, and a central container for the 250 rounds of ammunition.

With the guns removed, the internal space can be occupied by a 72 gal (325 lt) fuel tank, which can be used to feed the normal jet engine or the rocket motor. The rocket itself is only needed for very high altitude interception missions, and is fitted in a semi-recessed

CARTA MUESCADA

INDICADOR

ALMACEN DE CAMBIO DE BASES

ABOVE
The individual elements of the navigation computer
(via *Ala 11*)

ABOVE
The gun barrels are located along the bottom of the inlet trunking, just forward of the wing leading edge (S Mafé)

ABOVE RIGHT
The rocket pack is rarely used these days. Its place under the aft fuselage is generally occupied by an additional fuel tank, containing an Omera 60 oblique camera in the rear fairing. This is operated by the pilot through a foldaway sight on the left-hand side of the cockpit (S Mafé)

bay on the underside of the rear fuselage. When the aircraft is engaged on medium/low alitutude operations, the rocket-pack can be removed and replaced by a pallet containing another 120 gal (545 lt) of jet fuel, and an Omera 60 camera for oblique photography. This gives the Mirage IIIE a limited reconnaissance capability.

The wing is common to all production standard Mirage III/5 aircraft, and has a span of 27 feet (8.22 m) and an area of 375 square feet (34.85 m). The leading edge sweep is 60 degrees, and the thickness/chord ratio reduces from 4 per cent at the root to 3.5 per cent at the tip. The conical camber on the leading edge provides a more stable airflow at high Mach numbers, and at the sort of extreme, transitory angles of incidence likely to be encountered during combat. The whole cantilever wing is an all-metal torsion-box structure, with a stressed skin of machined alloy panels. Each side has two elevons and a trim-tab situated on the trailing edge to provide pitch and roll control, with pilot commands being transmitted by a combination of mechanical, hydraulic, electrical and electronic systems. The inner trim-tabs also act as stability augmentation devices. The air brakes—two each side, one above and one below the wing—are single hinged panels, hydraulically operated on demand. Each wing forms an

integral fuel tank holding 147 gal (670 lt).

The tricycle landing gear has low-pressure tyres to allow operations from poorly prepared, off-base facilities. Its retraction sequence is controlled hydraulically, with the nose wheel moving rearwards and the two main wheels folding in towards the centreline of the aircraft. On landing, the limiting speed for undercarriage deployment is 270 knots, and as soon as the wheels are fully locked down, the doors close to minimize drag. The nose wheel leg is equipped with a pair of landing/taxiing lights, but it has no steering system, so all ground manoeuvring has to be accomplished with differential mainwheel braking.

Engine
The Mirage IIIE is powered by a single SNECMA Atar 09C3/5 turbojet with integral afterburner. The engine is similar in most respects to the 09B that powers the Mirage IIIC, but it has a new compressor, a self-contained starter and an improved overspeed for high altitude performance. The nine-stage axial-flow compressor has a mass-flow of 150 lb/sec and a pressure ratio of 5.5:1. This feeds into an annular combustion chamber equipped with two burning cans, each one of which has a starting injector and an incandescent igniter. The gases pass through a two-stage, cooled turbine, before entering the afterburner which is integrally controlled by the throttle lever. The variable area exhaust nozzle opens and closes hydraulically on demand, or as part of the automatic approach-control system, which maintains a constant airspeed during landing by varying nozzle area in relation to commands from the autopilot and air data computer.

The maximum dry thrust of the engine at sea level is 9430 lb (4280 kg), rising to 13,200 lb (6000 kg) at 8400 rpm in full afterburner. The overspeed system—commanded by the air data computer—is engaged automatically from Mach 1.4 at 8710 rpm, and gives a power output at 36,000 feet (11,000 m)

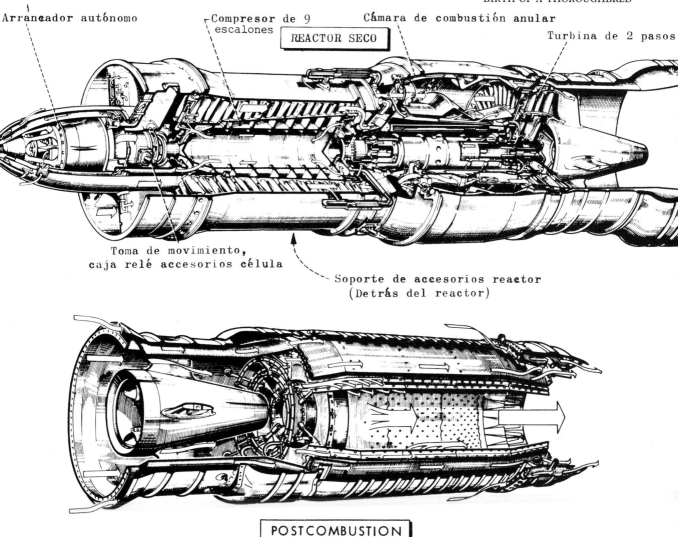

Arrancador autónomo

Compresor de 9 escalones

REACTOR SECO

Cámara de combustión anular

Turbina de 2 pasos

Toma de movimiento, caja relé accesorios célula

Soporte de accesorios reactor (Detrás del reactor)

POSTCOMBUSTION

ABOVE

Cutaway of the SNECMA Atar 09C. The 'dry' section (top) includes an autonomous starting unit, the accessory drive, nine-stage axial compressor, annular combustion chamber and two-stage turbine. The afterburner section is shown below (via Ala 11)

RIGHT

The multi-petal afterburner nozzle can be signalled by an on-board approach control system. This varies the nozzle area automatically, to provide a constant airspeed during the approach phase. The nozzle is also directly linked to the throttle for immediate take-off and combat power (S Mafé)

equivalent to a sea-level thrust of 14,110 lb (6400 kg). The autonomous self-start system on the 09C—which makes the aircraft independent of cumbersome air-start trolleys for off-base operations—consists of a tiny gas turbine located within the engine's nose cone. This is started by a low-power electric motor, and the exhaust gasses drive a free turbine connected to the Atar's rotating shaft. To ensure favourable airflow conditions throughout the aircraft's speed range, the intake geometry incorporates half-cone centre-bodies that move forward automatically above Mach 1.2. Because of their shape, these cones have been called 'souris' (mouse) inlets by generations of Mirage pilots. Although they improve the airflow at high speeds, they slightly restrict the intake during low-speed flight and taxiing, so auxiliary inlet doors located just above the wing root open automatically when required.

For high altitude interception missions the Mirage IIIE can be fitted with a SEPR.844 rocket motor. The single-chamber 844 burns normal JP-4 jet fuel (instead of the chemical fuels used by the SEPR.841), and uses nitric acid as the oxidant. This gives a fixed thrust at sea level of 3370 lb (1530 kg), improving to 3700 lb (1680 kg) at Mach 1.4 and 52,000 feet (16,000 m). The nitric acid is carried in an inverted 'saddle' tank that follows the contours of the lower fuselage to form part of the bolt-on motor assembly; the jet fuel is drawn from the tank in the gun bay. The motor is pump-driven from an accessory drive on the Atar, and enough nitric acid is carried to provide 80 seconds of continuous firing—although the rocket can be shut down in flight and re-lit up to three times.

The internal fuel supply for the Atar is located in two 113 gal (515 lt) tanks in the fuselage (amidships, wrapped around the inlet trunking), and two integral wing cells, each holding 147 gal (670 lt): there is also a small (13 gal/60 lt) negative G reservoir to cope with the demands of inverted flight. The gun bay and rear fuselage tanks provide additional internal capacity, but fitment of these depends on the role of the aircraft. Because of its relatively small internal capacity, the Mirage is rarely seen without external tanks. These are available in an unusually wide variety of sizes, including 110 gal (500 lt), 132 gal (600 lt), 181 gal (825 lt), 285 gal (1300 lt) and 375 gal (1700 lt). Most tanks are available in fixed and droppable form, and some of them have been developed by the Israelis to meet their special needs. In addition to the standard tanks, the aircraft can also carry RPK-17s, which are reinforced 110 gal tanks that double as weapons racks for up to four 550 lb (250 kg) bombs. The JL-100 weapons pod is also carried, and this holds 55 gal (250 lt) of fuel at the rear of a launcher for 18 2.75 inch air-to-surface rockets.

Weapons and navigation system

The heart of the Mirage IIIE's weapons and navigation system is the Thomson-CSF Cyrano IIbis multi-mode radar, which has an effective air-to-air range of 25 nm. For air-to-ground use one of two scales, 15 nm ('Visu-15') or 50 nm ('Visu-50'), is used, according to the height of the aircraft. The radar has a high-level navigation mode that makes use of the longer range-scale to recognize ground reference points such as coastlines, railways, built-up areas, etc. In the air defence role the Matra fire-control computer can be engaged as soon as a target appears on the radar display. It then ensures a correct pursuit curve by controlling the symbology on the gunsight display, allowing the pilot to manoeuvre into an advantageous attack position. During operational flying, radar search patterns are as brief as possible to avoid detection by the enemy, and the final lock-on emissions are left until the very last moment.

Besides the two 30 mm guns, the Mirage IIIE has five attachment points for external loads. The centreline station has a maximum load capacity of 2600 lb (118 kg), and is wired for the big MATRA R530 missile and several types of bomb: it also has the pipework and release circuits for fuel tanks holding up to 285 gal (1300 lt). The two inboard wing stations each have a capacity of 3700 lb (1680 kg) and are mainly used for carrying fuel tanks, although arming and release circuits for bombs are incorporated. The outer wing stations are relatively lightly loaded at 375 lb (168 kg) each, and are generally used to carry R550 Magic or AIM-9 Sidewinder air-to-air missiles, or LAU-32 seven-shot 2.75 inch rocket pods.

Flying characteristics

The Mirage was basically conceived as an interceptor, and its design was optimized to provide superior straight-line acceleration and climbing characteristics. The wing is exceptionally thin, and its delta planform allows good supersonic performance and excellent gust response, but it has a number of problems in the 'dogfighting' combat arena. It creates high parasite drag with increasing angles of attack, and this forces the pilot to engage afterburner to maintain a high turn-rate. This obviously leads to high fuel consumption, reducing both range and available combat time. On the plus side, the wing can be used as a big airbrake, and the Mirage can be flown to almost unbelievably low speeds before departure in the vertical plane.

A Mirage IIIE takes off at 160 knots with two 110 gal external tanks, and 180 knots with 285 gal tanks. Optimum climb speed is 450 knots. The aircraft is cleared to fly at 775 knots (Mach 1.25) at low level, but its speed is normally restricted to about 400/500 knots during training missions.

On returning to base, the Mirage slows down to 300 knots during the downwind leg and the landing gear is lowered at 220 knots before base turn. An approach speed of 190 knots is maintained on short finals, with touchdown achieved at a lively 160 knots. This high speed makes the landing phase somewhat delicate. The aircraft has to adopt a nose-high attitude for aerodynamic braking, and at the moment

ABOVE
The first of two Mirage IIIR prototypes flew on 30 October 1961. The nose was changed to accommodate the cameras (AMD/BA)

RIGHT
Detail of the centreline pylon for the Matra R530 missile. The disc brake on the right mainwheel is clearly visible (S Mafé)

of touchdown the tail is normally only 12 inches (30 cm) or so from the runway. Not surprisingly perhaps, even experienced pilots scrape the concrete from time to time!

Other Variants

Reconnaissance Mirages

At the start of the Mirage III's career, the need for a tactical reconnaissance variant had been studied. During the early 1960s the *Armée de l' Air* wanted a replacement for the Republic RF-84F Thunderflash—then in service with *Escadre de Reconnaissance 33* (ER33). An Operational Requirement was issued in 1960, and the first of two prototypes of the Mirage IIIR made its maiden flight on 30 October 1961. Sixteen months later the first production aircraft was delivered to ER 3/33 '*Moselle*' at Strasbourg AB, and deliveries continued to ER33 units until March 1965.

The IIIR was basically a IIIE airframe, although much of the simpler electronic equipment was derived from that used on the IIIC. As a dedicated

reconnaissance aircraft, it was not equipped with the Cyrano radar, but the nose bay was lengthened by 19 inches (53 cm) and re-shaped to accommodate a battery of five Omera 31, 40 or 60 cameras, with lenses ranging from 200 mm up to 600 mm. The cameras could be fitted in oblique, vertical and forward positions, and were carried in a variety of combinations, depending on the mission requirement. A radio-altimeter set the focus for the cameras, and photo-flashes were carried for night missions. The IIIR could take most of the weapon load carried by the IIIE, including the DEFA guns, and during its later operational life it was equipped with a Cyclope infra-red tracker in a ventral pod.

As good as it was, the Mirage IIIR was operationally limited because it lacked an effective all-weather capability. To overcome this problem, a new variant known as Mirage IIIRD was developed. This incorporated the improved Doppler navigation system and CSF 97 gunsight from the IIIE, and introduced automatic camera control in place of the manual system used on the IIIR. Twenty IIIRDs were ordered for the *Armée de l'Air* and deliveries to

ER33 were completed between July 1967 and Feburary 1969. In common with the IIIR, the IIIRD was later updated to carry a ventrally-mounted Cyclope IR tracker: this provided a thermal image of the terrain being overflown, irrespective of the weather conditions. The aircraft could also carry an SLR-1 (side-looking radar) pod on the centreline station, to gather radar images of the ground to the left or right of track.

By 1985 the Mirage IIIR had completely disappeared from service with ER33, having been replaced by the swept-wing Mirage F.1CR. Most of the survivors were put into storage, but a few, devoid of all their reconnaissance capability, were used by other *Armée de l'Air* units as advanced trainers. The IIIRD remained in service with ER 3/33 'Moselle,' for some time, but it was eventually replaced by the F.1CR.

Mirage 5F—the 'mud mover'

This variant was especially developed for the Israeli Government as the Mirage 5J, but delivery of the 50 aircraft ordered by the IDFAF was embargoed by the De Gaulle administration in June 1967. A number of Israeli technicians and engineers had been seconded to Dassault throughout the development phase of the project, and after the embargo was announced they all returned home to mastermind the production of the IAI Nesher (Eagle)—an 'unofficial' copy of the Mirage 5J. The prototype of the French aircraft made its maiden flight on 19 May 1967, and the Israel copy flew in September 1969.

The concept of the Mirage 5J was simple. It used the airframe and engine of the Mirage IIIE, but the expensive interception radar was omitted. The avionics suite was less comprehensive, and all the electronics were moved into the nose, following the pattern set by the trainers. This left the centre section equipment bay available for an extra 110 gal (500 lt) of internal fuel. Two additional weapons pylons were installed, making seven in all, and these could carry up to 8820 lb (4000 kg) of weapons and 220 gal (1000 lt) of fuel during ground-attack missions. The aircraft retained its full Mach 2 plus capability at altitude, and could still be used as a ground-vectored interceptor with simple missiles such as the Sidewinder or Magic.

Ultimately many variants and sub-variants were developed from the basic VFR-equipped aircraft, and the Mirage 5 rapidly gained a strong foothold on world export markets. The 50 aircraft ordered by Israel were all completed and stored in France until the two governments negotiated a satisfactory

The prototype of the Mirage 5, showing a selection of possible armaments, including the AS30 air-to-ground missile and JL-100 weapons pod (front row), and the reinforced RPK-17 bomb-carrying external tanks (AMD/BA)

financial settlement. They were then delivered to the *Armée de l'Air* in 1971 as Mirage 5Fs.

An interesting twist to this story developed from the 1978/79 crisis between Argentina and Chile, which nearly resulted in open warfare between the two countries. During the build-up of tension, both sides scrambled to update their armed forces, and Chile ordered a batch of Mirage 5s direct from France—including eight of the used 5Fs that were originally destined for the IDFAF. These were taken out of *Armée de l'Air* service (later replaced with new-built aircraft during 1983/84) and modified to Mirage 50FC standard before delivery to Chile in 1980. The Argentinians meanwhile, having been rebuffed by the French Government, were operating their first batch of ex-Israeli IAI Neshers (renamed Dagger in FAA service)—a virtually identical aircraft that had never been anywhere near France!

More power—the Mirage 50

The Mirage 50 was a logical development of the Mirage 5, with more power and improved equipment standards. The major difference between the two aircraft was the SNECMA Atar 09K-50 engine, which also powered some of the South African AF Mirage IIIs and the swept-wing Mirage F.1. The new engine developed 15,875 lb (7200 kg) of thrust with afterburner, compared with just over 13,600 lb (6200 kg) of the Atar 09C. This extra power, combined with a redesigned inlet splitter-plate and a new nozzle, improved the take-off capability of the aircraft

ABOVE

The more powerful Mirage 50 flew for the first time on 15 April 1979. The development aircraft was equipped with the Cyrano IVM fire-control radar, or the Agave system could be fitted as an alternative. The intake has a contoured splitter-plate (AMD/BA)

OPPOSITE

The Mirage IIING was a remarkable design exercise, but it seems certain that Mirage 2000 sales will prevent it going into full production. The modifications are also available as retrofits, but the Israelis now seem to have cornered most of the canard-equipped Mirage III update market (AMD/BA)

by up to 20 per cent, and provided significantly better climb rates and sustained-turn performance. The avionics suite could be adapted to meet customer requirements, and the options included a Cyrano IVM air-to-air fire-control radar, and the Agave anti-shipping attack-radar. The prototype flew for the first time on 15 April 1979, but despite its obvious potential the actual sales were very disappointing.

Mirage IIING, canards and fly by wire

The Mirage IIING (*Nouvelle Génération*) probably represents the peak of development for the Mirage III/5 family, but production of new-build aircraft has almost certainly been eclipsed by the even more advanced Mirage 2000. The NG was developed to

obtain more agility from the basic airframe, and much of the technology has been derived from progress made with the Mirage F.1, 2000 and 4000 series. The most striking external differences are the fixed, intake-mounted canards, and subtle leading edge extensions at the wing roots. These combine aerodynamically to relax the stability of the aircraft, thereby increasing its potential manoeuvrability. In order to maintain control throughout the now extended flight envelope, the IIING has been fitted with a digital command-computing 'fly by wire' (FBW) system, adapted from that used on the Mirage 2000. The nav/attack system was also upgraded to include a choice of Cyrano IV or Agave radars, an inertial navigation system (INS) and a full head-up display (HUD).

The canards were first flown on a modified Mirage 50 'K', piloted by Patrick Experton on 27 May 1981, and the FBW system—which involved the complete redistribution of electrical wiring on the aircraft—was initially installed in a Mirage 5 'mock-up' that had earlier been grounded following an accident. After the success of these trials, Mirage 50 (01) was sent to Dassault's St Cloud shop for modification in January 1982. The aircraft emerged six months later as the Mirage IIING, and was moved to the Istres Test Centre, where it was eventually flown for the first time on 21 December 1982.

The performance of the IIING is almost comparable with the J79-powered, Mirage-based, IAI Kfir C7, which also has canards and computerized flight controls. The aircraft is being marketed as the Mirage 50M, but despite regular demonstrations—including highly effective appearances at the Paris Air Show—none had been sold by late 1988. It now seems unlikely that Dassault will recoup its heavy investment in the project, unless it can persuade a number of existing operators to convert earlier aircraft to the new standard.

Experimentals

Apart from prototypes of the different variants, there have been a number of interesting experimental aircraft based on the Mirage III. The Mirage IIIT for example, was used as a flying test-bed for US-designed engines that were being built under licence by SNECMA. Initially it received a Pratt & Whitney TF-30 afterburning turbofan, which developed a thrust of 10,400 lb (4725 kg). This engine was designated TF-104B in France, and it flew for the first time in the Mirage on 4 June 1964, with test pilot Jean Corean at the controls. Later the more powerful TF-106 was fitted: this developed 13,250 lb (6000 kg) of thrust, and flew on 25 January 1965. The most obvious external difference between the Mirage IIIT and a standard production airframe was the much wider rear fuselage of the test-bed. The engine trials lasted for five years, and although a two-seat version of the aircraft was planned, it never actually flew.

Following the development by Rolls-Royce of the RB.108 lightweight lift engine, and its successful application in the remarkable Shorts SC1, the

On 4 June 1964, Jean Corean flew the Mirage IIIT for the first time. The aircraft was specially built to accommodate a range of engines, and its rear fuselage was much bigger than a standard Mirage III. It was initially fitted with a French-assembled Pratt & Whitney TF-30 afterburning turbofan (AMD/BA)

LEFT
The first tethered hovering trials of the Balzac V (001) were conducted on 19 October 1962. The aircraft was powered by eight Rolls-Royce RB.108 lift engines, and a single Bristol-Siddeley Orpheus 3 propulsion engine (AMD/BA)

ABOVE
The Balzac V's first full transition from hovering to forward flight, and then back into hover for a vertical landing, was completed on 29 March 1963 (AMD/BA)

concept of vertical take-off and landing (VTOL) became a fashionable target for European combat-aircraft designers in the early 1960s. Using the airframe of the Mirage III prototype (001), Dassault launched an experimental programme aimed at equipping the *Armée de l'Air* with an operational VTOL fighter. The fuselage of 001 was completely rebuilt to accommodate eight RB.108s, each developing 2200 lb (1000 kg) of vertical thrust, and a single Bristol-Siddeley Orpheus 3, rated at 5300 lb

(2400 kg) for conventional forward flight. The lift engines could be tilted through 30 degrees to aid transition. The programme was managed by Sud-Aviation, and on 12 October 1962 Dassault test pilot René Bigand achieved the first tethered hover. On 29 March 1963, a complete flight-cycle including vertical take-off, translation into forward flight and then back into the hover for a vertical landing, was successfully demonstrated. Unfortunately, on 27 January 1964, while exploring low-speed roll capabilities on the 125th test-flight, the aircraft stalled and crashed, killing its CEV test pilot, Jacques Pinier. Although the prototype was badly damaged, it was quickly repaired and put back into service to continue the trials programme. Then, on 8 September 1965, its luck ran out completely when it crashed again at the Istres Test Centre, resulting in the death of its American test pilot and the complete destruction of the airframe. By that time, the unfortunate aircraft—which had been nicknamed Balzac throughout its career—had virtually finished its trials programme, and provided Dassault with valuable experience of VTOL operations.

As the result of early trials on the first aircraft, two further research prototypes were designed as forerunners of a fully operational version. These were designated Mirage IIIVs, and were considerably bigger than the Balzac. The fuselage was lengthened by nearly 10 feet to 59.5 feet (18 m), and the wing chord was increased at the roots, resulting in a compound-sweep leading edge. To absorb the

ABOVE LEFT
This unusual airborne shot of the Balzac V shows the aircraft in conventional forward flight, with the lift engine inlets closed, and the bulky undercarriage fully retracted (AMD/BA)

LEFT
The Mirage IIIV used the same basic aerodynamic and structural formula as the Balzac V, but it was considerably longer and heavier. It was powered by eight Rolls-Royce RB.162 lift engines, and a SNECMA TF-104 turbofan (AMD/BA)

ABOVE
Mirage IIIV 01 began its hovering trials in February 1965, and by March 1966 it had completed its first full transition (AMD/BA)

vertical descent loads more securely, all three undercarriage legs were strengthened and fitted with twin wheels. The first prototype carried out initial hovering trials on 12 February 1965, and completed its first full transition on 24 March 1966. It was powered by a 13,890 lb (6300 kg) SNECMA TF-104 turbofan for conventional flight, and eight Rolls-Royce RB.162 lightweight turbojets, each supplying 3525 lb (1600 kg) of lifting thrust. The lift engines were mounted in pairs, under four rear-hinged, grill-type intakes.

The second IIIV flew on 22 June 1966, differing from the first principally in having an augmented Pratt & Whitney TF-30 turbofan as its main propulsion engine. This provided 18,050 lb (8200 kg) thrust in full afterburner, and on 12 September 1966 it pushed the aircraft up to Mach 2.04, after a near-maximum weight take-off at 26,450 lb (12,000 kg). Only two months later, on 28 November 1966, it crashed after taking off from Istres on a test-flight. The limited combat-range of VTOL aircraft with separate lift engines had already caused the *Armée de l'Air* to lose interest in the concept, and the accident simply drove Dassault to abandon the whole programme. Despite its overall failure, the Mirage IIIV was—and indeed still is—the only VTOL aircraft ever to have flown beyond Mach 2.

At that time Dassault was in the planning stage of a new Mirage family with swept and variable-geometry wings. These were all based on the Mirage III aerodynamics and operational experience, and were originally known as the Mirage IIIF1, IIIF2 and IIIG, but in reality they represented the birth of a new generation of aircraft, and as such fall outside the scope of this book.

One final experimental variant almost reached operational status. During 1967 the Swiss AF decided to replace some of its Hunter fleet and all of its ageing Venom fighter-bombers. Dassault, in co-operation with the Federal Aircraft Works at Emmen, proposed a modification to the Mirage that would allow a shorter take-off run with increased payloads, combined with tighter turning ability and a lower approach speed. This was to be the Mirage Milan, equipped with retractable foreplanes in the nose. At the start of the programme an ex-Israeli Mirage 5J was fitted with foreplanes that were adjustable from the ground only, and flight testing of these began during September 1968. The second test aircraft was a modified Mirage IIIR equipped with the necessary electrics to move the foreplanes in flight: this joined the trials programme in May 1969. The third and final prototype, an Atar 09K-50 powered Mirage IIIE, was fully equipped to production standard, including some elements of the nav/attack system developed for the Anglo/French SEPECAT Jaguar. This was dubbed Milan S01, and it flew for the first time on 29 May 1970, with Mitaux Maurovard at the controls. The test results with this aircraft were very good, and it seemed to be just what the Swiss were looking for. At its maximum weight of 30,800 lb (14,000 kg) the Milan could take off in just over 3800 ft (1180 m), and its low-speed handling and general combat manoeuvrability were much improved. During weapons trials at Cazaux the aircraft carried up to five 1000 lb (450 kg) bombs, with two 110 gal (500 lt) drop tanks and a pair of Sidewinders. Despite all the joint effort that had gone into producing the Milan, and its obvious success, the Swiss Government finally opted to buy a large batch of refurbished Hunters, and later acquired 110 Northrop F-5E/F Tiger IIs to replace the Venom.

There were also several proposed variants of the Mirage that never saw the light of day. These included the Mirage IIIK that was offered to the Royal Air Force, the carrier-capable Mirage IIIM for France's *Aéronautique Navale*, and finally the Mirage IIIW, a co-operative venture between Dassault and Boeing to compete with the Northrop F-5: this was an interesting idea, but the study was abandoned before any real progress was made.

ABOVE
The second Mirage IIIV (02) incorporated a more refined system of lift engine doors than 01 (page 39). These could be hydraulically closed and covered to produce a more streamlined external surface. The lift engines were virtually the same as those used on 01, but forward propulsion was provided by an afterburning Pratt & Whitney TF-30 turbofan (AMD/BA)

LEFT
This was the final configuration of the Mirage Milan (S.01), incorporating all the elements of a production-standard aircraft. The nose foreplanes are extended (AMD/BA)

Chapter 3
Service at home

The *Armée de l'Air* received about 450 operational Mirage III/5s of all versions, and by the beginning of 1988 over half of these had been withdrawn from use, sold to other air forces, or lost in accidents. The number of active aircraft continues to decline, as more and more squadrons are re-equipped with variants of the Mirage 2000. Units that have flown, or are still flying, the first-generation Mirage, are listed below in numerical order of the parent Escadre (Wing). Mirage squadrons were primarily assigned to the air-defence duties of *Commandement Air des Forces de Défense Aérienne* (CAFDA), or to the close-air support tasking of *Force Aérienne Tactique* (FATac). These assignments were liable to change occasionally, especially for those squadrons operating the later multi-role aircraft. Such changes are noted in the text where applicable.

2e *Escadre de Chasse* (Dijon-Longvic AB)

EC 1/2 'Cicognes'
This was the first *Armée de l'Air* squadron to be equipped with the Mirage IIIC, replacing its Mystère IVAs in July 1961. It was originally assigned to CAFDA, but then transferred to FATac in April 1968 after re-equipping with Mirage IIIEs. 'Cicognes' operated the multi-role IIIE for over 15 years, and then returned to CAFDA assignment immediately before receiving its first Mirage 2000C on 2 July 1984.

EC 2/2 'Côte d'Or'
The conversion of pilots onto the delta-winged Mirage was a specialized task, and the French Air Staff decided in April 1965 to activate a dedicated operational training squadron. This was EC 2/2, formed with three flights of aircraft instead of the usual operational complement of two. Assigned ad-ministratively to CAFDA, it was initially equipped with Mirage IIIBs and IIICs. During 1968 the unit's designation was changed to ECT 2/2 (*Escadron de Chasse et de Transformation*) to reflect its training role. The much-improved Mirage IIIBE trainer began to arrive in 1971, and the last Mirage IIIC was withdrawn in late 1978. During the period 1983–85 most of the Mirage IIIRs formerly operated by ER 1/33 and 2/33 (see page 47), were stripped of their reconnaissance equipment to serve as advanced trainers, and some of these were allocated to 2/2. As the only Mirage III operational conversion unit (OCU), the squadron also trained air and ground crews for most of the aircraft's export customers. The OCU role, together with most of the remaining Mirage III trainers, passed to EC 1/13 'Artois' in 1985, as a prelude to ECT 2/2's re-equipment to become the Mirage 2000 OCU in 1986.

EC 3/2 'Alsace'
This squadron replaced its ageing Mystère IVAs with the Mirage IIIC, starting in December 1961. To help with the pilot-training task (prior to ECT 2/2's formation) the unit was allocated a small number of two-seat Mirage IIIBs for a limited period. In April 1969 the squadron was reassigned from CAFDA to

ABOVE RIGHT
In July 1961, EC 1/2 'Cicognes' was the first unit to receive Mirage IIICs

RIGHT
For many years ECT 2/2 'Cote d'Or' performed the Mirage III/5 OCU role, both for the Armée de l'Air, *and for a large number of overseas students. Illustrated is Mirage IIIBE (268 2-ZL) during an instrument training sortie. The rear seat has a canvas hood above it* (AMD/BA)

FATac, disposing of its IIICs and preparing the pilots and technicians to operate the Mirage IIIE— the first example of which arrived on 27 September that year. 'Alsace' retained its multi-role capability and the tactical tasking for some 15 years, before finally relinquishing the Mirage III altogether, and returning to CAFDA command in September 1985 with the Mirage 2000C.

3e *Escadre de Chasse* (Nancy-Ochey AB)

EC 1/3 *'Navarre'*
A former F-100 Super Sabre unit based at Lahr, in West Germany, EC 1/3 received its first Mirage IIIEs in November 1965. By 30 August 1967 the squadron had relocated to Nancy, where it remains today, still operating the Mirage IIIE. Assigned to FATac, its main task is low-level defence suppression (the Wild Weasel role) with AS37 Martel anti-radar air-to-surface missiles. Secondary tasks include conventional strike-bombing, and all-weather interception using Matra R530 and R550 air-to-air weapons.

EC 2/3 *'Champagne'*
Like its sister squadron, EC 2/3 was equipped with Super Sabres before being converted to Mirage IIIEs from October 1965. It has the same assignment, role and weaponry as 'Navarre'.

EC 3/3 *'Ardennes'*
This strike squadron was activated with Mirage 5Fs (originally 5Js destined for Israel) in July 1979. Three years later the Mirages were replaced by SEPECAT

Jaguars for a short period, before the unit settled down with its current equipment, the Mirage IIIE. 'Ardennes' remains under FATac command.

4e *Escadre de Chasse* (Luxeuil-St Sauveur AB)

EC 1/4 *'Dauphine'*
In January 1967 EC 1/4 retired its last Republic F-84F Thunderstreak, and one month later received the first of its new Mirage IIIEs. The squadron was originally assigned to FATac with a primary role of low-level interdiction, but by the end of 1972 this had undergone a significant change. 'Dauphine' became one of the squadrons tasked with low-level nuclear strike, using the AN52 'special store'. Its secondary roles were conventional attack and all-weather interception. In July 1988 the Mirage IIIEs were

BELOW
These three camouflaged Mirage IIIEs are all from different units, and they all carry different armaments. From top to bottom they are: EC 2/4 'La Fayette' carrying an AN-52 nuclear store, EC 1/13 'Artois' with a Matra R530 air-to-air missile, and EC 1/3 'Navarre' with the Martel AS37 anti-radar missile (AMD/BA)

RIGHT
Mirage IIIE No 590 from EC 1/4 'Dauphine' based at Luxeuil. The greyhound is the insignia of SPA 81. During the summer of 1988 the squadron converted to the Mirage 2000N (EC 4 via Romero)

withdrawn, and replaced with Mirage 2000Ns. These are equipped to launch the new ASMP (*Air Sol Moyenne Portée*) nuclear missile.

EC 2/4 '*La Fayette*'

This is one of the most historic squadrons in the *Armée de l'Air*. After many years of F-84F operations, the ageing American fighter-bombers were traded in during October 1966 for multi-role Mirage IIIEs. In common with its sister squadron, EC 2/4 is assigned to FATac and currently has a nuclear deterrent role. The Mirage IIIE was replaced by Mirage 2000Ns in late 1988.

5e *Escadre de Chasse* (**Orange Caritat AB**)

EC 1/5 '*Vendée*'

Originally operating Super Mystère B2s, this squadron was re-equipped with Mirage IIICs in September 1966. It was assigned to the air-defence arena of CAFDA. Less than nine years after their arrival at Orange, the Mirage IIICs were replaced with Mirage F.1Cs.

EC 2/5 '*Ile de France*'

In common with '*Vendée*', EC 2/5 was re-equipped with the Mirage IIIC after operating the Super Mystère B2. The new aircraft started to arrive in November 1966, and were eventually replaced with Mirage F.1Cs in 1975. Tasking and assignment shared with EC 1/5.

10e *Escadre de Chasse* (**Creil AB**)

EC 1/10 '*Valois*'

Converted from Super Mystère B2s in August 1974. The Mirage IIICs were assigned to CAFDA and remained in service until replaced by Mirage F.1Cs in May 1981. After the disbandment of the 10e *Escadre de Chasse* in 1985, the squadron was relocated to Reims AB and changed its designation to EC 1/30.

EC 2/10 '*Seine*'

Operational with Mirage IIICs assigned to CAFDA in December 1968, following a period with Mystère B2s. After flying the Mirage for almost 12 years, the squadron was deactivated in June 1985.

ABOVE
*Mirage IIIC No 51 in the markings of Creil-based EC 2/10
'Seine'. The aircraft is seen in the blue-grey air superiority
paint scheme applied to all of the later air defence Mirages*
(ECPA)

LEFT
*Mirage IIIC coded '10-Lima Hotel' in the desert camouflage
of EC 3/10 'Vexin'. The squadron is based at Djibouti, in
East Africa, and is the only* Armée de l'Air *unit to be
permanently engaged on overseas duties* (via Christian
Boisselon)

RIGHT
*A pair of Mirage IIIEs from EC 1/13 over a heavily
forested area in early style camouflage* (EC 13)

EC 3/10 'Vexin'

This is the only fighter squadron of the *Armée de l'Air*
to be based permanently overseas. It was activated at
Creil in December 1978, and equipped with 10
Mirage IIICs in a striking 'chestnut and sand' colour
scheme for desert operations. The aircraft were also
modified to carry the Matra R550 Magic IR-guided
air-to-air missile. In January 1979 the squadron left
Creil for Djibouti Airport, on the East African coast
at the entrance to the Red Sea. Here it provides air
defence for this former French colony, helping to
police the skies in a highly sensitive area. The unit
was re-equipped with Mirage F.1Cs and F.1C-200s
in 1989 and was subsequently renumbered EC 4/30.

13e *Escadre de Chasse*
(Colmar Mayenheim AB)

EC 1/13 'Artois'

The first Mirage IIIC was received by this squadron
early in 1962, after a period operating Fiat-built
North American F-86K Sabres. The Mirage IIICs
were assigned to CAFDA, but during 1965 'Artois'

was re-equipped with the multi-role Mirage IIIE and
its assignment switched to FATac. The squadron's
primary roles at that time were low-level strike with
conventional weapons, and battlefield air superiority.
EC 1/13 is the longest continuously serving Mirage
IIIE squadron. From July 1986 it also became the
largest fighter squadron of the *Armée de l'Air*, when
the Mirage III OCU task was assigned to it following
ECT 2/2's re-equipment with the new Mirage 2000B.
As training aircraft began to arrive at Colmar, two
new flights had to be activated within the existing
squadron administration. The two original flights
(SPA 83 'Chimère' and SPA 100 'Hirondelle'—both
equipped with Mirage IIIEs) continue their normal
operational tasking, while the two new ones (SPA 155
'Petit Poucet' and SPA 160 'Diable Rouge') are both
equipped with Mirage IIIBs and IIIBEs for their
training role.

EC 2/13 'Alpes'

This was one of the earliest Mirage IIIC operators,
receiving its first aircraft in May 1962. The squadron
was also equipped with two-seat Mirage IIIBs from

June 1964 to June 1966, acting as a 'stand-in' OCU for the aircraft until the role was taken over by ECT 2/2. In April 1965 the operational Mirage IIICs were replaced by Mirage IIIEs, and these were used for 12 years, until they too were replaced by Mirage 5Fs that had been released by the re-equipping of EC 3/3. The squadron is assigned to FATac.

EC 3/13 'Auvergne'
For over four years the 50 Mirage 5Js under embargo which had been ordered by the IDFAF were stored at Châtaudun AB. During 1971 the French and Israeli Governments agreed a financial settlement of the affair, and the aircraft were purchased for Armée de l'Air service. They were redesignated Mirage 5F (for France), and immediately subjected to an extensive weapons and tactics trials programme by EC 24/118 of CEAM at Mont de Marsan. In April 1972 the first Mirage 5F was delivered to EC 3/13—a squadron specially formed at Colmar to operate these suprise acquisitions. Eight additional 5Fs were built in 1983 to replace a small batch modified to Mirage 50FC standard for Chile. 'Auvergne' is assigned to FATac.

33e Escadre de Reconnaissance (Strasbourg Entzheim AB)

ER 1/33 'Belfort'
This was the third squadron to be equipped with the specially adapted Mirage IIIR reconnaissance variant. The first arrived during January 1967, and the type was kept on strength as part of the FATac command until it was replaced by the Mirage F.1CR in November 1985.

ER 2/33 'Savoie'
The second FATac reconnaissance squadron to operate IIIRs. The initial deliveries were made in January 1964, and the type remained in service until the arrival of Mirage F.1CRs in July 1983.

ER 3/33 'Moselle'
The first production Mirage IIIR was received by ER 3/33 during June 1963. Five years later the squadron converted to the more advanced IIIRD, and the earlier aircraft were distributed between the other two 'recce' units. The re-equipment of 'Moselle' with

ABOVE
A formation of Mirage IIIEs and Mirage 5Fs from EC 13 form up into the number '13' while overflying Colmar AB (EC 13)

LEFT
EC 3/13 'Auvergne' was the first unit to receive ex-Israeli Mirage 5Fs. The aircraft pictured here is still in the old metallic lacquer finish (EC 13)

ABOVE RIGHT
This Mirage IIIRD of ER 3/33 'Moselle' displays its nose-mounted doppler antenna fairing

RIGHT
This camouflaged Mirage IIIR reconnaissance aircraft carries the double-headed axe insignia of ER 1/33 'Belfort' (AMD/BA)

Mirage F.1CRs was delayed by budgetary constraints, but it was finally achieved in 1988. All reconnaissance units are under FATac command.

Centre des Expérimentations Aériennes Militaires (Mont de Marsan AB)

EC 24/118
This unit, assigned to CAFDA, is in charge of all the operational trials work on *Armée de l'Air* fighter aircraft. Because it deals particularly with the formulation of tactics and procedures, it has operated every variant of the Mirage III/5 family in French service. EC 24/118 was redesignated EC 33/330 '*Côte d'Argent*' in October 1987.

Centre d'Instruction Forces Aériennes Strategiques (Bordeaux AB)

EE 2/328
This little-known squadron attached to the Strategic Air Forces has several Mirage IIIB and IIIB-RVs on strength. These are used for proficiency training by future Mirage IVA/P strategic bomber crews. The IIIB-RV has been specially modified with a dry probe, for practice air-to-air refuelling. The Mirage IIIB/IIIB-RVs have been passed to EC 1/13.

LEFT
Carrying the 'paper hen' insignia of ER 3/33 'Moselle', these three aircraft are all Mirage IIIRs

BELOW LEFT
Mirage IIIE No 512 carries the triangular badge of EC 24/118 (CEAM) while conducting evaluation trials with the Matra Martel anti-radar missile (AMD/BA)

Chapter 4
Aussie Mirages

During 1958 the Australian Government began an evaluation of potential replacements for the Avon powered CA.27 Sabre—then the standard equipment of RAAF fighter squadrons. A wide range of aircraft were originally assessed, but the finalists were the Lockheed F-104 Starfighter, Republic F-105 Thunderchief, Saab Draken, English Electric Lightning and Dassault's Mirage III. In 1960 the F-104 and Mirage were brought forward for further evaluation, and after an exhaustive analysis of both designs, the Mirage III was finally selected. The preliminary contract documents stated that the aircraft for Australia would be assembled under licence by the Government Aircraft Factories (GAF) in Melbourne.

The Rolls-Royce Avon series of engines was already being manufactured in Australia, and it seemed logical to use one of these powerplants if the technical difficulties could be overcome. A Mirage III (No 100) was therefore modified in France as an engine test-bed, and this flew on 13 February 1961 powered by a 300 series (RB.146) Avon, developing 13,220 lb (6000 kg) of dry thrust, and 16,000 lb (7257 kg) with afterburner. The increased power of

This Mirage III was fitted with a Rolls-Royce Avon Mk 67 engine for evaluation by the RAAF. Despite obvious improvements in both fuel efficiency and performance, the Australian Government decided against the modification for its production aircraft. The experimental prototype was an interesting hybrid machine, with the longer nose of the Mirage IIIE and the cranked tail of the earlier Mirage IIIC. It also had a number of modifications that were specific to the RAAF requirement, notably a Doppler radar mounted under the nose, and extra cooling air inlets around the rear fuselage. First flown on 13 February 1961, the Avon-powered aircraft was given the designation Mirage IIIO No 1, and named City of Hobart *(AMD/BA)*

the Avon improved the performance of the aircraft substantially, but the cost of the installation—especially the 'learning curve' problems of building a non-standard aircraft in Australia—was simply too high, so the modification was abandoned in favour of the original Atar.

From April to September 1961, two Australian missions including RAAF pilots and engineers, travelled to France to work on the final details of the contract and smooth out any engineering problems. For Dassault, the whole programme was an enormous challenge. It represented the biggest Mirage III export order so far, with the added complication of having to build, test and support the aircraft on the other side of the world. Company technicians had to train their Australian colleagues, then provide tools for the GAF assembly line and ship them to Melbourne, while nearly 120 small modifications asked for by the RAAF were incorporated into the airframe and systems. Finally, all the technical documentation had to be amended to reflect the engineering and procedural changes. It was a remarkably complex exercise, but it was completed with a degree of good humour on both sides, and it provided valuable experience for everyone concerned.

The initial contract included a first batch of 30 aircraft, followed by 30 more, and then a final batch of 40 to bring the overall order up to 100 machines. In response to the RAAF's requirements, the single-seaters were to be delivered in two different versions: 52 fighter/attack Mirage IIIO(A)s, and 48 Mirage IIIO(F)s—which were slightly less complex and optimized for the air-to-air role. The agreement specified that Dassault would build the first two aircraft in France, then supply the next six in the form of completely knocked down kits for quick assembly in Australia. These would be followed by smaller

sub-assemblies for two complete airframes, and finally some components would be supplied for the local construction of the next five. After the first 15 aircraft, all French involvement in the actual production line would cease, and the remainder of the run would be assembled entirely by GAF. Dassault-owned companies, acting as sub-contractors to GAF, would continue to supply a limited range of specialized equipment, as would some of the other Australian companies involved in the programme.

In mid-1963, a group of RAAF pilots under the command of Sqn Ldr Bill H Collins, was sent to France to begin conversion training in the Mirage with EC 1/13 'Artois' at Colmar (this was before the activation of ECT 2/2 as the Mirage OCU). After their basic course, they went on to more advanced flying with CEV at Istres, and with CEAM at Mont de Marsan. Meanwhile, back home in Australia, the GAF assembly line for the Mirage was beginning to take shape.

The aircraft were to be assembled at the GAF plant at Avalon, near Melbourne. The company was responsible for building several components and sub-assemblies from scratch, as well as the final assembly, ground tests and flight trials. The Melbourne-based Commonwealth Aircraft Corporation (CAC) was principal sub-contractor to GAF, and was responsible for large sub-assemblies such as the wing, fin, part of the fuselage and the Atar engine. Hawker

de Havilland built the remainder of the fuselage; Dunlop Australia supplied the landing gear and tyres; and Normalair (Australia) Pty the environmental system.

Dassault handed over its first complete aircraft on 9 April 1963. This was flown to Australia aboard an RAAF C-130 Hercules, and loaned to GAF as a production pattern. The second French-built example (A3-2) remained with Dassault for some time to enable the technical documentation to be completed. When this was done, the aircraft was sent to Australia for reassembly and testing. The first GAF-assembled Mirage IIIO completed its maiden flight from Avalon on 16 November 1963. The aircraft was in the hands of Sqn Ldr Bill Collins, and the flight—which was the first ever for a Mirage in Australia—lasted 75 minutes, and was watched by Dassault test pilot, Jean-Marie Saget. Two more flights were recorded in November, and another in December.

A3-1, the French-built pattern aircraft, made its first flight in Australia on 11 January 1964. During February it was sent to RAAF Darwin, where Bill Collins made several flights in the tropical environment to test the resistance of systems and electronics to high levels of humidity and temperature. The next series of tests—which involved the same aircraft, was at the high altitude, high Mach edges of the flight envelope, and these too were trouble-free.

The initial delivery rate from GAF's assembly line was very disappointing. During the nine months between 2 January and 21 September 1964, only six aircraft were completed and flown (A3-4 to A3-9), representing an average output of only nine aircraft per year! The main reason for the delay was the slow 'acclimatization' from relatively uncomplicated aircraft to the highly sophisticated Mirage. The fact that the aircraft was French, and therefore entirely metric in origin, made things even more difficult because the Australian industry was historically linked to the Imperial measurement techniques used in British and American aircraft. There were also problems with the supply of parts and sub-assemblies from subcontractors in both France and Australia, which

added further delays to an already difficult situation. As these problems were resolved, the programme slowly gathered momentum, until the planned delivery rate was finally achieved. On 25 September 1967 A3-50 was delivered, and just over a year later, on 4 November 1968, the contract for single-seat aircraft was completed with the delivery of A3-100.

All Mirage IIIOs were handed over to the customer without armament and radar, because the RAAF itself was responsible for installing these. The IIIO(A) was equipped with the Cyrano II*bis* air-to-air/air-to-ground radar, plus a pulse-Doppler navigation radar—which differed from the standard Mirage IIIE's set in having the antenna radome flush with the lower fuselage profile. The simpler IIIO(F), which was optimized for air-to-air missions, was fitted with a Cyrano IIA radar. After a year or so of service, it was realized that this difference between the two aircraft was uneconomic and operationally unsound. It was therefore agreed that all surviving IIIO(F)s should be modified to IIIO(A) standard, and the first of 43 aircraft to be updated arrived at GAF's Avalon plant on 16 October 1968.

It took no time at all for the RAAF to realize that the Mirage could be a 'hot' and unforgiving machine in particular flight situations—especially for an inexperienced pilot. A conversion trainer was considered vital, and a two-seat derivative of the Mirage IIIE was ordered. This aircraft was known in

BELOW LEFT
The first few Australian-built Mirages suffered considerable production delays, mainly because the local aircraft industry was not geared up to handle such a sophisticated machine (AMD/BA)

BELOW
The Mirage IIIO(F) was optimized for the air-to-air interception role, and was not originally equipped with a doppler navigation system. This policy was later reversed, and all the aircraft were brought up to a common standard (RAAF)

France as the Mirage IIIBE, but the Australians changed the designation to IIID (for Dual), and all subsequent export two-seaters were given this shortened designation by Dassault. The initial RAAF order was for 10 trainers, the first of which had its maiden flight on 6 October 1966, after being fully assembled in France. The remaining aircraft were constructed by GAF using fuselages supplied by Dassault, and the last of these flew in July 1967. An order for a further six was placed in October 1970, and the very last Australian-built Mirage, a IIID numbered A3-116, rolled off the Avalon line on 1 December 1973.

During the 1970s a small number of RAAF Mirages were converted into reconnaissance aircraft. This was done by removing the Cyrano radar and fitting in its place a mount for cameras, control equipment and film magazines. The primary camera was a panoramic Fairchild KA-56-B1, with 75 mm lenses and a 770-frame film cassette, but a 75 mm low-level camera could be fitted as an alternative. The standard aircraft nose was replaced by a modified

TOP
A3-8 was one of the first Mirage IIIO(F)s to enter day-to-day service with the RAAF. The aircraft is seen here in the early style trim of No 2 OCU at RAAF Williamtown, NSW and carries a pair of AIM-9B Sidewinders (RAAF)

ABOVE
One of the Mirage IIID two-seat trainers is seen here landing at Williamtown, carrying No 2 OCU's dramatic black/yellow striped tail. The instructor (rear seat) has his hands on the instrument panel coaming—indicating that the student is flying the aircraft (RAAF)

RIGHT
This panoramic shot of Sydney Harbour was taken by No 77 Sqn RAAF, using a Mirage IIIO(PR) modified to accept the Fairchild KA-56B-1 reconnaissance camera. Sydney's famous opera house can be seen on the left, and the harbour itself on the right. The road in the centre leads down towards the harbour bridge (RAAF Williamtown)

Mirage F.1-type radome, with appropriate windows set into its surface. The aircraft could also carry an optional reconnaissance system in place of the 30 mm guns. This consisted of a Vinten F95 camera-pack, containing two 100 mm low-level cameras, offset to the vertical axis of the aircraft to give as wide a field of view as possible. The converted aircraft were designated Mirage IIIO(PR)s, and were all flown by No 77 Sqn at RAAF Williamtown.

Due to their relatively high utilization, the Australian Mirages were likely to run out of operational hours before their replacements could be established in service. It was therefore decided to embark on a Life Of Type Extension (LOTE) programme during the early 1980s. This involved fitting new spars and wing skins to claw back some of the fatigue life; modification of the Atar 09C5 engine; installing a Martin-Baker OH-6 zero-zero ejection seat; and updating the weapons system to include a Thomson-CSF 97K gunsight and make the aircraft compatible with the Matra R550 Magic IR-guided air-to-air missile.

Midway through the LOTE programme the McDonnell Douglas F/A-18A Hornet was selected as a replacement for the Mirage, and this inevitably meant that the delta's period of front-line service was coming to an end. The run-down began in earnest on 17 May 1985, when the first two F/A-18Bs arrived at Williamtown after a record-breaking non-stop flight from NAS Lemoore in California. These were soon joined by the first locally manufactured examples, and production is currently building towards the planned total of 57 F/A-18As and 18 two-seat F/A-18Bs. The Aussie Mirages were finally retired in February 1989, but at least two will be preserved in the RAAF Fighter Display Centre at Williamtown. One of these is A3-3, which was the first of the

type to be assembled in Australia. It was handed over to the RAAF in December 1983, and was finally withdrawn from service by No 77 Sqn in May 1987 with 3200 hours on the airframe: the aircraft is now painted in the colours of No 2 Operational Conversion Unit.

Although a few of the remaining Mirages have already been spoken for as gate-guardians or exhibits at other museums, the majority are stored at Williamtown and Woomera awaiting disposal. The Defence Department would like to see most, if not all, sold to other politically acceptable countries, but the competition for such orders is bound to be fierce. France, which has a similar stock of retired aircraft and a far more effective after-sales service, has already sold used Mirages to Brazil and Venezuela—both originally thought to be likely customers for the Australian aircraft.

RAAF Mirage III units

No 2 Operational Conversion Unit

The OCU was still basically a Sabre unit until four instructors returned to Williamtown in April 1963, following their Mirage conversion training with EC 1/13 in France. A Mirage Flight was then set up within the OCU administration, and former Sabre technicians underwent conversion to the new aircraft in September that year. No Mirages were actually received until 13 January 1964, and the instructor pilots had to pass their time on ground school duties, teaching theories and systems to their colleagues. As the number of aircraft slowly built up—albeit with some spares provisioning problems—Mirage Conversion Courses began on an experimental basis. In 1966 the unit received its first two-seat Mirage IIIDs, and the instruction began to take on a more

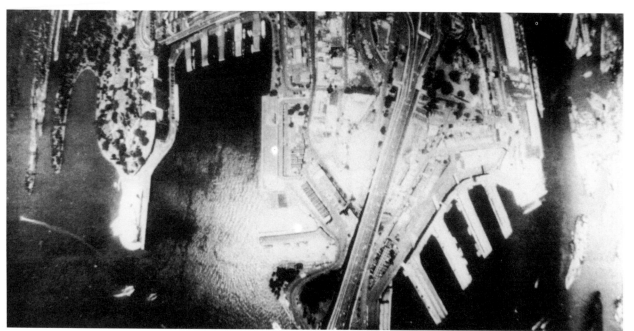

TOP
On 17 May 1985, the first two RAAF F/A-18B Hornets arrived in Australia, accompanied by a US Air Force KC-10A Extender. Two Mirage IIIO(A)s from No 77 Sqn provided an escort for the last stage of their journey into RAAF Williamtown (RAAF)

ABOVE
Another variation on the theme of No 2 OCU's markings, showing the unit's tiger head emblem over the yellow and black tail design (RAAF)

Seen overflying Singapore, this formation includes a Mirage IIIO(A) from each of the four operating units during the late 1970s. From top left, the markings are those of No 75 Sqn, No 77 Sqn, No 3 Sqn and No 2 Operational Conversion Unit (RAAF)

ABOVE
Mirage IIIO(A)s A3-87 from No 3 Sqn and A3-65 from No 75 Sqn, photographed during a training flight over northern Malaysia. Both squadrons are now fully converted to the F/A-18 Hornet (RAAF)

definitive form, with all future Mirage pilots undergoing a 22-week conversion course before being posted to an operational squadron. The OCU disbanded during the last few months of 1984, and all the Mirage training commitments were passed over to No 77 Sqn, which was also resident at Williamtown. In May 1985 the OCU was reactivated as the training squadron for the F/A-18 Hornet. Then and now, the OCU role includes reinforcement of front-line squadrons in times of crisis.

No 3 Squadron
The first No 3 Sqn Mirage was received at Williamtown on 27 July 1967, and eight months later it was fully up to strength. The unit redeployed to RAAF Butterworth in Malaysia during March 1968, and remained there in company with No 75 Squadron until returning to Williamtown in 1984 to prepare for re-equipment with F/A-18 Hornets.

No 75 Squadron
This was the first operational RAAF squadron to re-equip with Mirage IIIs. The unit transferred its Sabres out to other squadrons during November 1964, and began conversion courses with No 2 OCU. The first aircraft arrived on 12 January 1965, but due to early production problems the squadron was not fully up to strength for many months. On 15 May 1967 the squadron departed to Butterworth, via Darwin, and while serving in Malaysia it provided permanent detachments (shared with No 3 Sqn) to Tengah, Singapore. On 11 August 1983 the squadron returned from Butterworth to Darwin, and finally disbanded as a Mirage unit on 30 September 1988. On the following day, 1 October, it was officially reformed as an F/A-18 squadron at RAAF Tindal, some 300 km south of Darwin.

No 76 Squadron
A former Sabre unit, No 76 Sqn was equipped with Mirages only for a very short time. Defence cuts implemented by the Australian Government led to the number of fighter squadrons being reduced, and No 76 was disbanded at Williamtown in 1973.

No 77 Squadron
This squadron had a remarkable combat record in the Korean War. It was equipped with the usual two flights of Mirage IIIs at Williamtown in 1969, and a third flight was added later to operate the RAAF's tactical reconnaissance Mirages. Following the appearance of the F/A-18 Hornet, the squadron grew even bigger as it assumed responsibility for Mirage conversion and continuation training from No 2 OCU. At one time the squadron was operating about 40 aircraft, including most of the two-seat trainers, and it retained a Training Flight for the Mirage well into its own operational conversion to the F/A-18. The first Hornets arrived in 1987, and the squadron is now fully up to strength on the type.

No 79 Squadron
This unit was activated at RAAF Butterworth, Malaysia, on 31 March 1986, to replace temporarily the two squadrons that had moved out to convert to the F/A-18. During its short period of operation, most of its Mirages carried a variation of the new air-superiority grey colour scheme, some with irregular patterns of dark grey over the top surfaces, others with symetrical shapes like a chevron. The squadron was finally disbanded on 30 June 1988, and most of its aircraft were stored to await disposal.

Air Research and Development Unit
During the introductory phase and throughout the normal service life of the aircraft, the ARDU had a varying number of Mirages on strength. Operating from Edinburgh, South Australia, the unit conducted most of the armament and equipment trials on the Mirage, including compatibility tests with the Paveway laser-guided bomb and its illuminator pod. An ARDU pilot flew the last Australian Mirage sortie in February 1989.

A pilot's impression

Sqn Ldr David Piettsch is a highly experienced fighter pilot with more than 1800 hours on the Mirage III. He is currently an F/A-18 instructor at Williamtown, and was one of the hand-picked group of fighter instructors selected for Hornet training with VFA-125 at NAS Lemoore. He still has fond memories of his Mirage III days:

I joined the RAAF as a direct-entry aircrew cadet at Point Cook in 1969. After receiving my wings as a graduate from the Basic Flying Training Course there on the piston-engined CA-25 Winjeel, I underwent a jet conversion course and advanced training to become a fighter pilot.

I flew Sabres for 12 months before being posted to Butterworth, where I flew the Mirage for four years. I returned to Australia for a three-year stint as a flying instructor with the FTS at Point Cook, before going to RAAF Williamtown for a further five years of Mirage operations.

Flying the Mirage was a memorable experience in my Air Force career, and although the F/A-18 is a world apart operationally, the Frenchy delta will remain engraved on my memory for ever. It was a real fighter pilot's aeroplane; very responsive, and almost immune to turbulence thanks to its aerodynamic finesse—but it did have some defects! The engine was somewhat underpowered, and the aircraft was a little tricky during landing or entering a flat spin. But at medium to high altitude it could be flown as though it were an extension of the pilot. Of course it was short-legged compared to the Hornet, but I can assure you that once strapped in to that narrow (but not uncomfortable) cockpit, one felt like a real ace!

Carrying the ARDU badge on its fin, A3-76 was used for compatibility tests with the Paveway II laser guided bomb system (Texas Instruments via PG)

Chapter 5
The Israeli connection

During the period of squadron service by its Ouragan, Mystère IVA and Super Mystère B2 fighters, the IDFAF maintained a close working relationship with the *Armée de l'Air* and the French aviation industry—particularly with Dassault and SNECMA. An Israeli military delegation was invited to inspect the Mirage III in 1957, only a matter of months after the aircraft's first flight. Even at that early stage the officials were clearly impressed by its potential, and the IDFAF watched its subsequent development with increasing interest. Egypt, Iraq and Syria were all in the process of acquiring Soviet-made MiG-21 interceptors, and the new Mirage was seen as the only practical answer to the threat posed by these Mach 2.0 fighters.

On 23 June 1959, Danny Shapira, chief test pilot for the IDFAF, made the first of a series of evaluation flights in the third preproduction Mirage IIIA. During that initial sortie he reached Mach 1.2 in the aircraft, and on the third flight he had the distinction of becoming only the twelfth pilot in France to achieve Mach 2.0. The evaluation team was headed by Gen Ezer Weizman, the IDFAF's Chief of Staff at that time.

The reports from Shapira's evaluation were so enthusiastic that the IDFAF decided to acquire Mirage IIIs as quickly as possible, and Weizman announced a requirement for 100 aircraft. This proposal was followed by an impassioned debate in the Knesset—and indeed within the IDFAF itself—because some people expressed the view that the (then) high price of US 2 million dollars per aircraft could be more effectively spent on a larger number of less advanced machines. As an interim measure, the Government finally agreed to buy 24 Mirages for the interceptor role, and use the existing Mystères and Super Mystère B2s as fighter-bombers. Weizman was far from happy about this decision, and continued to demand the Mirage for both roles.

ABOVE
Col Danny Shapira did a huge amount of test flying for the IDFAF and IAI. He is seen here with the prototype Mirage 5J—the order for which was subsequently embargoed by the French government. (Dassault)

Throughout the underlying political discussions, the IDFAF had been working on a military level to define its operational requirements more accurately. The Mirage IIICJ (J for *Juif*, or Jewish) began to emerge from this process as a multi-role fighter, rather than sticking to the original French concept of a rocket-boosted point defence interceptor. For service in Israel the rocket motor was considered unnecessary, but the aircraft would still carry the two 30 mm cannon and the centreline (R530) stores station. In addition, the Israelis wanted extra bomb racks and missile rails, the clearance of which would be completed by Shapira in France.

Internal debates about the size of the order ended abruptly in January 1961, when Zvi Tsur was appointed Chief of Staff of the IDFAF. He agreed to compromise by accepting a reduced order for 72 Mirages, and this arrangement was ratified by the Knesset. The aircraft were immediately ordered from Dassault, but a new obstacle then emerged, just after the intergovernment contract was signed by Shimon Peres and the French Minister of Defence. The increasingly turbulent nature of Middle Eastern politics—and probable pressure from the Arab nations involved—led the French Foreign Minister to refuse his vital sanction to the deal. For a while it looked as though the whole order was in jeopardy, but President De Gaulle finally stepped in and gave his personal approval to the contract. The final agreement involved 76 aircraft, all powered by the SNECMA Atar 09B3 engine. The bulk of the order consisted of 68 'standard' Mirage IIICJ multi-role fighters, but four two-seat Mirage IIIBJ trainers were also included, together with four unarmed, single-seat Mirage IIICJ(R) reconnaissance aircraft. The reconnaissance variant would be fitted with a more rounded, interchangeable nose, housing US-manufactured cameras for low, medium and high altitude photography.

During 1961 six pilots were sent to France for conversion training. These were in two teams of three, and would ultimately form the nucleus of two squadrons (a plan that was subsequently modified to include the conversion of a third squadron). The first team consisted of Maj Shmuel Sheffer with Capts David Ivri and Dror Avnery, and the second was led by Maj Joe Allon, and included Capts Amos Lapidot and Ezra Aharon. Shmuel Sheffer and Joe Allon were both highly experienced commanding officers of existing Mystère squadrons.

On completion of their own training, both teams returned to Israel to act as instructor pilots and organize the squadrons. The third team followed later. The first unit to convert was the famous No 101 Sqn at Hatzor AB, previously equipped with Mystère IVs. The second was a former Meteor F8/FR9 unit based at Ramat David AB, which has subsequently been identified as No 117 Sqn. The third was No 119 Sqn at Tel Nof AB, which was formerly equipped with Meteor NF13s and Vautour IINs. The first two Mirages arrived at Hatzor on 7 April 1962, after being ferried from the manufacturers by Shapira and a French pilot.

Initially the IDFAF Mirages were not camouflaged, and each squadron could be identified by its own individual markings. No 101 Sqn used a red and white striped rudder, and a badge representing a skull with a winged helmet. No 117 Sqn had a red line painted along the fuselage, and a badge depicting the plan-view of a white jet inside a red circle. The tail-fins of No 119 Sqn were decorated with a red arrowhead, and the squadron badge consisted of a black bat over a white cloud, all enclosed in a red circle.

Mirage deliveries to Israel—including the uniquely configured Mirage IIICJ(R)s—were finally completed in 1964. The squadrons all embarked on an intensive training programme, honing their

TOP
The second squadron to re-equip with Mirages was No 117 Sqn based at Ramat David AB. In pre-camouflage days its aircraft could be identified by a red line along the fuselage, as seen here on No 725. The squadron badge on the fin has not been censored in the usual way, but the design is too indistinct to be useful (IDFAF via David Eshel)

ABOVE
The third IDFAF unit to convert was No 119 Sqn at Tel Nof AB, and all its aircraft carried a red arrowhead flash on the fin. The squadron badge has been censored. Aircraft No 787 was one of four Mirage IIIBJ trainers delivered to the IDFAF, and this picture must have been taken after the Six Day War because an RWR has been installed just above the rudder (IDFAF)

Squadron badges are all too frequently obliterated by Israeli censors, but the designs for No 101 Sqn (left) and No 119 Sqn (right) are now known

tactical and operational skills to a fine edge in preparation for the inevitable combat sorties against Arab MiGs. During this work-up period a number of shortcomings were discovered in the aircraft, most of which were directly related to the high temperatures encountered in the region. The most serious of these was a mysterious sequence of in-flight engine failures. This problem caused at least six known accidents, but fortunately not all of the aircraft were written off. The reason for these failures remained undetected until Maj Ran Peker lost his engine

ABOVE
A Mirage IIICJ from No 101 Sqn takes off for a training sortie during the War of Attrition. The aircraft is painted in the camouflage scheme adopted for combat missions, and carries six 'kill' markings just forward of the intake (IDFAF)

BELOW
Overhead view of one of four Mirage IIICJs that were converted into reconnaissance aircraft. These machines, together with a handful of specially modified Vautours, provided the backbone of IDFAF recce capability until the RF-4E Phantom IIs arrived (IDFAF)

while returning from a reconnaissance sortie over Port Said. He tried hard to regain his home base, but was forced to eject at very low level. The pilotless Mirage then glided on towards a 'perfect' wheels-up landing in a ploughed field, sustaining only moderate damage in the process (it was later repaired). An examination of the engine and its control system soon revealed that a fuel pump had failed because it was unable to sustain frequent exposure to such wide temperature variation. Once this was understood, a quick fix was devised, and the overall problem ended immediately.

Another serious shortcoming was the poor reliability of the Cyrano 1*bis* radar, which regularly overheated, and had a mean time between failures of only five hours! It was also operationally limited, with poor low-level performance and an apparent inconsistency in its combat-ranging function. This latter problem was only discovered after an exhaustive analysis of early combat results. It was found that the range obtained by the radar was indeed true, but it was being corrupted before presentation to the weapons sight. A group of technicians under the leadership of Maj Ephraim Ashcenazi, himself an experienced combat pilot, traced the problem to the transformation box between the radar and the Thomson-CSF sight. Only after this was fixed did the Mirage start scoring in combat. Despite all the time and effort that went into keeping the radar serviceable, it was never 100 per cent effective. After

A Rafael Shafrir 2 IR-guided AAM with cruciform steering vanes on its nose. Mirages and Neshers were credited with approximately 100 Shafrir 2 kills, and the missile was also used successfully by F-4Es and Super Mystères (Rafael)

the Six Day War the IDFAF removed it from most of the Mirage fleet, and simply fitted a ballast weight in the empty radome. The aircraft that did retain the radar had it pegged in the rangefinder-only mode.

There were also early difficulties with the aircraft's hydraulics. Caution lights on both systems (Hyd-1 and Hyd-2) frequently gave false warnings, terminating missions prematurely and causing unnecessary maintenance effort. Several aircraft also suffered nosewheel collapse during taxiing, and the behaviour of the afterburner clamshell nozzles was somewhat erratic, with one set of 'petals' cycling towards the 'open' position, while the other set was closing.

Despite these early difficulties, the Israelis were basically very pleased with the Mirage. Operational experience progressively resolved most of the problems, and as maintenance procedures improved, so the aircraft itself became more reliable. The IDFAF soon obtained Government permission to go ahead with the development of the long-range interdictor Mirage 5. A firm order for 50 was placed with Dassault, together with options on another 50. Deliveries were scheduled to begin in October 1967.

Shafrir

Towards the end of 1963, Rafael's Shafrir 1 IR-guided air-to-air missile was pressed into service. Its introduction was hurried through before full completion of the development programme, and as a result it was far from being a reliable weapon. Work on the Shafrir started in the late 1950s, and it took five years of trials and effort to turn it into an 'acceptable' device. One of the main problems was its relatively small warhead, which was not effective enough to

achieve a high kill rate with anything other than a direct hit. Unfortunately the seeker system was not wholly reliable, and could never be depended upon to provide that degree of accuracy. Many rounds of Shafrir 1 were fired during the 1967 Six Day War, but the missile's success rate was far lower than expected.

Shafrir 1 was obviously an unpopular weapon with Israeli pilots, and the Matra R530 was not much better. The missile itself was accurate enough, but its acquisition and launch parameters were so tight that it was rarely used—particularly in a fast-turning dogfight. Most of the air-to-air victories scored before 1969 were achieved with the Mirage's two 30 mm cannon.

Rafael started work on an improved Shafrir missile in 1963, and the development period lasted for about five years. The initial batch of Shafrir 2s reached the IDFAF during the first half of 1969. They were quickly put to good use during the so-called War of Attrition, with the first of 13 confirmed kills during that particular conflict coming on 24 July 1969. Since then, the Mk 2 weapon has completely restored Shafrir's reputation, achieving a much better kill rate than any other air-to-air missile of the period. During the brief Yom Kippur War of October 1973, Shafrir 2s destroyed no less than 102 enemy aircraft in a wide variety of combat situations.

During the early 1970s a number of US sources made extravagant claims that the Shafrir was a direct copy of the Sidewinder missile. Some of the technology used in the two weapons is similar, but the charge of copying has never been supported by any evidence and is clearly unfounded. The second-generation Shafrir was already in service with the IDFAF when the first Sidewinders arrived in Israel. The missiles are totally different in size; their IRseekers, sensor-gyros and servo mechanisms also vary considerably, as do their internal layout, warhead and fusing systems. The IDFAF acquired its first batch of AIM-9Ds in 1970, mainly because the Israeli missile was still being virtually hand-built at the time. This failure to use mass-production techniques pushed up the price of Shafrir, and significantly reduced its delivery rate. Under the circumstances, the Sidewinder buy was inevitable.

Nesher

After Israel's crushing defeat of the Arabs in the Six Day War, France imposed its arms embargo—initially on the delivery of the 50 Mirage 5Js, but later on military equipment of any description. This even had the effect, from December 1968, of denying access to all spares and systems improvements for the existing Mirage III fleet. The embargo was a formidable blow to Israel, and its own relatively inexperienced industry was forced into an ambitious expansion programme to fill the gap. One of the earliest results of this effort was the Rafael Mahut weapons-delivery computer, which was designed to enhance the bombing accuracy of the Mirage III during air-to-ground operations. Results of 12-Miliard were obtained in a series of tests that involved dropping 50 bombs from various heights and angles. The development programme ended in 1970, but by that time the F-4E Phantom II was well established in squadron service and the Mirage's role was focused more on interception missions. As a result, the Mahut system was never installed. One major product that did go into service was the Elta EL/M-2001 ranging radar, which was specifically designed for air-to-air combat at low altitude. This excellent new radar was not available in production quantities until 1973, and by then the indigenous Nesher was the main beneficiary.

The multi-role Nesher (Eagle) was perhaps the most remarkable outcome of the French sanctions. It was virtually a direct copy of the embargoed Mirage 5J, but manufactured entirely in Israel by Israel Aircraft Industries (IAI). When De Gaulle stopped delivery of the original Mirages, all the Israeli engineers that were working on the project in France returned home and began to set up an 'alternative' production line at IAI. The whole programme was shrouded in total secrecy at the time, but it is now known that Tel Aviv received a good deal of unofficial help from *Armée de l'Air* and Dassault engineers, who between them managed to provide exact manufacturing drawings and the necessary tools and jigs. At the same time, *Mossad*, the shadowy Israeli intelligence gathering service, was making contact with Alfred Frauenknecht, an engineer working for the Sulzer organization in Switzerland. Sulzer was building the Atar 09C under licence, and Frauenknecht supplied the Israelis with many blueprints of both the engine and the aircraft. He was

subsequently caught by Swiss police, and received a four-year prison sentence in return for his illicit activities.

Since the mid 1960s, in addition to its typical military overhaul work, IAI had been legitimately producing spare parts and components for the IDFAF's Mirage IIIC fleet. Beit Shemesh, the company's engine division, had also started building some Atar 09C3 components as part of an offset arrangement for the Mirage 5J contract. When the aircraft was embargoed, the 'official' engine component agreement lapsed, but clandestine work continued in Israel. The first complete engines were produced in 1968, initially with most of the components openly imported from France, but as the restrictions on military supplies began to tighten, more and more sections were copied and manufactured in Israel.

The prototype Nesher made its first flight in September 1969, piloted by the then chief test pilot of IAI, Danny Shapira. This was a fairly basic vehicle, which did little more than prove the aerodynamic limits and bring together some of the systems that had been tested separately in a modified Mirage IIIBJ. The definitive Nesher was first flown on 8 January 1971, again by Shapira. All subsequent production aircraft were powered by the copied Atar 09C3, which was, by 1971, wholly manufactured by Beit Shemesh. Apart from a few differences in detail, the Nesher was an exact duplicate of the French Mirage 5J, with its electronics bay in the nose and the 110 gal (500 lt) fuel cell in the space immediately behind the cockpit. It was fitted with a Martin-Baker JM6 zero-zero ejection seat. Most of the early aircraft were delivered with only a basic avionics package, because development of the combat electronics suite had lagged behind that of the airframe and engine programme. As soon as the equipment was made available, the 51 Nesher As and ten Nesher Bs (dual) were updated to squadron standard.

Deliveries started in May 1971: the first recipients were Nos 101 and 117 Sqns, which operated the Nesher along with their Mirage IIIs (No 119 Sqn was by then converting to F-4E Phantom IIs). In late 1972 a third unit—known as 'E' Squadron—converted to the Nesher at the new Etzion AB in Sinai. The markings of this new squadron consisted of a black and yellow checkered rudder, and a badge depicting a black bird over a yellow circle. A fourth unit, the former Ouragan squadron at Hatzor also converted to the Nesher during this period. The primary role of all Nesher units was interception and air superiority.

With the influx of the Nesher, Nos 101 and 117 squadrons became 'composite' units—operating several different versions of the delta-winged fighter at the same time. They each had French-built Mirage IIICJs, some with and some without radar, and some re-engined with the Atar 09C in place of the original 09B: some of the aircraft had even been rebuilt after accidental or combat damage, using part French and part IAI-manufactured components. Even the Neshers were not completely standard: some used French-supplied engines assembled in Israel, others used engines partly manufactured by Beit Shemesh, and the later batches used all-Israeli engines—a truly cosmopolitan group! Whenever possible, for both training and operational sorties, aircraft from similar 'batches' were flown together to avoid problems with performance variations. The fastest and less problem-prone aircraft were generally allocated to the 'hottest' pilots.

Production of the Nesher came to an end in 1975, by which time deliveries of the J79-powered Kfir were well under way. As the squadrons were re-equipped with Kfirs, the Neshers were stored to await disposal. Eventually the Argentinian Government bought 39 flyable examples, and another 20 broken down into spares. These were all delivered in two batches, during 1978–79 and 1981–82. The Nesher had completely disappeared from IDFAF service by 1983.

A new engine

As the French embargo tightened, it became clear to the Israelis that continued reliance on a 'French' engine could pose serious problems to the IDFAF, especially in the longer term, if aircraft needed updating or improving. It was therefore decided to look elsewhere for a suitable powerplant, and while the Nesher was being designed around a copy of the Atar, two groups of IAI engineers examined possible alternatives. Their work began in 1968, with one team looking at the General Electric J79, and the other concentrating on the Rolls-Royce Spey. After much deliberation the J79 was finally selected, mainly for political and economic reasons, rather than any technical superiority. In April 1969, the IDFAF loaned a Mirage IIIBJ (No 988) to IAI for a trial installation of the new engine. The first engine runs were completed in August 1970, and on 21 September, Danny Shapira flew the aircraft for the first time.

Kfir

As a result of their design work on the re-engined Mirage, IAI engineers put forward a suggestion for a J79-powered, enhanced-performance Nesher. This aircraft was called Raam (Thunder), and the first production examples could have been made available

in November 1973. After examining the basic proposal, the IDFAF saw considerable merit in the idea, but decided to go for a much more sophisticated machine altogether. A new proposal was requested for an aircraft with computerized weapons-delivery and navigation systems, pressure refuelling, liquid oxygen instead of the gaseous systems used on the Mirage and Nesher, and individual flight systems that were widely separated to ensure increased survivability. In November 1971 it was agreed that a

single prototype Raam should be built to prove the concept, but its series production was abandoned in favour of the more ambitious project.

Initially the new project was given the name Rackdan (Dancer), but this was changed to Kfir (Cub Lion) on the direct order of Gen Benjamin Peled, the then Commander-in-Chief of the IDFAF. The Kfir's airframe was firmly based on that of the Mirage/Nesher line, but the rear fuselage was slightly shorter, and of larger diameter, in order to accommodate the J79 engine. A large dorsal airscoop was installed at the base of the fin to supply cooling air to the afterburner, and the landing gear was strengthened and provided with longer-stroke oleos. The cockpit area was extensively changed, and a considerable amount of Israeli-made avionics equipment was fitted. To take maximum advantage of the more fuel-efficient J79, the internal tankage was slightly rearranged, and its capacity was increased to a total of 713 gal (3243 lt).

The prototype of the Kfir—which was in fact a conversion of Nesher No 712—was flown for the first time in June 1973. Production aircraft did not reach operational squadrons until well after the 1973 war, but variants of the design went on to become vital components of the IDFAF's combat capability. The development of the aircraft is briefly recorded here for completeness, because it was originally based on the Mirage structure. However, continual development of the Kfir airframe has now taken it several

BELOW LEFT
The IAI Nesher was basically a copy of the Mirage 5, developed and produced in Israel with some covert French assistance. A total of 61 Neshers were built by IAI between May 1971 and late 1974; they were excellent fair-weather air superiority fighters. The fin has a yellow and black identification triangle and the Shafrir pylons are empty as this aircraft taxies back from a combat mission during the Yom Kippur War (IDFAF)

BELOW
Nesher No 712 was converted into the Kfir prototype, and flew for the first time in this new form in June 1973. The wider rear fuselage and short jet pipe are both necessary in order to fit the J79 engine into the original narrow fuselage. The air scoop at the base of the fin is also characteristic of the Kfir (IDFAF via David Eshel)

steps beyond the initial Mirage concept, and as such, it falls outside the scope of this book.

Raam

The prototype Raam (a conversion of Nesher No 788) finally made its maiden flight on 4 June 1973, piloted by Assaf Ben-Nun. Right from the start its performance was extremely good, and it was flown to Mach 1.0 for the first time only 17 days later. Mach 2.4 was achieved on 10 December 1973, and on 16 December it reached a height of 75,000 feet. After its initial aerodynamic trials, it was converted to test canard control surfaces for the updated Kfir C2—a programme that it shared with the J79-powered Mirage IIIBJ. The Raam first flew in this new configuration on 23 March 1975, piloted by Mennachem Shmul, but it was lost only eight weeks later when it crashed into the Mediterranean on 25 May: the pilot ejected safely. Its place on the test programme was taken by a converted Kfir C1 (No 714).

Mirages updated ...

After the 1973 Yom Kippur War, the surviving Israeli Mirage IIIs were put through an important update programme. The aircraft progressively passed into the IAI workshops on a rotational schedule that finally lasted over 18 months. All the original Atar 09Bs were replaced by the more powerful 09C; the wings were re-skinned and additional stores stations were fitted: the inboard pylons were wired to launch AIM-9 or Shafrir 2 missiles (making it possible to carry four AAMs in total) and improved avionics were installed, including a state-of-the-art Radar Warning Receiver (RWR), new VHF radios and a dorsal blade-antenna. Some of the aircraft also received a new 'air-superiority grey' camouflage scheme.

... and finally retired

During the early 1980s, with the F-15 Eagle equipping two squadrons and the F-16 Fighting Falcon in the process of re-equipping three more, the IDFAF finally decided to retire its veteran Mirage IIIs. The last operational sorties were flown in 1982—20 years after the aircraft first entered Israeli service. By that time, after so many years of combat losses as well as normal attrition, there were relatively few of the original 76 aircraft available for disposal. Nevertheless, the Argentinian Government, desperate to replace its Falklands losses, managed to acquire 22 operational airframes (a similar deal involving redundant Israeli A-4 Skyhawks was vetoed by the United States). The Argentine purchase included 19 Mirage IIICJs and three two-seat Mirage IIIBJs, together with a smaller number of single-seat aircraft broken down into spares.

The Mirage had served the Israelis exceptionally well, not only in the combat arena, but also as the unwitting spur to the development of an effective aircraft industry. Many pilots carry irreplaceable memories of the Mirage, and stories of its combat performance are still held in high regard within the IDFAF—especially for those squadrons that operated the aircraft so successfully.

Of the original three squadrons, No 119 converted first, becoming an F-4E Phantom unit during 1971.

No 101 Sqn converted to the Kfir in 1975, initially with the Kfir C1, followed by the canard-equipped C2, and then the much-improved C7 variant. No 117 Sqn was re-equipped with F-16s in 1980, but some Mirages and Neshers were retained by a 'shadow' squadron which was administered by No 117 Sqn until F-16 deliveries were completed in 1982. A number of this special unit's aircraft carried markings that included a blue rudder and a black-and-white chevron.

Three members of the Mirage family are now preserved in the IDFAF Museum:

LEFT
This IAI-modified Mirage IIICJ is equipped with the Atar 09C engine and updated Israeli avionics, as shown by the dorsal blade antenna. It is painted in the 'air superiority grey' camouflage scheme (IDFAF)

BELOW
A pair of Israeli Mirage IIICJs, probably from No 101 Sqn, flying near Massada. No 755 was sold to Argentina in the early 1980s, and No 778—which was credited with two 'kills' in combat with Arab aircraft—is believed to have been reduced to spares (via AMD/BA)

No 111. A Mirage IIICJ that was presented to the Museum on IDFAF Day in 1983. The aircraft is painted to represent a combat veteran with 13 kills (seven Egyptian and six Syrian) to its credit, but during its active service days it was only ever photographed with one such 'kill' marking. The 13 now applied may be for display purposes only, although at least two other Mirages (No 159 and No 458/758) have been credited with 13 kills each.

No 712. Built in Israel as a standard production Nesher, but subsequently converted into the prototype Kfir. First flown as Nesher in 1971, and then as the Kfir in June 1973.

No 988. Modified two-seat Mirage IIIBJ with General Electric J79 engine. First flown by Dassault in France, but re-engined in 1970. Also fitted with canards for research into Kfir C2 aerodynamics; first flight in this configuration was in July 1974. Since it was re-engined in 1970, this aircraft has carried the nickname 'Technology'.

Chapter 6
Neshers and Mirage IIIs in combat

Early skirmishes of the MiG slayers

Air-to-air

During the period between 1963 and 1965, Israeli Mirages were involved in a number of inconclusive engagements with Syrian AF MiG-17s and MiG-21s, and with Jordanian AF Hawker Hunters. Their lack of early combat success was directly attributable to the failure of the Cyrano radar-ranging function, and to inadequate development of the indigenous Shafrir 1 air-to-air guided missile. The Shafrir was to remain troublesome until the second generation weapons were made available in 1969, but the aircraft itself began to score an increasing number of victories with cannon fire as soon as the radar problem was resolved.

On 14 July 1966, a formation of four Mirages from No 101 Sqn covered IDFAF strikes into Syria, in response to an artillery barrage that had been launched against Israeli territory. Two Syrian AF MiG-21s were scrambled, and the Mirages engaged them. Captain (now Brig Gen, retired) Yoram Agmun was No 4 in the formation, and after some tight manoeuvring he positioned his aircraft about 1000 feet behind one of the MiGs. He fired his 30 mm guns and missed. Closing to about 500 feet, he fired again, and this time his burst impacted on the MiG's starboard wing-root, which broke away from the fuselage trailing smoke and flames. The pilot was seen to eject. This was the first 'kill' achieved by an IDFAF Mirage III, and the aircraft involved was

Four Mirages from No 101 Sqn on patrol over the Negev Desert. The aircraft are still in their natural metal finish, with very early red and white squadron identification markings (IDFAF)

No 159, which was eventually destined to have a remarkably colourful career.

The second successful combat was on 15 August 1966. A number of Syrian MiG-17s attacked an Israeli patrol boat on the Kinneret Lake, while MiG-21s acted as their top cover. Mirages were scrambled and a dogfight developed, in which Capt Yehuda shot down a MiG-21 with gunfire. The Syrian aircraft fell into the lake, but this time the pilot failed to escape.

On 13 November 1966, some Royal Jordanian AF Hunters were intercepted over Samoa. Maj Ran Peker, one of the Mirage squadron commanders, found himself involved in an eight-minute dogfight with one of these aircraft—perhaps one of the longest man-to-man encounters in the history of jet fighter operations. He chased the Hunter at very low level, for what must have seemed like an eternity from the Mirage cockpit. The Jordanian aircraft was expertly flown by a pilot later named as Miwafac Scati, and despite the performance differences between the combatants, it took Peker the full eight minutes to get the target more or less steady in his sights. When he did open fire, he scored several hits on the fuselage and wings, and the Hunter's fuel tanks began to burn. Scati straightened up and tried to hold the aircraft level but suddenly the Hunter rolled violently and smashed into a canyon wall.

On 29 November 1966, two Egyptian AF MiG-19s tried to intercept an IDFAF Piper Cub flying over Nitchana, just inside Israel's southern border. Two Mirages from No 101 Sqn were launched in response, and both MiGs were destroyed. The Mirage pilots both fired their R530 missiles—one of which missed its target completely, but the other scored a direct hit, blowing the EAF fighter to bits and killing its pilot instantly. The second MiG was shot down with 30 mm cannon fire, by the Israeli pilot who had already scored the R530 kill.

On 7 April 1967 the Israeli Mirage pilots had their best day so far. In three separate engagements, six Syrian MiG-21s were shot down, all of them with

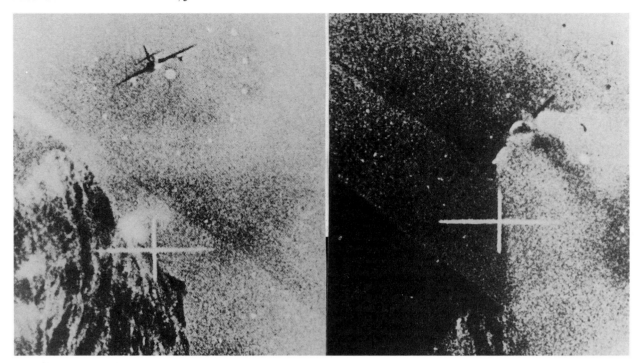

gunfire. The first battle, involving two Mirages and four MiG-21s, took place between Kuneitra, on the Golan Heights, and Damascus: two of the MiGs were destroyed. The second skirmish of the day occurred over the northern end of the Golan Heights, and resulted in the destruction of another MiG-21. Finally, in the last engagement, three more Syrian MiGs were drawn into the open and shot down, all of them crashing on Jordanian territory. Four of the six victories were later claimed by No 101 Sqn, and among the successful IDFAF pilots were Ezra Dothan and Ran Peker.

Up to June 1967, a total of 11 air-to-air victories had been scored by the Israeli Mirages, with no combat losses to themselves. One aircraft was lost however, when it ran out of fuel while returning from an inconclusive battle with RJAF Hunters.

Air-to-ground
The Israeli Mirage IIIs are best remembered for their excellent air-to-air combat record, but they also performed well in the demanding surface-attack role. Their first operational use in this guise took place in November 1964, when Capt Ezra Dothan led four Mirages of No 117 Sqn (then under the command of Maj David Ivri) to attack Syrian installations on the Golan Heights. The results from that raid were good, but it was still considered more profitable to use the Mirage as top cover for some of the more specialized ground-attack aircraft, so further raids were not exactly encouraged. This situation was generally maintained until 1967, when Israel reacted to increasing tension in the area. This was the year of the Six Day War, and the ground-attack capabilities of the Mirage were used to devastating effect.

Six Day War

During May 1967 the Egyptian leader, Col Nasser, insisted that a post-Suez UN Peacekeeping Force be withdrawn from the Sinai Peninsula. He also effectively closed the Straits of Tiran, cutting off the southern end of the Gulf of Aqaba, and denying open access to Israel's only southern port at Eilat. On 30 May, Egypt and Jordan signed a defence co-operation pact, and on the following day, Iraqi troops were welcomed into Jordan to bolster the combined Arab forces.

Not unnaturally, the Israelis began to feel boxed in by these manoeuvres, and the threat of attack from all sides began to look very real. By early June, the military situation was being reassessed almost hourly, and it seemed increasingly certain that the country was facing an attack of monumental proportions. Based on the clearest possible evidence of a massive build-up and reorganization of Arab forces, it was decided that Israel should seize the initiative immediately, and strike at the enemy before his preparations were complete. The ensuing battles became classic demonstrations of the effective projection of air power, and the tactical brilliance of the plan is still discussed in military colleges all over the world. The campaign overwhelmed the Arab forces so rapidly, that it was later to become known as the Six Day War.

Day 1 (5 June 1967)
The Mirages started the war not in their familiar air-to-air role, but as ground-attack aircraft forming part of a much-practised pre-emptive strike against Egyptian AF bases. To achieve the maximum

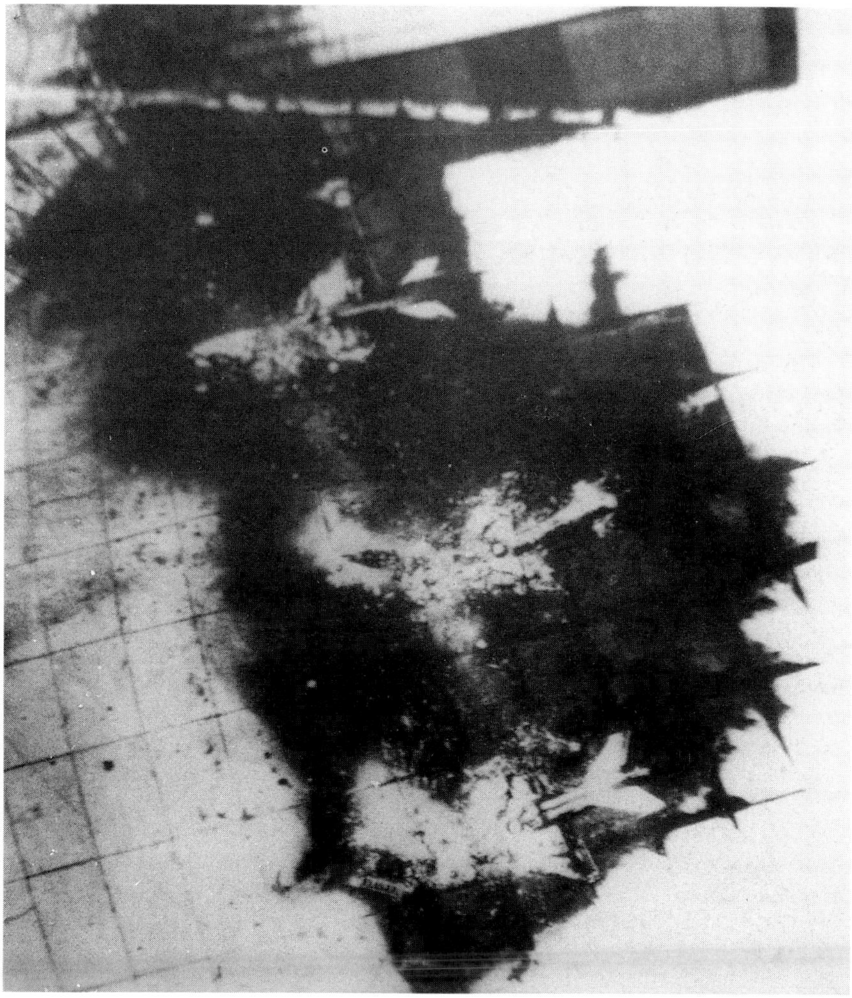

LEFT
Ran Peker's victory of 13 November 1966, as seen through the gunsight of his Mirage. In the left-hand picture the port external tank of the Hunter has just taken a hit, and the right-hand picture shows the port wing and starboard external tank 'torching' as vapourized fuel is released into the airstream by the Mirage's cannon shells. Seconds later, the Hunter crashed and exploded (IDFAF)

RIGHT
These three MiG-21s were among many Egyptian aircraft destroyed by the first wave attack on Inchas AB (IDFAF)

possible surprise, the first wave of aircraft was launched at 07:45 hrs. The Mirages were divided into flights of four, and they approached their targets at very low level to avoid detection until the last possible moment. After a brief 'pop-up' manoeuvre to drop two cratering bombs each on the runways, the pilots were authorized to make three strafing runs on parked aircraft, before clearing the area for the next formation. Each attack lasted 10–15 minutes, and at least one Mirage formation did *five* strafing runs before leaving Inchas AB at the mercy of an attacking Super Mystère squadron. Each Mirage unit left four of its aircraft on intercept-alert back at home base, but for the first three hours they were left without any 'trade'; only when the second wave of Israelis attacked at about 10:00 hrs did the Egyptian AF rise to offer any resistance. The reserve Mirages were then quickly launched to intercept the Egyptian fighters.

The bases attacked by Mirages in the first wave were as follows: Inchas, led by Maj Ran Peker; Abu Sueir, led by Maj Amihai; Beni-Suef, led by No 117 Sqn, who were followed by No 101 Sqn; Bir Gafgafa (also known as Meliz AB to the Egyptian AF, and when later occupied by the IDFAF it became Refidim AB), No 101 Sqn; Cairo West, a formation from No 101 Sqn, led by Capt Oded Marom and Maj Amos Lapidot; Faid, No 117 Sqn; and Bir Tmade, No 101 Sqn. Most attack leaders experienced some degree of navigation difficulty because of the morning mists, but each formation found its target, and the Egyptians were taken completely unawares. Only one air-to-air kill was recorded by the first wave of Mirages: a top cover pair from No 101 Sqn shot down an Il-14 transport that was unlucky enough to be acting as an airborne command post over the Jabel Libni area.

The second wave of attackers launched at about 09:30 hrs. The Egyptian AF, although badly mauled by the first raids, managed to scramble a few of its remaining interceptors, and a number of dogfights developed over the Abu Sueir area. Capt Eythan Carmi and Lt Giora Rom of No 119 Sqn were each credited with two kills, although Carmi had to abandon his Mirage later due to fuel starvation. Over the Nile Delta, Capt Yair Noyman of No 101 Sqn was shot down by a MiG-21, but one of his squadron colleagues evened the score by destroying an Egyptian aircraft. The second wave of Mirages attacked the following bases: Abu Sueir, led by Ran Peker; Cairo West, No 101 Sqn; Cairo International,

No 101 Sqn; Helwan, No 101 Sqn; Bilbeis, No 101 Sqn; and finally El Minaya, No 101 Sqn, led by Lt Col Zoric Lev.

The third wave took off at about noon, and this time the Royal Jordanian AF was also attacked because its Hunters had earlier raided Kfor Sirkin AB, and because Jordanian artillery had opened up on Israeli targets. After attacking Ardaka AB on the Red Sea coast the Israeli formation, led by Maj Ran Peker, was intercepted by four Egyptian AF MiG-19s. During the battle that followed Peker was credited with two kills, Lt Arnor got a third, and the fourth broke up and exploded after trying to land on the bomb-damaged runway. A second Israeli formation bound for Ardaka was diverted to Amman, and became the first unit to attack the RJAF base adjacent to the civilian airfield. A Mirage pilot from No 119 Sqn was credited with a Jordanian Hunter during this strike. At about the same time (around 14:00 hrs) Capt Ori Aven-Nir, second-in-command of No 117 Sqn, shot down another Hunter—only this time it belonged to a hapless Lebanese AF pilot who strayed into the battle area after allowing his curiosity to get the better of him! Luckily he was able to eject from his aircraft over Rayak AB in Lebanon.

The fourth wave got airborne in the early afternoon (around 16:00 hrs), and among the bases attacked by Mirages were Egypt's Cairo West, led by Ran Peker; and the Syrian AF facilities at Damascus El-Maza, led by Maj Giora Forman; and Damascus itself, led by Maj Amihai. During these raids two of the Mirages were lost to ground-based AA fire. Lt Shar was killed, but Maj Amihai managed to eject over

Israeli territory, despite being wounded: he was later replaced as squadron leader by Capt Ori Aven-Nir. The Syrian tactical airfield known as T4 was also attacked that afternoon. Led by Capt Eythan Carmi, this raid was intercepted by a Syrian AF standing patrol, but the Mirages downed both of the defending MiG-21s. Capt Asher Snir and Lt Giora Rom were credited with one MiG each. The No 101 Sqn machines attacking Cairo West managed to evade several SA-2 surface-to-air missiles launched against them. During the late afternoon and early evening, Mirages were also used to attack Jordanian artillery batteries near Jenin, and to escort helicopters searching for IDFAF aircrews who had been forced to abandon their aircraft over enemy territory.

By the end of the first day of the war, the IDFAF had virtually destroyed the Royal Jordanian and Egyptian Air Forces, severely damaged the Syrian Air Force, and struck at the Iraqi Air Force forward base known as H3. The most conservative estimates put the number of Arab aircraft destroyed on the ground at over 300. No 101 Sqn claimed 30 including 13 Tu-16 bombers during the raids on Cairo West, and at least three MiG-21s in air-to-air combat.

No 101 Sqn claimed at least 30 Arab aircraft destroyed by the end of the first day, including most of the Egyptian strategic bomber force caught on the ground at Cairo West airfield. Here a Tu-16 'Badger' burns fiercely, while another appears to have escaped damage (IDFAF)

Day 2 (6 June 1967)

After their marauding raids into enemy territory on the first day of the war, the Mirages were mainly used for air superiority missions on the second day, protecting the IDF ground forces as they advanced across the Sinai. During the early morning a lone Iraqi AF Tupolev Tu-16 bombed Ramat David AB, causing only light damage and a few craters out on the perimeter. The *Badger* was quickly intercepted by a Mirage, which launched a Shafrir 1 missile. Despite receiving a direct hit (rare enough in itself), the bomber was only damaged by the small warhead and continued to fly away. It was finally shot down and credited to the crew of a Bofors L/70 40 mm AA gun.

Shortly after the Tu-16's visit—but unrelated to it—four IDFAF Vautours took off to strike again at H3, the Iraqi forward base that may well have been the bomber's temporary home. The Vautours were escorted by two Mirages led by Capt Yehuda Corn. The formation was intercepted above H3 by standing patrols of MiG-21s and Hunters, and although Corn himself was credited with one of each type destroyed, the sortie was regarded as a tactical failure.

Also in the early morning, Egyptian AF Sukhoi Su-7 fighter-bombers (which had only recently been delivered to Egypt) attacked the IDF forces occupying El Arish AB in the Sinai. This raid was intercepted by Mirages, and three of the Su-7s were shot down. The Mirage was also used to attack Syrian artillery and heavy mortar positions that were shelling settlements just inside the Israeli border. The AA activity in the area was considered to be particularly heavy, and two aircraft were forced to make emergency landings as a result of damage caused by this gunfire. The first of these incidents occurred in the morning, after the aircraft had attacked a Syrian forward command post at Kuneitra, and the second (flown by Lt Giora Rom) followed a raid on a stronghold near the Bnot-Ya'akab bridge. During the air-to-air combats on 6 June, No 101 Sqn was credited with the destruction of four Su-7s, two MiG-19s and a MiG-21.

Day 3 (7 June 1967)

The third day of the war saw the last and least successful raid against the aggressive Iraqis at H3. This time four Mirages, led by Maj Ezra Dothan, escorted the four attacking Vautours. As on the two previous raids, the formation was 'bounced' by defending Iraqi Hunters, and two of the Vautours were lost—the leading IIN and a single-seat IIA. One of the Mirages was also shot down, but its pilot, Capt Gideon Dror, managed to eject and was captured. All three IDFAF aircraft had fallen victim to the tactical skills of RAF-trained Iraqi pilots. As far as the Israelis were concerned, the only positive thing to come out of the whole raid was a single Hunter claimed by Dothan.

At about noon, four Mirages escorted an assault force of airborne troops in Super Frelon and Sikorsky S-58 helicopters, to occupy Sharm el Sheikh, in the south of the Sinai peninsula. Two of the aircraft bombed and strafed the area before the heliborne landing, while the pair on top-cover duties shot down two MiGs that were on their way to attack the force.

Later in the day, Maj Dothan and Yehuda Polak were sent on a reconnaissance mission to locate the four missing aircrew at H3. They failed to do so, but on their return leg, while flying at well over 30,000 feet above Gabel-Droz in Syria, Dothan received a direct hit from a Soviet-made AA-2 *Atoll* air-to-air missile. The weapon had been fired by a clever Syrian AF MiG-21 pilot, who had managed to get within range entirely undetected. Although badly damaged, the Mirage was still flyable, and Dothan nursed it back to make a safe landing at an Israeli forward airstrip.

During the afternoon, a formation of Mirages destroyed an Egyptian radar site in the Ardaka area, on the Red Sea coast. Three Mirages were also sent to attack Egyptian armour between Ras-Sudar and Sharem, but on the way they encountered two MiG-17s that were in hot pursuit of a pair of Israeli Super Mystères. The Mirages immediately engaged the MiGs, and Lt Giora Rom shot them both down, achieving his fourth and fifth kills of the conflict.

Day 4 (8 June 1967)

The Mirage squadrons maintained their air superiority role throughout 8 June, but by that time enemy air activity had decreased noticeably. Lt Giora Rom conducted two long patrols over the Sinai region, and failed to make contact with a single Egyptian aircraft. Other areas did at least see some activity. Lt Col Zoric Lev, an ex Mirage squadron commander, achieved his first kill when he shot down an Egyptian MiG-17 over Romani, and Capt Ahud Hankin destroyed a Syrian MiG-21 with gunfire at point-blank range—an action that nearly cost him his life, because his own Mirage was badly damaged by debris from the exploding MiG. During the third and fourth days of the war, Mirages flown by Capts Benjamin Rommach and Baruch David were both shot down by SA-2 surface-to-air missiles: both men were killed.

During the late afternoon, two Mirages patrolling the Romani area were diverted to provide air cover for Israeli naval forces. An unidentified ship had been seen near the coast at El Arish, and several torpedo boats were sent to intercept it. The overflying Mirage pilots could see no flags or other identification, so they made a number of strafing runs without any retaliation from the ship. Short of fuel, the Mirages broke off the engagement and returned to base. They were replaced by a pair of Super Mystère B2s, which attacked the unfortunate ship with napalm. One of the Mystère pilots reported seeing the letters 'CVT' on the hull, and an alert IDFAF operations officer realized that it was an American vessel, and called the aircraft off. This message somehow failed to get

through to the naval forces, and six torpedoes were fired at the intruder. After the attack an American flag was finally seen, and the ship was identified as the USS *Liberty*—an intelligence-gathering unit of the US 6th Fleet. The torpedo boats immediately offered every assistance, and a Super Frelon was sent to evacuate the wounded. Perhaps understandably, the American captain refused to have the Israelis anywhere near his ship, preferring to wait for the US Navy helicopters that were already on their way. The whole incident—which killed over 30 of the ship's company—came very close to provoking a massive retaliation from the 6th Fleet's strike aircraft.

Day 5 (9 June 1967)

With IDF troops occupying Sinai and the West Bank area so completely, Egypt accepted the terms of a UN ceasefire at 04:35 hrs on 9 June. Syria tried to do the same, but Israel was not prepared to accept any agreement that left Arab forces in control of the vital Golan Heights region. At 11:30 hrs IDF forces launched an all-out attack on the Golan defences, forcing Syrian troops back to defend Damascus. Most of the air activity to support the offensive consisted of ground-attack sorties by Mystères, Super Mystères, Magisters and Ouragans. Mirages were involved in limited air-to-air combat further south, over the now occupied Sinai Peninsula. Capts Hankin and Avi Lanir made contact with two MiG-17s while escorting Vautour bombers to the Mitla Pass, and while Hankin shot one of them down fairly quickly, Lanir had to chase the other one until it finally crashed in the Cairo area!

Day 6 (10 June 1967)

By the end of Friday 9 June, IDF ground forces had

pushed nearly four miles into Syria, and during the night paratroopers were dropped behind the Syrian lines, further isolating the already beleaguered Golan defensive positions. Additional airborne landings were made on 10 June, and while these troops moved on towards Kuneitra—the Syrian High Command HQ, some 20 miles inside the border—the Golan area was again attacked by Israeli air and land forces. The war was now rapidly drawing to a close, and the last significant action involving Mirages occurred while Capt Eythan Carmi was leading Lt Col Shmuel Sheffer (the Tel Nof AB commander) to attack Syrian forces in the Sheikh Maskin region. Sheffer was hit by AA fire, and although wounded, he managed to eject at very low level. A rescue mission was mounted, and while the vulnerable helicopter removed Sheffer from a highly dangerous area, two Mirages strafed Syrian troops to prevent any interference with the operation.

Ceasefire

The end to hostilities was finally negotiated by the United Nations on the evening of Saturday 10 June, leaving Israel firmly in control of the Golan Heights. The Mirage squadrons had entered the war in good shape, with 65 aircraft fully operational. At the end of the conflict, the IDFAF confirmed an overall total of 58 air-to-air victories, and Mirages were credited with 48 of these, all of which were achieved by gunfire (Shafrir 1 missiles were used many times in air battles, but they failed to achieve a single kill). The tally of confirmed Mirage victories comprised nine MiG-17s, 12 MiG-19s, 15 MiG-21s, five Su-7s, five Hunters, an Il-14 and an Il-28. Two Arab aircraft also crashed independently while being chased at low level by Mirages: these are not included in the totals shown above, nor are the many aircraft destroyed on the ground during raids on Arab airfields. This figure is difficult to fix exactly, but gun-camera and photo recce evidence suggests that the total could be as high as 120 machines of all types. Lt Giora Rom emerged as the leading air-to-air 'Ace' with five confirmed victories: others, including Capt Asher Snir and Lt Menachem Shmul, were credited with three apiece, and quite a number of pilots were credited with two. The top-scoring unit was No 119 Squadron, which also had the lowest casualty rate, with only two Mirages lost and both pilots recovered. Twelve of the victories were achieved by No 117 Sqn. Numerous accounts of the war have established the myth that some Israeli pilots flew up to eight missions on 5 June. This is simply not true. The maximum number of missions flown on any day was four, and even this figure was achieved only by the most senior pilots.

'Their finest hour'
IDFAF Mirages between 1967 and 1973

The period between the end of the Six Day War in July 1967 and the start of the Yom Kippur War in October 1973 has been likened to an extended Battle of Britain, with the Israeli State borders under attack from all directions. This was particularly true during the so-called War of Attrition in the Suez Canal area between March 1969 and August 1970. This was the longest of the Middle East conflicts up till then, and it came very close to developing into a wider international issue when the Soviet AF began to take a more active part in the confrontation. Until the arrival of the first F-4E Phantom II in September 1969, the Mirage played a dominant role in the air-to-air fighting, and the period has become known as the 'finest hour' for its pilots.

The first air combat after the Six Day War took place on 8 July 1967, when two Mirages intercepted four MiG-21s in the Port Said area. A battle developed, and one of the Soviet-made interceptors was claimed. A week later, on 15 July, the Shafrir 1 missile was finally credited with its first kill. Maj Ran Peker led four Mirages to intercept eight MiG-21s in the Suez Canal area, and during a running fight towards the west, he shot one of them down over the Nile Delta: the Shafrir was launched at a range of about 1250 m, and scored a direct hit. Two other MiGs were also downed by cannon fire. Later that day, a Sukhoi Su-7 and a MiG-17 were shot down in separate combats, while on the debit side a Mirage was destroyed by Egyptian AA guns. The Su-7 pilot ejected safely over the Sinai and was taken prisoner by the IDF.

There were no further incidents until 10 October 1967, when an Egyptian MiG-21 was shot down with

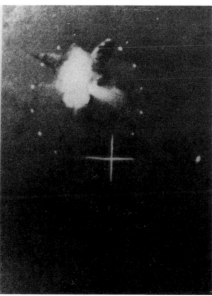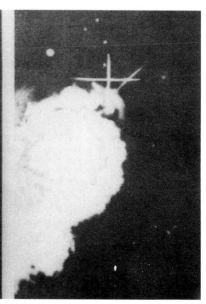

LEFT
The War of Attrition has been likened to the Battle of Britain, and fast turn-round times were essential if the Israeli Mirages were to remain on effective alert. The weapons trolley is used to lift heavy 30 mm ammunition (IDFAF)

RIGHT
Mirage IIICJ No 779 basks in the sun at one of the Sinai bases. The dust covers on the intakes are a vital precaution in desert conditions, despite the aircraft being fully armed with Shafrirs and held on instant readiness (IDFAF via David Eshel)

BELOW RIGHT
A good example of deflection shooting, as an EAF MiG-21 is cut to pieces by a well aimed burst of 30 mm gunfire from an Israeli Nesher. This kind of passing shot is far from easy, because accurate judgement of the relative velocities of the two aircraft is needed (IDFAF)

gunfire by a Mirage. A short time later, during the night of 21 October, a formation of Mirages helped in the search for survivors from the Israeli Navy destroyer *Eylath*, which had been sunk by *Styx* surface-to-surface missiles off the coastal region of Romani. Despite its poor air-to-air performance, a few of the Mirages had retained the Cyrano radar for surveillance missions, and its ability to detect even the smallest objects on the sea was put to good use during this lengthy search operation. Some of the aircraft patrolled the area to provide top cover for the rescue helicopters, while others launched parachute-type flares for illumination.

During this time the Soviets were providing massive aid to the depleted air forces of Egypt and Syria, while their pilots were learning new tactics to enable them to master the aggressive Israelis. This reorganization was certainly reflected in subsequent engagements, because until 10 December 1968, there were no conclusive combats. On that day, a pair of fighter-bomber MiG-17s were intercepted south of Sharm el-Sheikh, and one was hit by Mirage cannon fire before crashing into the sea. The Mirages were part of a four-ship detachment that had been based at Refidim AB in the occupied Sinai since late 1967. They were moved there in order to catch just such a raid of Egyptian low-level marauders.

On 12 February 1969, over the relatively quiet northern front near Kuneitra, a Syrian AF MiG-21 was shot down with cannon fire. Just twelve days later, IDFAF ground attack aircraft undertook a massive raid against PLO targets in Syria. Mirages were used for top cover protection of the raiders, and they downed two MiG-17s that were probably flown by Palestinian pilots. On 3 March, an Egyptian AF MiG-21 was shot down by a Mirage from No 101 Squadron, over the Great Bitter Lake.

The War of Attrition

Gamal Abdel Nasser, the Egyptian President throughout this period, felt that Arab honour had been torn to shreds by the Israelis, and steadfastly refused to accept any kind of settlement or diplomatic moves towards restoring peace to the area. He clearly wanted revenge, and by early 1969 he felt strong enough to attempt to regain the Sinai by military action. Thus began the conflict that became known as the War of Attrition—started to all intents and purposes on 8 March 1969, when Egyptian artillery on the west bank of the Suez Canal initiated a co-ordinated bombardment of Israeli positions on the other side. Air activity in the region increased sharply, and No 101 Sqn established Mirage detachments at a number of Sinai air bases in order to improve reaction times. The aircraft were used as interceptors, for 'planned air combat' (the classic ambush technique), for reconnaissance, and to provide top-cover for attacking aircraft.

On the first day of the conflict four Egyptian MiG-21s were intercepted at low level over the Sinai, and one was shot down. The pilot ejected and was subsequently taken prisoner. On 14 April another four EAF MiG-21s were spotted by two Mirages. The Egyptians turned towards their own secure territory, but the Israeli pilots chased them until one of the MiGs was hit, exploding over Egyptian soil seconds after the pilot was seen to eject. On 5 May,

another MiG-21 was added to the mounting score of No 101 Sqn, and on 21 May another formation of four MiG-21s was intercepted, this time by four Mirages. After a short skirmish one of the MiGs was shot down over Egyptian territory, and then a second had its wing blown off by Mirage gunfire, giving one of the Israeli pilots his fifth kill. The action switched to the north on 29 May, when the Syrians tried their hand at challenging the IDFAF. The raid was not a success, and one of the intruders was downed with a Shafrir missile over the Kuneitra area, its pilot managing to eject safely within Syrian-controlled territory.

On 17 June four reconnaissance Mirages, led by Amos Amir, penetrated deep into Egypt and broke the sound barrier at very low altitude over Cairo. In the process they smashed windows all across the capital, and for several minutes scared its citizens half to death! This was a very public display of air superiority, and Nasser was furious that such a thing could be allowed to happen. He reacted swiftly to the operation, and instantly dismissed the Chiefs of Staff of both the Egyptian Air Force, and its Air Defence Command.

The Israelis also started Operation 'Rimonim' in June. This phase of the conflict saw IDFAF Mirages systematically flying into Egyptian territory south of Suez city, in order to draw the MiG-21s into open combat. The route was carefully chosen to avoid the formidable array of surface-to-air missile batteries installed along the Suez Canal, and the selected SAM-free battle area was so wide-ranging that it was called 'Texas' by the Israeli pilots. Within the space of a few days, nine MiG-21s were downed by this operation. The first aircraft was shot down with gunfire on 24 June, with only a few 30 mm rounds expended before the MiG's rear exploded in spectacular fashion. On 26 June four more were destroyed in three separate combats, two with cannon and two with air-to-air missiles. A single aircraft was shot down on 2 July, rapidly followed by another pair, all of which fell victim to Mirage guns.

It was clear that the IDFAF enjoyed total air superiority at that time, and this was well understood by the Egyptian AF. Under the circumstances, any EAF aircraft attempting to cross the Suez Canal was inviting disaster. July had seen a major escalation of the war, and the IDFAF was used to provide a quick-reaction 'flying artillery' in the Canal Zone. Whenever the Egyptian Army opened up on Israeli troops, the Sinai-based squadrons would mount immediate and devastating reprisal attacks. The relatively quiet northern border also exploded into action briefly on 8 July, and seven Syrian AF MiG-21s were shot down in two separate engagements.

On 20 July 1969, Operation 'Boxer' was mounted by the IDFAF. This consisted of attacks on Egyptian positions along an axis from Kantara to Port Said. The Egyptian AF rose to the challenge, and several dogfights developed in which two MiG-21s, two MiG-17s and an Su-7 were downed by Mirages.

During these battles, a Mirage from No 101 Sqn was shot down by an *Atoll* AAM launched from a MiG-21; the Israeli pilot managed to eject over Sinai. Four days later, seven Egyptian aircraft—four Su-7s, two MiG-17s and a MiG-21—were claimed in air combat, by anti-aircraft fire, and by Hawk SAMs. The day was significant because one of the kills was made by a Mirage equipped with Shafrir 2 missiles. This weapon was to become the most reliable AAM to enter service with the IDFAF, and before the 1973 Yom Kippur War it would be credited with 13 confirmed kills.

The next Egyptian AF offensive occurred on 11 September. During the morning EAF MiG-17s and Su-7s—with MiG-21s as top cover—tried to attack the Israeli-controlled northern part of the Canal Zone. One of the MiG-21s was destroyed in combat with Mirages over Kantara. Later, the EAF turned its attention to the Ras Massala area, where a MiG-21 and an Su-7 were brought down. The IDFAF's reprisal for these raids was swift and decisive. During the afternoon attacks were made against Egyptian positions near the Nile Delta, and the escorting Mirages engaged defending MiG-21s in combat, and shot three of them down. One of the Egyptian pilots achieved a significant success when he shot down Capt Giora Rom, the IDFAF's top scorer during the Six Day War. Rom was hit by an 'Atoll' AAM, but he managed to eject safely over Mansura, and was taken prisoner. During an air battle on 6 October, two more EAF MiG-21s were destroyed: both were hit by cannon fire, but in each case the pilot was seen to eject over Egyptian territory.

During September 1969, the first four McDonnell Douglas F-4E Phantom IIs had been delivered to Hatzor AB, and the arrival of this outstanding 'heavy duty' fighter signalled a new era for the IDFAF. The Phantom achieved operational status very quickly, and on 11 November its first kill was recorded in the shape of a MiG-21 shot down near Suez city. Two MiG-21s were also brought down by Mirages on the same day. (Because of the confused nature of modern air combat—particularly when missiles are involved—it is possible that individual victories will be claimed by both Phantom and Mirage squadrons.) On 27 November, a single EAF MiG-21 was added to the increasing Mirage tally as the result of a chase that started in the Ismailia area, and concluded with the Egyptian pilot ejecting about 40 km west of the Canal. On the northern border with Syria, Mirages bagged two more MiG-17s and a MiG-21 near Damascus: one of the MiG-17s was credited to Israel Aircraft Industries' chief test pilot, Menachem Shmul, who was more recently involved in the flight-test programme of the IAI Lavi fighter.

The first air combat of the new year took place over the Canal Zone on 4 January 1970, when two Egyptian MiG-21s were claimed by Mirages: four days later, three Syrian AF MiGs were shot down in

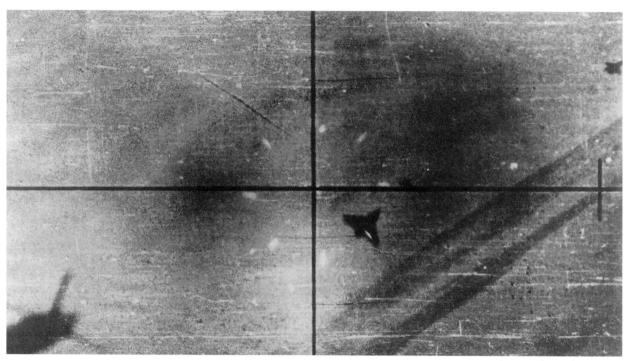

ABOVE
The Israeli pilots did not have it all their own way! Here a Mirage in hot pursuit of an EAF MiG-21 seems unaware that he too is about to be caught by the pipper of an Egyptian gunsight (EAF)

RIGHT
During the heat of battle, a Syrian AF pilot defected with this MiG-17. It was rapidly repainted in Israeli markings and test flown by Danny Shapira. For obvious reasons, it was always escorted by at least one Mirage (IDFAF)

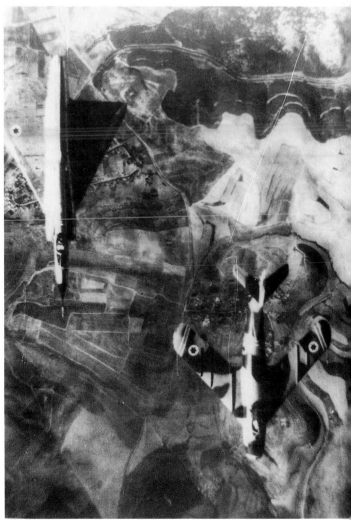

the Seikh Maskin area. On 2 February, four Mirages led by Ori Aven-Nir (then CO of a Mirage squadron), were sent to intercept a formation of Syrian AF MiGs. One of the Israeli aircraft exploded after a direct hit from a heavy calibre AA shell, and its pilot, Shlomo Weintraub, was killed instantly. The pre-planned ambush was abandoned.

On 8 February, Egyptian MiG-21s tried to intercept IDFAF Phantoms on a deep penetration strike. Two of the MiGs were shot down in the Nile Delta area, at least one of them with gunfire from a Mirage. Next day, in another air battle over the Canal, a MiG-21 was shot down, but a Mirage from No 119 Sqn was also lost—probably downed by an *Atoll* AAM. Its pilot, Lt Avi Keldes, ejected and was taken prisoner. The Egyptian AF again tried to intercept long-range IDFAF strikes on 26 February, and this time a big dogfight developed between the MiG-21s and the escorting Mirages. Three of the MiGs were shot down, all with gunfire. During March 1970 a further seven Egyptian MiG-21s were destroyed in a variety of combat situations.

Action over the Syrian border flared up again on 2 April, and three MiG-21s were shot down during a battle over the Golan Heights. An Israeli F-4E from Hatzor AB was also lost on that day. On 25 April, Amos Amir destroyed an Egyptian Il-28 bomber while on night patrol off Port Said. He later reported that his Cyrano radar was switched off at the time—a tactic frequently used at night because it eliminated the green glare of the screen. Mirage pilot Ashir Snir used an AIM-9D Sidewinder to bring down a Syrian AF MiG-17 over Lebanon on 12 May, and the Israelis believe that the pilot of this aircraft could have been the Syrian AF squadron commander who planted sonic booms over Haifa in January 1970, duplicating the supersonic Mirage 'raid' on Cairo some six months earlier.

Ambushing the Russians

The complete air superiority enjoyed by the IDFAF during 1969, and the success of Israeli F-4E deep penetration raids against targets well inside Egypt, forced President Nasser to ask the Russians for even more assistance. He made a quick visit to Moscow on 24 January 1970, and a month later a complete Soviet Air Defence Division was moved by air and sea into Egyptian bases. Some political and military observers were surprised at the speed of the Soviet response, but their answer lay not in any Soviet willingness to help the Egyptian people, but rather more in the acquisition of an immediate foothold in the strategically important eastern Mediterranean region.

The first units to arrive were the SAM systems, equipped with the latest variants of the SA-2 *Guideline* and SA-3 *Goal* missiles. These were deployed to defend Cairo and Alexandria, as well as the gigantic Aswan High Dam and hydroelectric power complex financed mainly by the Soviet Union. The first missile sites were operational by 15 March. This sinister development did not go unnoticed in Israel, and Brig Gen Modechai Hod, the IDFAF Chief of Staff and a definite hard-liner as far as the prosecution of the war was concerned, wanted to attack these new threats as quickly as possible. The Defence Minister, Moshe Dayan, resisted, and told him it would be unwise to take any pre-emptive action against the SAM sites at that time, because it would cause wider international problems for the State of Israel. In the wake of this controversy, the IDFAF abandoned the deep penetration raids carried out by the Phantoms, and concentrated instead on attacking Egyptian targets on the west bank of the Canal.

The Soviet fighters arrived during April. Consisting of about two regiments with mixed materiel, the deployment included at least 75 of the latest MiG-21MFs, 16 MiG-25 *Foxbats* and a similar number of Su-15 *Flagon-Ds*. This considerable force was split between Beni Suef, Mansura, Kom Awshim and Khatamiya—all providing cover for the Cairo area and its approaches, including some high-value military complexes—and the air base at Giancalis, near Alexandria, protecting both the city and its vital naval facilities. All the Soviet aircraft wore EAF camouflage and markings for obvious reasons, but the personnel of the entire Air Defence Division were Soviet citizens. In overall charge of the operation was Gen Vasily Okoniev, formerly a commanding officer of the Moscow Air Defence Division.

The first Israeli-Soviet encounter took place on 18 April, when MiG-21s tried to intercept a pair of Phantoms on a recce sortie. The IDFAF pilots had been given orders to avoid all combat with the Soviet-flown fighters (they knew who was who by monitoring radio traffic), so the F-4s made good their escape and returned to base. The Canal area was always treated as a 'free-fire' zone by the IDFAF, allowing its pilots to attack in response to Egyptian artillery barrages, and to counter the sporadic low-level raids by EAF fighter-bombers. On 14 May, two Egyptian MiG-21s were downed, and on the following day another was destroyed—in both instances by Mirages that were acting as escort to attacking A-4 Skyhawks. During mid-May, the EAF launched several attack sorties against Israeli positions in Sinai. These raids caused little harm, and seemed likely to have been training missions for inexperienced Egyptian pilots. Two raiding MiG-17s were shot down on 15 May, and a further pair were dispatched on the following day—all in air combat, and probably all by Mirages. The next engagement was on 3 June, as IDFAF strike aircraft were attacking the west bank of the Canal. As usual, the Egyptian MiG-21s rose to intercept them, but the defenders were 'bounced' by a Mirage top cover formation, and three of them were destroyed without loss to the Israelis.

While the conflict continued in the Canal Zone, the situation in the Golan Heights area was hotting up, with frequent artillery and tank duels towards the end of June. This short period of bitter fighting became known as the Three Day War. Most of the action involved ground forces, but air battles did occur, and on 25 June a Syrian MiG-21 was claimed. On the next day the IDFAF was particularly successful, with two MiG-17s and two MiG-21s destroyed in air-to-air combat.

By late June 1970, the Soviets had moved some of their early warning radars closer to the Canal Zone, thus providing a faster reaction time for the SAMs and interceptors. SA-2 and SA-3 batteries had been detected near Kathamiya, and on 30 June the IDFAF was finally authorized to attack the sites. The ensuing raid was partially successful, but two Phantoms were lost in the process, and three crewmembers were captured. The fourth man managed to evade the Egyptian troops, and was rescued by a CH-53 helicopter. During July the Israelis continued to

Nesher No 524 taxies past a burning truck after one of the sporadic EAF raids on Israeli installations in the Sinai (IDFAF)

attack the SAM and radar sites on the west bank of the Canal, but as the Soviet air defence system moved closer, air combats naturally decreased sharply. There were, however, some engagements, and on 10 July three EAF MiG-21s were shot down—at least one of them by Mirage gunfire. On 27 July, two Egyptian MiG-17s attacked Israeli positions in Sinai, but during their escape they were jumped by Mirages, and after a breathtakingly low-level chase, both were shot down over Egyptian territory.

Meanwhile it seemed that a ceasefire was near, after US mediation in the conflict. No serious encounters with Soviet MiG-21s were recorded until 23 July, when two of them tried to pounce on IDFAF A-4s attacking targets near Suez city. The Skyhawks jettisoned their bombs and turned for home with the MiG-21s in hot pursuit. The chase went deep into the Sinai, until the Soviets were forced to disengage due to diminishing fuel levels. Before disengaging, one of the MiGs launched a K-13A *Atoll* AAM, which exploded close to an A-4, causing enough damage to force its pilot to make an emergency landing at Refidim AB.

It was clear that the IDFAF wanted to teach the Russians a lesson before any ceasefire came into effect, and Mordechai Hod obtained authorization for an 'ambush' operation that forced the Soviet interceptors into battle. The operation was originally planned for 29 July, but political considerations delayed it for 24 hours. The plan involved four Mirages simulating a recce flight over the Soviet-patrolled area. As soon as the defending MiGs were scrambled, reinforcements—in the shape of four additional Mirages and four Phantoms—would be called in from their holding orbits to join the fray. Aircrew for the mission were carefully selected from among the best in the Mirage and Phantom squadrons.

By 14:15 hrs on 30 July, the decoy Mirages were over the chosen area, finishing their first 'recce' run. About seven minutes later, just as they were starting a second run near Ras Arab in the Gulf of Suez, the Soviet interceptors appeared. Up to 24 MiG-21s had been scrambled, most of them from Beni Suef, but including some from Khatamita and Kom Awshin. Battle was joined at about 30,000 feet, and the first to score was Mirage pilot Asher Snir, who launched both of his Shafrirs in quick succession at the same MiG-21. The aircraft was hit and exploded in a brilliant flash, but miraculously the pilot managed to eject. His 'chute opened almost immediately, and he had a grandstand view of the continuing fight as he slowly descended with aircraft all around him!

The combat was a little confusing, with many near misses, but the highly experienced Israeli pilots quickly got the upper hand. The Phantoms dispatched two MiG-21s in rapid succession, and these were followed by another, shot down by a Mirage. Then Snir's Mirage was damaged by shrapnel from an *Atoll* near-miss, and he had to abort the operation—landing safely some time later at Refidim AB in Sinai. One more MiG was destroyed by Mirage gunfire, before the Soviets disengaged and all the aircraft returned to their bases—although some of the Mirages and Phantoms had to land at Refidim to top up with fuel. Of the five Soviets shot down, two ejected safely, two ejected but were wounded, and one was killed. The Soviets were aggressive, and handled their nimble fighters well, but their tactics seemed ineffective against a group of 'aces' with such a tremendous level of experience. Shortly afterwards a ceasefire came into effect, and the 30 July air battle proved to be the last major action of the War of Attrition. According to figures published in the *IDFAF Magazine* (which can be considered to be official), the conflict encompassed 97 air combats, during which the Israelis claimed 101 enemy aircraft shot down, against the loss of only five of their own.

The skirmishes continue

The end of the War of Attrition did not mean that the air war against Israel's Arab neighbours had ceased, although the next actual combat was not recorded until about two years later. On 13 June 1972, two Egyptian MiG-21s were shot down 40 km north of Port Said, when they tried to intercept an IDFAF RF-4E Phantom II on a reconnaissance sortie. Both

fairly rapidly—mainly because the Syrian pilots obviously lacked the tactical awareness of the Israelis. During the fight, one of the Mirages was brought down by an *Atoll* missile, and its pilot managed to eject safely over the Mediterranean. While he was being rescued by a CH-53 helicopter, another wave of MiGs tried to disrupt the operation, and four more were shot down by an Israeli escort formation of Mirages and Neshers. Of the 13 confirmed victories that day, ten were credited to Mirage IIICJs, two to IAI Neshers and one to an F-4E Phantom. One of the Syrian pilots was rescued from the water by the Israeli CH-53.

The Yom Kippur War

The scale of the concerted Arab attacks at the start of the 1973 Yom Kippur War caught the Israelis by surprise. The Jewish Day of Atonement is an intensely holy festival, and many of the military personnel were either stood down completely, or operating at a lower state of readiness during the 24-hour period of penitence and fasting. At 14:00 hours on Saturday 6 October, massive simultaneous attacks were launched by the Egyptians on the Suez front, and by the Syrians over the Golan Heights region.

The Egyptian assault began with a 1000 gun artillery barrage directed against IDF positions on the Sinai bank of the Suez Canal. This was quickly followed by an Egyptian Army crossing of the Canal itself, in very large numbers and at four separate locations. At the same time, a strike force of over 220 aircraft attacked Israeli military installations all across the Sinai.

On the northern front, the Syrian AF carried out raids against Israeli positions on the Golan plateau, and helicopters landed commando-style troops on the lower slopes of Mt Hermon. After a difficult climb, these troops managed to seize the Israeli observation posts on the mountain, depriving IDF commanders

of the EAF pilots ejected over the sea. During this period, the northern front was also active, especially when the Syrian AF attempted to defend the Palestine Liberation Organization (PLO) against attacks by the IDFAF. On 9 September 1972, three SAF Su-7s were destroyed in air combat after conducting a counter-attack against IDF positions on the Golan Heights: two were brought down by Mirages, and the other by a Phantom. Two more Syrian MiG-21s were shot down on 9 November, one of them by a Mirage-launched AAM. On 21 November, as the result of two separate air battles, six Syrian MiG-21s were destroyed—five of them by Mirages and one by an F-4E.

The new year began with increasing tension in the Golan Heights region, and on 8 January a major incident developed which accounted for another six Syrian MiG-21s. The Syrian AF had then lost 17 aircraft—most of them to Mirages—over a three-month period, without bringing down a single Israeli fighter. That record in itself was bad enough, but the last big air battle before the Yom Kippur War was to prove even more decisive. Four Israeli reconnaissance Phantoms, escorted by eight Mirages, were intercepted by a formation of 16 Syrian AF MiG-21s. Battle was joined over international waters just off the Syrian coast, and nine of the MiGs were shot down

of their early warning of future attacks.

At the outbreak of war, the IDFAF had four Mirage/Nesher squadrons. These were No 101 Sqn and 'H' Sqn at Hatzor AB; No 117 Sqn at the northern base of Ramat David; and 'E' Squadron, based at Etzion in SE Sinai—just west of the Israeli port of Eilat. Both E and H Sqns were equipped exclusively with Neshers, but the other two units were operating a mixture of both types. For this reason, combat report concerning No 101 Sqn and No 117 Sqn might confuse the two aircraft types. Reports relating to the single-type 'E' and 'H' Sqns should be correct.

The first air-to-air combat on 6 October took place at 14:00 hrs, just seconds after the start of hostilities. Four Neshers from 'E' Squadron were patrolling the Tasa-Om-Hashiba area, only a few miles east of the Canal, when they intercepted part of the first wave of Egyptian raiders—a formation of eight Sukhoi Su-7s. During the battle that followed, four Su-7s were shot down. The leader of the Israeli group downed one with a Shafrir missile, and another was destroyed by gunfire. Maj Irmi, the second-in-command of the squadron, accounted for the other two, one with guns and one with an AAM. Among the Egyptian pilots killed in the action was Capt Adel Sadat, the young half-brother of Egypt's President, Anwar Sadat.

Ten minutes later, Maj (reserve) Eythan Carmi, flying a No 101 Sqn Mirage (No 159), intercepted an AS-5 *Kelt* cruise missile that was bound for Tel Aviv after being released from an Egyptian Tupolev Tu-16. Carmi fired an air-to-air missile, which missed, and finally had to shoot it down with gunfire—not an easy thing to do with such a small target carrying a 2200 lb warhead! About 25 of these weapons were launched against Israeli targets during the war, and all but five were shot down by air or ground defences.

During the late afternoon and early evening, the Egyptians conducted a big heli-borne operation to insert commando raiding parties at key points in Sinai. Large numbers of Mil Mi-8 *Hip* helicopters were involved, but these proved to be extremely difficult targets for the high-speed Nesher, and only one or two were brought down. Meanwhile, on the northern front, flying activity was relatively subdued, and No 117 Sqn was credited with only one Syrian MiG all day.

On 7 October the IDFAF undertook a major but confused effort to attack Arab air-defence missile and gun systems. The initial attacks were made against Egyptian targets, but the emphasis then switched to a series of raids against the Syrians. Only a few Mirages and Neshers were left in the Sinai for interception duties. During the morning, the second-in-command of No 101 Sqn was slightly injured in a take-off accident involving Mirage No 159: the aircraft—which was badly damaged in the crash—was eventually repaired by IAI. It had already been credited with 12 kills, and went on to notch up a total of 13 before the end of its operational life. The same squadron also lost two Mirages in combat that day, both on the southern front, and both after their respective pilots had shot down an Egyptian aircraft. The two Israelis ejected safely over the Sinai, and were recovered by helicopter. With most of the action on the northern front, No 117 Sqn claimed an assorted bag of 11 Syrian MiGs and Su-7s during the day, but 'E' Sqn remained on alert in the south with virtually nothing to do. Its commanding officer eventually urged the IDFAF Operations Staff to pass the squadron some ground-attack missions, and they ended the day strafing Egyptian crossing points on the Suez Canal at the request of OC Southern Command.

During the early morning of 8 October, 'E' Sqn Neshers were tasked to attack Syrian positions at Jabel-Druz, but returned to the Suez area immediately afterwards to continue the interception of Egyptian raiders. Later that morning the squadron commander downed a MiG-17, and his wingman accounted for another two from the same formation. During the afternoon, over the Nile Delta, the CO scored again—this time a MiG-21—and Asef Ben-Nun (an IAI test-pilot flying as a reservist) shot down a second MiG in the same battle. A Mirage from one of the other squadrons was also lost in this engagement.

At 09:00 hrs that morning, a pair of Neshers detached on interception-alert at Refidim AB (formerly Bir Gafgafa), in central Sinai, scrambled to challenge six low-flying Su-7s that were clearly heading in to attack the airfield. Intercepting the Sukhois at high speed, the Neshers closed in and the leader launched a Shafrir at a range of about 1000 metres. The missile failed to make contact because the Egyptian pilot saw it coming and broke away at the last moment. The Nesher pilot also turned hard, and positioned himself on the Sukhoi again before launching his second Shafrir at a range of only 600 metres. This time the missile found its target, and the tail of the raider disappeared in a brilliant flash just before the aircraft slammed into the desert floor. Meanwhile the second Nesher had brought down another Su-7 with a missile, and a third had crashed into the ground while taking panic evasive action, although no ordnance had been fired at him.

Two squadrons of Iraqi AF Hunters were temporarily deployed to Egypt to assist in the war effort, and during the afternoon of 8 October, Lt Col Oded Morom—an ex-Mirage squadron commander—intercepted four of the aircraft attacking Tassa Camps. He managed to shoot down one of the Hunters, but flying debris fragmented his canopy and he had to make an emergency landing back at base. Another Mirage from the same formation downed two more Hunters, while the fourth fell victim to IDF AA fire. The Iraqis later admitted the loss of all four aircraft. Other kills credited to No 101 Sqn during the day included a MiG-17, three MiG-21s and four Su-7s. No 117 Sqn on the other hand, had a very quiet day, and made no claims at all.

At 04:00 hrs on 9 October, at least two Syrian Army FROG (free rocket over ground) unguided SSMs struck Ramat David AB, damaging a building that housed an A-4 squadron's administrative offices. One pilot was killed, and four others—including the squadron CO—were wounded. Later that day 16 F-4Es, escorted by No 117 Sqn Mirages, carried out a reprisal raid on the Syrian Army and Air Force staff and headquarters buildings in Damascus. The Mirages shot down six of the defending Syrian fighters, and returned the following day to claim another eight.

The CO of No 101 Sqn, Lt Col Avi Lanir, was forced to eject from his Mirage after an air-to-air combat over Syria on 13 October. Although the ejection was successful, he was taken prisoner and

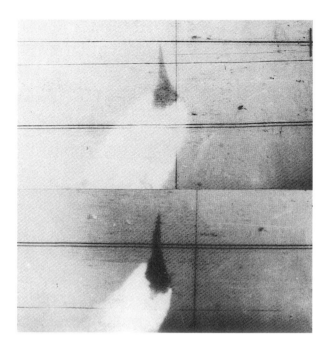

eventually tortured to death by the Syrians. Lanir was replaced by the officer who had crashed only six days earlier in Mirage No 159. Despite having a badly injured hand, the new CO insisted that he could not lead the squadron effectively unless he was declared fit to fly. With obvious misgivings, the medical branch did finally clear him to fly, and he promptly dumbfounded his critics by shooting down another Syrian MiG.

On 14 October, four Neshers from 'E' Sqn were patrolling over the Port Said area, when they were directed across to the Nile Delta to help a formation of Israeli F-4Es. The Phantoms had been 'bounced' by a group of Egyptian AF MiG-21s, and the Neshers arrived on the scene just in time. The squadron CO quickly dispatched two of the MiGs, one with a Shafrir and the other with gunfire, while Asef Ben-Nun got one with his guns. Another Nesher from the formation destroyed the fourth MiG with a Shafrir missile.

During the afternoon of 15 October, four Neshers escorted four Phantoms to attack Damascus International Airport, which was still being used to mount raids into Israel. A previous attack on the airport had been intercepted by the Syrian AF and aborted, but the return visit was far more successful and achieved its objectives. All the aircraft were recovered safely, although one of the Neshers was slightly damaged by an SA-3 missile that exploded too close for comfort.

Air combat is always a chancy business, and a curious incident that occurred on 18 October proved just how much luck is sometimes involved. A pair of Mirages were scrambled from Refidim AB to intercept a formation of Egyptian MiG-17s. One of the Mirage pilots managed to shoot down two of the MiGs in quick succession—one with a Shafrir and

LEFT
This gun-camera sequence shows the destruction of a Mirage hit by MiG-21 gunfire. Although it is undated, this is believed to show the Mirage lost over the Nile Delta on 8 October 1973. If it is, the pilot managed to eject safely (EAF)

ABOVE
This dramatic shot was taken from the ground, and shows part of the dogfight that took place on 8 October 1973, near Refidim AB in central Sinai. The EAF Su-7, its engine ablaze, is desperately trying to gain height, while the Nesher in the background is turning for another firing pass (IDFAF)

RIGHT
Taken from the gun camera of a Nesher, this frame shows an Egyptian MiG-21 lurching skyward as most of its tail is blown away by Israeli cannon fire. The position of the MiG's flaps shows that the pilot was trying to turn when he was caught (IDFAF)

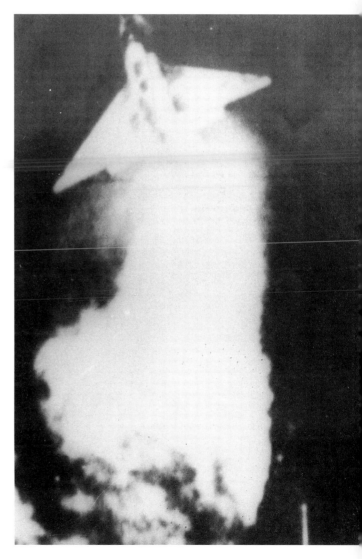

one with a Sidewinder (both weapons were sometimes carried). The second Israeli pilot unwittingly flew directly into the fireball from one of the exploding MiGs, and emerged from the other side virtually undamaged by debris, but with his aircraft badly singed and almost completely black! Practically unable to see through his fire-damaged canopy, he nursed the aircraft back to Refidim and had to be talked down by his colleague.

During the closing stages of the conflict Israel regained the initiative, and the Egyptians threw everything into a desperate effort to stop the IDF advance. Large air battles were more and more common along the southern front, and Arab aircraft became easy pickings for Israeli pilots. A reserve Lieutenant Colonel (who cannot be named under IDFAF rules because he is still on active service)

achieved phenomenal success in a very short time, and emerged from the war as the IDFAF's leading ace—despite the fact that he was a senior staff officer who would normally be expected to fly only on emergency appointment. On 18 October he shot down an Egyptian Mi-8 helicopter that was being used to bomb an Israeli bridgehead across the Canal with napalm! On 19 October, in roughly the same

LEFT
This Mirage IIIBJ clearly illustrates the large black and yellow identification markings. These were repeated on the upper and lower surfaces of each wing, and provided instant recognition of an Israeli aircraft in the confusion of a fast-moving dogfight. This particular aircraft is fitted with the Atar 09C engine, as can be seen from the modifications to the rear fuselage (IDFAF)

BELOW
At the end of its operational life with the IDFAF, Mirage IIICJ No 159 had notched up 13 victories over Arab aircraft—a record equalled only by No 409. The aircraft is seen here in the markings of No 101 Sqn, carrying three big external tanks and the usual ID markings (IDFAF via David Eshel)

area, he was credited with two Su-7s and two Su-20s in two consecutive sorties. He followed this with the destruction of four MiGs (three with guns and one with an AAM) during a single sortie on the afternoon of 20 October, and then, on 24 October, he was credited with three more kills only hours before the final ceasefire. These brought his personal tally during the Yom Kippur conflict to 12, and his total score—including those achieved as a young fighter pilot—to a magnificent 17.

On 21 October, four Neshers from 'E' Sqn were patrolling over the Faid area, when they intercepted some Libyan AF Mirage 5s that had been drafted in to help the Arab cause. One of these was damaged by a Sidewinder missile, and then finished off with cannon fire. Earlier in the day, during a battle near the Bordavil area, two No 101 Sqn aircraft intercepted four Libyan Mirages that were flying over the Mediterranean, but clearly heading towards the Sinai. The Libyans broke hard to the right at low level, and jettisoned their underwing bombs and tanks into the sea. One of the unfortunate pilots over-manoeuvred and hit the water with his starboard wingtip, which instantly pulled the aircraft down into the sea, raising a huge plume of spray as it exploded on impact. After a chase out to the west, the Israeli No 2 shot down two of the remaining Mirage 5s in

quick succession, one with gunfire and the other with a Shafrir. The only survivor made good his escape at high speed and very low level.

The appearance on the scene of these Libyan Mirages caused a potentially dangerous visual identification problem. To avoid mistakes in the future, Israeli machines were repainted to include large yellow/black triangles on the upper and lower surfaces of each wing, and on each side of the vertical tail. These dramatic markings served their purpose, but were removed during the late 1970s when the Egyptians began to have border clashes with the Libyans, and applied similar (yellow/orange) ID markings to their own Mirages.

A UN ceasefire agreed for 22 October failed to materialize, mainly because the Israelis wanted to retake and secure the observation posts on Mt Hermon, and press home their attacks on the Egyptian 3rd Army and the vital airfield at Kasfarit. The last big air battle of the war took place on 24 October, as Israeli attack aircraft hammered Egyptian ground forces near Suez, and the EAF tried to beat them off. UN observers confirmed that at least five Egyptian and two Israeli aircraft were shot down on the final day, but conflicting claims from each side suggest that their combined losses may well have been in the region of 15–20.

A fragile ceasefire was finally secured by UN negotiators during the early afternoon of 24 October. At the end of the war, despite 18 days of bloody fighting and huge losses on all sides, the actual military position was little changed. The initial Israeli claims of more than 400 enemy aircraft shot down in air-to-air combat, were later reduced to 277 after the gun-camera films and missile results from 117 separate battles had been analysed. The main

roles of the Mirage and Nesher squadrons throughout the war were fighter-escort and interception, and between them they were responsible for well over half the confirmed kills. No 117 Sqn was credited with 55, 'E' Sqn with 42 (without any loss to themselves, and No 101 Sqn with about 48. The Hatzor-based all-Nesher squadron claimed 25 kills.

The Shafrir 2 guided missile—used only by the Mirage and Nesher—was highly successful and achieved a total of 102 confirmed kills. Remarkably, only a handful of Mirages and Neshers were lost to enemy action during the war, but of course their air-to-air role normally kept them clear of the formidable array of Arab ground-based defences. Consequently they suffered much less than the ground-attack F-4, A-4 and Super Mystère units.

With the introduction of the Kfir C1 in 1975 and the McDonnell Douglas F-15 Eagle in 1976, the Mirages and Neshers were relegated to a secondary role in Israeli air defence. The last conflict in which they were involved was the 'Peace for Galilee' operation in June 1982, when they were used for rear-area patrol duties without achieving any real results. At that stage, their pilots could only watch in awe as the new breed of F-15 and F-16 fighters mauled the Syrian AF.

Between their introduction in 1966 and the end of the Yom Kippur War in late 1973, the Mirage and Nesher were credited with over 300 confirmed victories, nearly 200 of which were achieved with the 30 mm cannon. Of the 100 or so AAM kills, by far the most significant number involved the Shafrir 2, but the Shafrir 1 and Sidewinder were also successful in limited numbers. Throughout the long career of the Mirage, only one confirmed kill was credited to the original Matra R530 radar-guided missile.

A close-up of the forward fuselage 'kill' markings show that ten of No 159's victims were Syrian aircraft, and only three were Egyptian. The difference lies in the number of tiny stars on the lighter ring of each roundel (IDFAF via David Eshel)

Chapter 7
Alpine Mirages

Switzerland, in common with Sweden and neighbouring Austria, has adopted a long-term policy of armed neutrality, using modern weapons and equipment to ensure its security. The Swiss AF and Anti-Aircraft Command (*Kommando Der Flieger Und Fliegerabwehrtruppen*), is a Corps-strength unit of the Swiss Army, which now operates nearly 300 combat aircraft, and is recognized as one of the best equipped and best trained air arms in Europe. This standard has been achieved despite having only six full-time professional squadrons (*Staffeln*) in the Surveillance Wing (*Uberwachung Geschwader*): all other squadrons are part-time militia units. Three squadrons of Mirage IIIs, together with another three squadrons equipped with Northrop F-5E/Fs, form the backbone of Surveillance Wing air defence operations.

The story of the Mirage III in Swiss AF service began nearly 30 years ago. Towards the end of 1960, after an extensive series of evaluations which included the F-104 Starfighter, F11F Tiger, J-35 Draken and Mirage IIIA and IIIC, the Chief of the General Staff proposed the acquisition of up to 100 Mirages. This proposal was passed on to the Federal Military Department, and the Swiss Government gave its formal approval of the order during the summer of 1961. The majority of the aircraft were to be assembled by the nationally owned Federal Aircraft Works at Emmen.

The Swiss Mirage IIIS was developed from the French AF multi-role Mirage IIIE, but the two aircraft are substantially different in detail. On the Swiss version, the Doppler navigation system—which is of questionable accuracy over mountainous terrain—was removed altogether, and the Cyrano II*bis* fire-control radar was replaced by the Hughes TARAN 18 (Tactical Attack Radar and Navigation). This equipment was specially developed for the Swiss AF, and it virtually duplicated the air-to-air

range, search and track functions of the Cyrano. The American radar was also more compatible with the chosen Falcon missiles, and with Switzerland's FLORIDA ground-based early warning and control chain, which was developed by Hughes under a separate contract. The compatibility aspect was vital to the success of the whole air-defence network, because the Mirage was to be data-linked into the ground stations. When it entered service, the TARAN 18 had better look-down capabilities than any other radar in Europe, and it incorporated an effective terrain avoidance system. These were both valuable assets for operations over and between the mountains.

The main all-weather armament chosen for the Swiss Mirage was the radar-guided Hughes AIM-26B Falcon, which meant abandoning the bigger and heavier Matra R530. Some of the early Falcons were acquired direct from Hughes, but most of the stock came from Sweden, where the missile is assembled under licence as the Saab RB-27. For shorter range interceptions the IR-guided Sidewinder was selected, and a number of variants, including the AIM-9B/E/J/P/P3 and L, have been operational during the long service life of the aircraft. For the rarely used attack role (only about ten per cent of training missons are devoted to it), the Mirage IIIS can carry a variety of free-fall bombs, and the Matra AS30 air-to-surface missile. Following the late 1980s update programme, the Matra missile will gradually be replaced by the Hughes Maverick, which is already carried by the Swiss AF Hawker Hunters.

To allow for Switzerland's unique operational situation, a number of important systems and structural modifications were incorporated in the Mirage IIIS. The landing gear, fuselage and wings were all strengthened, in order to spread the stress of steep approaches into small valley-floor airfields. Provision for four JATO bottles on the rear fuselage

LEFT
One of the two original Dassault-built Mirage IIIS airframes for Switzerland (J-2302) is prepared for a test flight from Bordeaux-Merignac. The aircraft was delivered to the Swiss AF in June 1964, and a month later it was on its way to the United States, where it conducted a two-year test programme related to the Hughes Taran 18 weapons system (AMD/BA)

BELOW LEFT
This overhead view of J-2330 illustrates the early metallic finish on Swiss Mirages. The mountainous terrain below the aircraft is not really suitable for Doppler navigation systems because random echoes often occur in deep valleys. The profusion of lettering on the wings is a result of the multi-lingual society in Switzerland and the need to print everything in French and German (Swiss AF)

BELOW
J-2301 was the first (French-built) Mirage IIIS. The aircraft is seen here during early trials with Dassault, equipped with two Falcon and two AIM-9B Sidewinder missiles. The two-position nosewheel leg is fully extended (AMD/BA)

gave the extra thrust needed for short take-offs and a steeper-than-normal climb-out. The aircraft was also fitted with an unusual two-position nosewheel leg, which could be 'pumped up' to lower the tail while the aircraft was passing through the blast-proof doors of a 'Kavern' mountain shelter. The nose radome also folds sideways to save space in these massive hangars, which are concealed under the bedrock of the Alps themselves.

The Swiss tactical reconnaissance variant, the Mirage IIIRS, carries a slightly different TARAN 1S navigation and terrain-avoidance radar, as well as a typical 'recce' nose, equipped with a battery of vertical and oblique Omera cameras. The aircraft retains the AIM-9 system for self-defence and certain fighter missions, together with the two 30 mm Defa cannon that are common to all Swiss Mirages.

Preparation for manufacture under licence was started shortly after the 1961 Parliamentary approval. It was soon evident that the cost of the project would far exceed the programmed calculations, mainly because so many modifications were required. The estimates for the full 100 aircraft programme jumped from SFr 830 million to SFr 1447 million in just one year! In 1963 the Parliament renewed its interest in what had become known locally as 'The Mirage Affair', and a Committee of Enquiry was set up to examine the whole contract. After lengthy investigations, the Committee could find no fault with the capabilities required of the proposed Mirage IIIS, but on purely financial grounds the total order was cut to 55 aircraft—bringing the overall value of the contract roughly back into line with the original estimate.

It was finally agreed that the Swiss AF would acquire one Mirage IIIC direct from France for early trials, followed by 36 Mirage IIIS interceptors and 18 Mirage IIIRS tactical reconnaissance aircraft. On the face of it, this massive reduction in the order should have saved a considerble amount of money, but by the time cancellation charges were paid to all the

ABOVE
One of the early Swiss-built Mirages is seen here on finals. Its auxiliary inlet doors are open

RIGHT
The first two-seat Mirage IIIBS trainer (U-2001) seen here without any external tanks. This configuration inevitably means a short flight—perhaps 40–45 minutes at best (Swiss AF)

licencees—many of whom had already planned for a 100 aircraft programme—the actual savings were minimal.

The single Mirage IIIC was acquired from Dassault in 1963, and preliminary investigations began immediately. Throughout the manufacturing period of the IIIS and IIIRS models—and for much of their service lives—this 'prototype' aircraft was used for systems trials by the Department of Flight Tests at Emmen. Later in its life it was given an all-over red colour scheme, and a decorative flower was painted on its belly. The aircraft was finally retired from service in 1981, and put on show in the Swiss AF Museum at Dubendorf.

Very early in the trials programme it became clear that a dual-control aircraft would be needed to ensure optimum pilot familiarization. Two Mirage IIIBS two-seaters were therefore ordered direct from Dassault, bringing the overall total up to 57 aircraft. These two were hybrid IIIB/D airframes, with the forward fuselage of a Mirage IIIB and the Atar 09C3 of the IIID. Both were delivered in 1964, and pilot training courses began almost immediately. One of the trainers was written off as the result of an engine-related accident in April 1969, and by the end of that year a replacement had been acquired. This was followed by the delivery of a fourth Mirage IIIBS in 1972—an aircraft that was assembled jointly by Dassault and Federal Aircraft Works from available spare parts. Finally, in January 1982 and February 1983, two Mirage IIIDS airframes were delivered from France, making a total of six two-seaters out of the overall total of 61 Mirage IIIs supplied to the Swiss AF.

The four surviving two-seaters (two of each variant) are flown from Payerne AB, where they form a small OCU flight within the administrative framework of the Mirage squadrons. The OCU's main role is the conversion of newly posted full-time pilots for the interceptor or reconnaissance squadrons, but it also conducts refresher courses for militia and reserve pilots who are being posted to the operational units.

The Swiss AF acquired a total of 36 Mirage III interceptors. The first two were assembled by Dassault and delivered in February and June 1964. The remaining 34 came from the Federal Aircraft Works, and all deliveries were completed between October 1965 and February 1969. The second French-built aircraft (J-2302) was sent to the United States in June 1964, where it spent about two years— mostly at Holloman AFB, New Mexico—conducting trials with the TARAN 18 weapons system and the Falcon air-to-air missile.

The first 24 production aircraft had been delivered by March 1968, and at that time *Fliegerstaffeln* 16 and 17 were both activated at Payerne. After a few teething troubles (mainly with the TARAN radar) the Mirage settled down superbly, and the whole weapons system proved itself well matched to Swiss requirements. Despite operating difficult missions in a very demanding environment, only three interceptors had been lost in accidents up to the end of 1988. The two squadrons currently have about 24–26 operational machines between them, while the

ABOVE LEFT
J-2330 carries the badge of 16 Staffel *on the fin. Two Falcon missiles are normally carried, on short rails either side of the centreline. The Sidewinders on the outer rails are clearly AIM-9Js* (Swiss AF)

LEFT
Two Mirage IIIS interceptors and two Mirage IIIBS trainers are seen here on the OCU flightline at Payerne AB. The lack of external tanks and weapons is typical of machines used for training (Swiss AF)

ABOVE
Two Mirage IIIS interceptors carrying the insignia of 17 Staffel. *J-2336 has a 'Geronimo' badge on the nose* (Swiss AF)

remainder are on a rolling programme of depot-level maintenance, major overhauls or involved in trials. Although normally based at Payerne, the squadrons maintain a virtually permanent detachment at Stans, and also deploy regularly to 'Kavern' airfields at a number of 'secret' Alpine locations.

A former Mirage IIIS pilot had this to say about the aircraft and some of the joys of mountain flying:

The specially developed Mirage IIIS was, and indeed still is, a good interceptor and air superiority fighter. The TARAN 18 fire-control and navigation radar is a marvel in itself, and in the late 1960s it was the best air-to-air radar in Europe, with real multi-target engagement capability. Of course all this had a price, and it must be said that the Mirage IIIS cost almost twice as much as the standard Mirage IIIE/Cyrano combination.

Our FLORIDA Ground Environment System can be linked in times of crisis or war to the NATO NADGE system. As in WW2, we are very keen to enforce our hard-won neutrality, and to this effect we maintain a pair of Mirages on QRA (Quick Reaction Alert) 24 hours a day, 365 days a year. Most 16 and 17 *Staffeln* pilots have experienced quite a number of QRA scrambles, because we are in the middle of some of the world's most congested air

ABOVE
You can almost hear the thunderous noise in the valley as J-2306 gets airborne in full afterburner, and with the aid of six JATO bottles (Swiss AF)

ABOVE RIGHT
'Flying over the Alps is incredible, with its narvellous scenery of glaciers and eternally snow-capped mountains ...' (Swiss AF)

RIGHT
The first of the 18 Mirage IIIRS reconnaissance aircraft (R-2101) was built by Dassault, but the remainder were assembled by the Federal Aircraft Works. The prototype carried this early unpainted finish, apart from the black camera nose (Swiss AF)

space, and foreign civilian and military 'strays' are frequent.

One of the more interesting experiences for a Mirage IIIS pilot is to conduct an operational exercise from a 'Kavern' airfield. The massive underground hangars, excavated out of the mountains themselves, are each capable of holding about two dozen aircraft, plus several months'

reserve of ammunition, fuel, spares, and food for all the personnel involved in keeping the unit up to strength. The massive steel and concrete hangar doors weigh more than 100 tons each, and are proof against blast damage and NBC contamination. The only things visible from the air are the runways and taxiways, and even these have been toned down to blend with their surroundings. All air traffic control facilities are provided by a mobile control tower.

'Kavern' exercises often involved JATO-assisted take-offs, and this is one experience a pilot will never forget! When full afterburner is selected, the JATO-button is pushed and things start to happen *very* fast, with the pilot pressed hard into his seat pan as the aircraft gets airborne impossibly quickly. No amount of training can fully prepare you for the breathtaking sensation of pressing that button for the first time. After that, the experience becomes rather more familiar, but it could *never* be described as dull!

Landings at these small airfields are also very interesting. Because of the surrounding mountains, the regular procedure involves steeper-than-normal approaches, and pilots are instructed to a high standard of accuracy to ensure that their main wheels touch down as close to the threshold as possible. This punishing operational technique was the main reason behind Switzerland's decision to strengthen the wing, centresection and undercarriage of the Mirage.

Flying over the Alps is incredible, with its marvellous scenery of glaciers and eternally snow-capped mountains—but it does have its problems. Weather conditions in particular, can change very quickly, and during low-level intercept missions down in the valleys and among the mountains, there can be very little radar warning of trouble up ahead. Everything is visual, and you have to use all your experience and concentration to stay ahead of the game. Strong turbulence can also be a problem at low level, but the gust-response of the Mirage's delta planform is very good, so the stability of the aircraft is rarely disturbed.

Mirage IIIS pilots frequently conduct dissimilar air combat training (DACT) exercises with F-5E/F Tigers and Hunters. In order to upgrade this kind of activity and make it more realistic, the Swiss AF has been renting time slots at NATO's Instrumented Air Combat Range at Decimomannu on Sardinia. At 'Deci' all the participating aircrews can hone their tactical appreciation and combat skills in completely unrestricted air space, and 'fight' against a wide variety of aicraft flown by pilots of different nationalities and levels of experience.

The prototype of the reconnaissance Mirage IIIRS (R-2101) was built by Dassault, and it flew for the first time on 5 November 1964. The aircraft remained in France for almost three years before final delivery, conducting development trials on the camera nose and TARAN 1S radar system. The remaining 17 aircraft were all manufactured by the Federal Aircraft Works, and delivered to *Fliegerstaffel* 10 between

A Mirage IIIRS with the grey/green tactical camouflage that was applied soon after the aircraft entered service. The 10 Staffel *badge—a stylized eagle's head—can be seen on the fin* (Swiss AF)

J-2302 was the first Mirage IIIS modified under the update programme, and it flew for the first time with canards on 23 August 1983. This shot shows the aircraft departing from Emmen during the early test programme (F + W)

RIGHT
The Mirage assembly/overhaul line of the Swiss Federal Aircraft Works at Emmen. In the foreground is the unique Mirage IIIC (J-2201), while the background includes four Mirage IIIRS reconnaissance aircraft and three interceptors. The sharp-eyed will also spot the Vampire FB.6s (F + W)

BELOW
All the update modifications, including the new paint scheme, were carried by J-2301 (F + W)

March 1968 and June 1969. This squadron is the only recce unit attached to Surveillance Wing of the Swiss AF, and the Mirages replaced some ageing de Havilland Venom Mk.1Rs in operational service.

Although the Venom was withdrawn from *operational* use in the late 1960s, a special training flight of six aircraft was retained by the squadron until 1984, to teach newly posted pilots the raw techniques of reconnaissance flying before they progressed onto the more advanced Mirage. About 50 per cent of the pilots are full-time professionals, with the balance being made up of militia reservists (the interceptor squadrons have a higher proportion of full-time people, leaving about a third of the aircrew places to be filled by reservists). *Fliegerstaffel* 10 is based at Dubendorf, near Zurich, but it also keeps detachments at Payerne, Sion and Stans. Although they have been in service for over 20 years, only three Mirage IIIRSs have been written off to date.

On 8 January 1969, a Federal Aircraft Works test pilot, Emil Otth, while engaged on a test flight in Mirage IIIRS R-2101, took the opportunity to celebrate the fiftieth anniversary of the first mail flight between Dubendorf and Berne, which was completed on 8 January 1919 in a Hafeli D.H.3 biplane. Otth's anniversary flight was made on a direct north-east to south-west route, cutting diagonally across Switzerland. He took off at 14:04 hrs from Dubendorf, and four minutes later he was climbing through 37,000 feet (11,000 m) over Romanshorn, and going supersonic in sector 3. Mach. 2.0 was reached at 14:12 hrs over Grosshochstetten, and seven minutes later he commenced an instrument approach to Payerne AB. Without landing, he returned to Dubendorf along the same route, for a touchdown at 14:44 hrs.

Mid-life update programme

Federal Aircraft Works has been co-operating with the Swiss AF for several years on a mid-life improvement programme (known as ISMA, for Improved Swiss Mirage Aircraft), which should allow the Mirage to stay in service at least until the turn of the century. The modification programme was started in 1987, and the final aircraft should be delivered back into service by 1990 if the defence budget allowance remains at its 1988 level.

The modifications are being applied in two stages, depending on the tasking of the aircraft. *All* Swiss Mirages—interceptors, trainers and reconnaissance

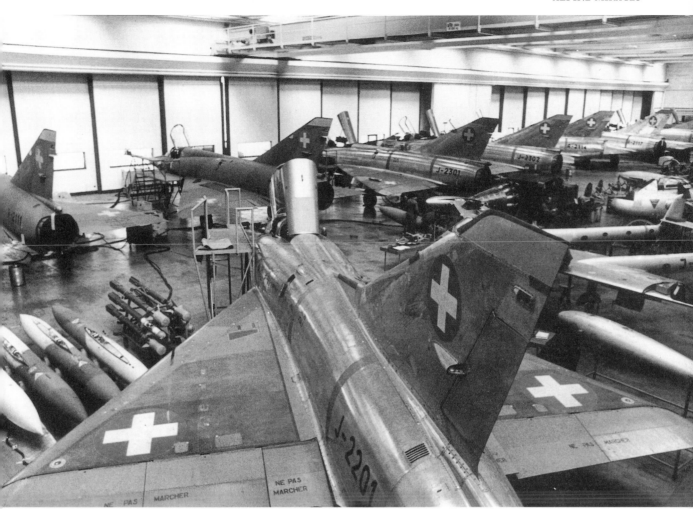

aircraft—are receiving a new Martin-Baker SRM Mk 4 rocket-powered zero-zero ejection seat; strengthening of the wing and airframe; a new low-visibility grey camouflage scheme; an active/passive electronic countermeasures suite; a radar homing and warning receiver, and an improved IFF/SIF and VHF radio package. The aircraft will also be modified to make use of the Israeli-developed 110 gal (500 lt) wing-mounted drop-tanks, and 181 gal (825 lt) centre-line drop-tank. These will be used in place of the standard 110 gal tanks, which are bolted on to the airframe and are removable only on the ground.

The modifications to the 30 Mirage IIIS interceptors and four IIIBS/DS trainers will go one stage further, and incorporate a number of aerodynamic and systems changes designed to enhance their manoeuvrability in combat. The most notable of these are intake-mounted canard surfaces, which were developed in co-operation with Israel Aircraft Industries. These are about 30 per cent smaller than the canards used on the Kfir, but they operate in conjunction with Swiss-designed strakes leading back from the nose of the Mirage IIIS. These aerodynamic improvements have dramatically increased the sustained turn-rate of the aircraft throughout the speed range, making it possible to retain control at much higher angles of attack (AoA). Because of this new freedom of manoeuvre, it has been necessary to fit an audio and visual AoA warning system, to tell the pilot if the aircraft is about to depart from controlled flight. This is particularly important during the high G turns experienced during combat. Swiss pilots who have flown the modified aircraft are delighted with the changes, and some have even reported that its manoeuvrability now roughly matches that of the current generation of fighters!

The first prototype of the modified aircraft was J-2302, which flew on 23 August 1983, and became the Federal Aircraft Works test article. This was joined some time later by the Air Force evaluation aircraft (J-2301), which carried all the modifications, including the new two-tone grey paint scheme.

In October 1988 it was announced that Switzerland is to buy 34 McDonnell Douglas F/A-18 Hornets to replace the Mirage IIIS in the high-level interceptor role. Delivery of the new fighters is unlikely to occur much before 1992/93, but when they do arrive the Mirage will be relegated to low-level air defence duties.

Chapter 8
Iberian Mirages

By the late 1960s, it was becoming obvious that the F-86F Sabres in service with the *Ejército del Aire* were nearing the end of their operational lives. The world was rapidly moving into the supersonic era, and if Spain wanted to keep up with the best in Europe, she had no choice but to re-equip with a new breed of fighter. After a long evaluation of all the available alternatives, the Mirage III was finally selected.

A contract was originally placed in 1968 for 30 Mirage IIIEE (the extra 'E' for *España*) single-seat fighters, and 6 Mirage IIIDE dual-seat operational trainers. This order was later reviewed due to budgetary constraints, and the number of fighters was reduced to 24. The Manises/Valencia-based fighter wing was due to receive all 30 aircraft.

Initial crew training began at Dijon-Longvic AB in France, when a group of Spanish pilots and technicians joined an aircraft-familiarization course with ECT 2/2—the Mirage III OCU of the *Armée de l'Air*. This completed, the first eight Spanish aircraft were flown to Manises in June 1970, and assigned to 101 *Escuadrón*. While deliveries were building up, 103 *Escuadrón* was activated as the second Mirage unit, but just after the arrival in Spain of the last aircraft, *Ala de Caza* No 11 was formally commissioned with two new squadron banners. The original units—numbers 101 and 103—were both disbanded to form 111 *Escuadrón* (callsign *Dolar*) and 112 *Escuadrón* (callsign *Rublo*). One of the two-seat aircraft was lost in 1971, but a replacement was

Twenty-four Doppler-equipped Mirage IIIEEs were ordered for the Spanish AF. This particular example, seen at Manises AB in April 1988, carries two 375 gal (1700 lt) drop tanks, and has the new individual coding system below the cockpit. The new codes dispense with the earlier squadron numbering system (S Mafé)

ordered, bringing the total number of Mirage IIIs acquired by Spain up to 31.

In Spanish service the aircraft are designated C.11 for the fighter version, and CE.11 for the two-seat trainer. *Ala de Caza* No 11 forms part of MACOM (*Mando Aéreo de Combate*—or Air Combat Command) which is the primary Spanish AF defensive/offensive organization. The Command disposition includes three additional wings, equipped with Mirage F.1s, F/A-18 Hornets and RF-4C Phantom IIs plus a computerized early warning chain, and a Flight of ELINT/ECM Casa C-212 Aviocars. (The Spanish F-4C interceptors have already been phased out following the F/A-18's arrival, but the RF-4Cs will remain operational until a recce pod for the Hornet becomes available in about 1995.)

Ala 11's major training commitment is now concentrated on ground-attack sorties, with 75 per cent of the flight time being given over to this role (a complete reversal of the pre-F/A-18 tasking). About 10 per cent of the total flying activity is devoted to night sorties, because all pilots have to maintain full day/night standards in order to be declared 'combat ready'.

As its contribution to the interception alert force, *Ala* 11 continuously provided two fully armed Mirage IIIEEs, readied for take-off within five minutes and 30 minutes respectively from dawn to dusk, and 30 minutes and one hour respectively during the night hours. These aircraft carried loaded cannon and live AIM-9P-3 Sidewinder missiles, and were available on QRA readiness 365 days a year. Early in 1989 this commitment was passed to the Zaragoza-based F/A-18s of *Ala* No 15.

Only once have the Mirages of *Ala* 11 been placed on a war footing. This was during the autumn of 1975, when Spain was involved in a confrontation with Morocco over the former territory of Spanish Sahara. For one week in November of that year, 12

aircraft were maintained at a high state of readiness, fully prepared for rapid deployment to the disputed area. Fortunately the issue was resolved through diplomatic channels, and the military on both sides were stood down.

During his normal training, an average *Ala* 11 pilot will fly 15–20 hours per month. The majority of this time will include some element of ground attack work, but sorties are also devoted to the ground-attack task, navigation exercises, aircraft handling skills, weapons release, etc. One of the more enjoyable experiences for any combat pilot is maintaining his gun qualifications, which for *Ala* 11 pilots means a series of air-to-ground exercises over the range or air-to-air gunnery against TDU target darts towed by the Phantoms of *Ala* 12. The gun has always been the classic fighter pilot's weapon, and because ammunition is comparatively inexpensive, live-firing exercises involving both air and ground targets occur with reasonable frequency. This is not so with guided weapons. Modern missiles are so costly that most pilots will only fire perhaps two or three in a lifetime, and even those will generally be obsolete or time-expired rounds that would otherwise be scrapped. Most of the art of successful missile combat is in finding the target in the first instance, and then releasing the weapon at the correct time to achieve a positive engagement. Training is therefore concentrated around the interception task, and the aircraft carry inert weapons that 'tell' the pilot when he has achieved a successful lock.

Realistic combat training is provided by regular participation in national and international defence exercises. In addition to the purely national 'Red Eye' exercise (which is held monthly), the Mirage IIIs are involved in 'Poop Deck' with the US Navy's 6th Fleet, and in the French 'Datex' and 'Navipar' exercises. They also take part in 'Daga' maritime

ABOVE LEFT
Seen on the intake of one of the squadron's Mirages, the badge of Ala de Caza No 11 (S Mafé)

ABOVE
About ten per cent of the total flying activity is devoted to night operations (S Mafé)

ABOVE RIGHT
Accidents are comparatively rare for the Mirage fleet—but they do happen. This Ala 11 *aircraft (111-6) suffered a wheels-up landing on 15 May 1972, but it was quickly covered in foam to prevent fire, and eventually returned to active service after a long period of repair* (Ala 11)

exercises with the Spanish Navy and its air arm, the *Arma Aerea de la Armada*. Exchange visits with other NATO air forces are a common feature of *Ala* 11's operations. The overall programme of visits, exercises and a heavy commitment of daily training flights, keeps the Mirage III fleet very busy. The last available figures indicate that the type had accumulated well over 71,000 flight hours with the Spanish AF, and up to the end of April 1989 only eight aircraft and two pilots had been lost in accidents— a good record for such a demanding aircraft. No 112 *Escuadrón* was disbanded in 1989 as the Mirage modernization programme significantly reduced fleet availability.

Flying the Mirage III

During the past ten years, I have had the opportunity to fly five times in the Mirages of *Ala* 11, logging a total of five hours and 45 minutes flight time in the process.

7 August 1979

My first sortie was an interception exercise involving three aircraft, a single-seater and two operational trainers. The single-seat aircraft (111-11/C.11–21) was flown by Capt Rodrigez; one of the trainers (112-13/CE.11-26) was crewed by Capts Pujals and Romero, and I was to fly in the back seat of 111-14/CE.11-27, flown by Maj Carretero.

We discussed the sortie plan, safety procedures, radio frequencies, etc. in the crew room, and then contacted *Pegaso*—the GCI radar control at Torrejon—to inform them of our planned 10:05 hrs (Zulu) departure time. We also relayed the callsigns we would be using, which were *Dolar 09* for ourselves, and *Rublo 21* and *Rublo 22* for the other two aircraft. It was a warm and sunny day, perfect weather for flying as we left the crew room and headed out towards the flight line.

While Maj Carretero completed his usual external walkaround, I climbed into the rear seat of 111-14. A ground crewman followed me up the ladder, and helped me to find and fasten all the straps, and then connected the anti G, oxygen and radio systems. He carefully removed the safety-pins from the emergency canopy release, the ejection seat, and the external stores jettison system, and handed them all to me for stowage in the flight box. Carretero joined us to check that everything was in order, and then strapped himself into the front cockpit. Once settled, he was on the intercom, telling me that the canopy was about to be closed and to keep clear of the rail. The canopy then hissed down into place, edged forward a little, and locked itself. My immediate impression was of the narrowness of the closed cockpit, but the Martin-Baker seat was surprisingly comfortable.

Carretero again came over the intercom, advising me that he was starting the engine: a series of noises from the rear of the aircraft signalled the start, and the cockpit began to pressurize. Some brief final checks, and then it was a thumbs-up signal to the ground-crewman standing to our left, and we were waved out of the parking spot. The other two aircraft were already taxiing in front of us, heading for the 'last chance' area at the head of runway 30. We were all carrying 880 gal (4000 lt) of JP-4 in fuselage and external tanks.

After a short delay we lined up for a formation take-off. Carretero applied the brakes and selected full power, and as soon as the formation leader nodded his head, the brakes were released and the afterburner engaged. The Mirage leapt forward at a terrific rate, and a glance at the ASI a few seconds later registered 140 knots. The nosewheel was lifted for rotation, and at 175 knots we were airborne, with the gear coming up almost immediately as the engine was moved back into dry power. A slight bank to the left to move away from other traffic in the vicinity, and the formation was soon climbing rapidly on a heading of 240 degrees towards the intercept training area over Albacete province. 'Pegaso' cleared us to 30,000 feet, and we established the cruise at Mach 0.92.

During the climb I quickly appreciated the superb vision from the rear seat. The noise level in the cockpit was very low, with only a slight humming sound from the pressurization unit just behind me. GCI control cleared our aircraft up to a more economical FL350, while the other two broke away to conduct a separate part of the sortie.

Carretero now began some aerobatics, including barrel rolls, a loop and an Immelmann turn. After he had finished, with the aircraft once more in a normal attitude, control was passed to me, and for a short time I tried my hand at some more rolls and a chandelle. The Mirage is a big aircraft, and its high rate of roll and general responsiveness were

remarkable. Next came some ACM (air combat manoeuvres) as we both kept a sharp look-out for the other two Mirages, which had finished their individual exercises and were now being vectored towards us for a stern missile attack.

The incoming 'attackers' were sighted in our 5 o'clock, some 2000 feet below us and closing fast. Carretero rolled inverted and made a split-S manoeuvre, pressing me hard against the seat-pan and forcing my suit to inflate as it took the strain of our 5 G turns. We soon had one of the opposition in our 10 o'clock, trying hard to disengage by going into a barrel roll. We managed to position even closer to our quarry, and at 1800 m Carretero called 'Fox-2' as he simulated a Sidewinder launch. The engagement was concluded, and we rendezvoused with the other aircraft some 30 miles SE of Manises, to fly some exhilarating aerobatics in formation.

After more than an hour in the air, we lined up in echelon for a run-and-break over the airfield, and all too soon we had taxied back to dispersal. In the back seat of 111-14 was a new convert to the Mirage—the aircraft was everything they told me, and more!

28 April 1982
An air-to-ground mission in Mirage IIIDE 111-15/CE.11-29, with Capt Romero as pilot. The aircraft carried two 285 gal (1300 lt) drop tanks, and two LAU-32 2.75 inch FFAR pods on the outboard stations. Take-off was timed at 09:05 hrs, and we landed one hour and 20 minutes later.

1 February 1983
The same aircraft as in August 1979 (111-14), and again with Capt Jesús Romero at the controls. This was a practice air-to-ground sortie, in company with 112-05/C.11-10 flown by Maj Ferrero (the CO of 112 Escuadrón), and 111-12/C.11-23 flown by Lt Ibañez. After the attack phase of the mission, I was able to fly the aircraft for a short time as we returned to Manises. I normally fly Spanish-built 'Colometa' ultra-light

ABOVE
The author's sorties were all flown aboard two-seat Mirage IIIDEs. This particular aircraft, newly coded 11-71, is about to depart for a training sortie. The auxiliary intake doors are, unusually, open (S Mafé)

BELOW
Gun-camera view of a practice combat high over the Mediterranean. The 'enemy' is a Mirage F.1 from Ala de Caza 14 *which is about 1700 metres away—optimum range for a Sidewinder shot (*Ala 11 *via Muñoz)*

ABOVE RIGHT
Capt Jesús Romero, seen here beside one of Ala 11's aircraft at Manises in February 1983, participated in four of the author's Mirage sorties (Romero)

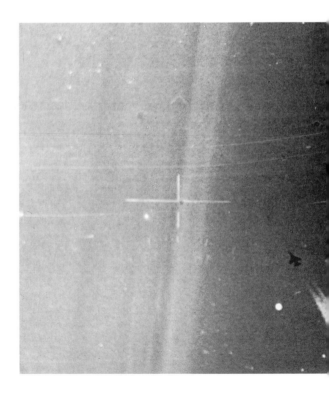

aircraft, and the differences between the two could not be more pronounced! In spite of the Mirage's relatively poor thrust/weight ratio—especially in dry power only—the French delta is a true fighter pilot's aeroplane, with sparkling manoeuvrability and an excellent positional sense. The ever helpful Jesús Romero demonstrated a short tactical landing on our return to Manises. The braking parachute was deployed while still airborne (just) over the threshold, and the nose was held high to use the big delta wing as an aerodynamic brake. The additional vigorous use of wheel brakes brought the aircraft to a halt after about 3000 feet—which is nowhere near as good as modern fighters, but not at all bad for a fast jet based on 1950s technology.

2 February 1983

Flying in the Mirage III is becoming something of a routine! For this trip I was in the back seat of 112-14/CE.11-28, piloted by Jesus Pinillos—one of the most accomplished fighter 'jocks' I have ever known (in 1988 he was appointed as CO of one of the two F/A-18 squadrons at Zaragoza). The sortie was planned around some DACT manoeuvres against two *Ala* 14 Mirage F.1s, and our flight leader was Capt Bestard in 112-05/C.11-10. Dogfighting in a clear blue sky at 30,000 feet was spectacular, with some gut-wrenching 6 G turns as we positioned for a kill on the F.1 leader. Just as we were about to call the shot, his wingman came out of nowhere and called a 'Fox-2' on us. Having been 'destroyed' we knocked it off, and waited for 112-05 to join up with 112-09/C.11-18—the third aircraft from our formation, piloted by Lt Gutierrez. All three in contact again, we

continued towards the Caude air-to-ground range, where we fired four 2.75 inch FFARs with smoke-marker warheads. We made our operational run as though we were attacking an AA site, at 250/400 feet and 400–500 knots over the uninhabited area surrounding the range. Then the aircraft pitched up—really spectacular stuff—inverted into zero G, with all the dirt from the floor floating around us. Pinillos located the rocket circle on the range below, and started a 30 degree dive, rolling through the vertical again before loosing off the first round. The release of the first rocket came as something of a surprise to me in the rear seat, because the sharp noise of its departure from the left pod was clearly audible, even through the canopy and helmet. We made a separate pass for each rocket fired. The first round impacted slightly to one side of the target; the second was an absolute spot-on bull's-eye; the third was obviously a defective round—probably with a tail-fin not deploying properly—because it began to corkscrew wildly as soon as it left the pod; and the fourth smacked into the circle, not far away from number two. What a splendid day!

18 February 1985

This sortie was in Mirage IIIDE 112-15/CE.11-30, with my good friend Jesús Romero as pilot. Our call-sign was *Dolar 13*, and we flew in company with 112-14/CE.11-28 (Maestre/Grau) as *Dolar 14* and 112-09/C.11-18 (Nuñez) as *Dolar 15*. This was a ground-attack training mission, with a little inter-service co-operation thrown in, and we carried 880 gal (4000 lt) of JP-4 and a pair of 2.75 inch rockets. Taxiing out to runway 30 in a calm wind, we stopped at the 'last chance' check area to allow the armourers to remove safety pins from the rocket pods, and arm the cannons of *Dolar 15* so that he could do some gun-qualification passes on the range. Taking off on time, we joined up in cruise formation and remained together throughout the transit, until it was time for us to split up for our individual range exercises. Romero was required to fire only two rockets, each on a separate pass: one of them was off target, but the second was well inside the circle. During the pull-out at the end of each pass we were subjected to just over 4.5 G, and although this is uncomfortable, it feels totally insignificant alongside the sheer exhilaration of being on board a jet fighter. After the range work we crossed the coastline and headed out to sea, dropping down to low level for the benefit of a Spanish Navy corvette that was exercising her ESM and fire-control radars. After about 20 minutes of these low passes, I began to understand some of the problems faced by the *Grupo* 6 Dagger pilots during the Falklands War.

Facelift for the Spanish Mirage IIIs

In 1983 the Spanish Government agreed to buy 72 McDonnell Douglas F/A-18 Hornets, with deliveries extending over a four-year period, starting in 1986. These aircraft were destined to re-equip Torrejon-based *Ala* 12 (replacing the F-4C Phantom II), and to activate a new *Ala* 15 at Zaragoza. *Ala* 15 was the first Hornet wing to commission, and many former Mirage III pilots were among its initial aircrew cadre.

At that time, it seemed certain the the days of the Mirage III in Spanish AF service were numbered. Some rumours even suggested that *Ala* 11 would be disbanded altogether once all the F/A-18s had been delivered, leaving the aircraft to be sold off to Argentina or Brazil. Such a plan would have been financially attractive, but it would also have led to

an unacceptable decrease in the Spanish Air Force's capability.

In 1985 it was decided to explore the possibility of upgrading the Mirages, and an initial approach was made to Israel Aircraft Industries. A more detailed study was carried out in 1986, and this proposed that one aircraft should be sent to Israel to act as a prototype for the conversion, while the remainder would be upgraded in Spain. The total cost of the programme was US 177 million dollars.

While the IAI offer was still being considered, Dassault entered the arena with its own proposal to modernize the fleet, bringing with it a lot of political pressure to have the work completed in Europe. Under the Israeli offer, Spanish industrial participation (Ceselsa) would amount to 60 per cent of the total workshare, whereas the Dassault scheme would allow only 40 per cent (managed by CASA).

In the event, neither scheme was fully adopted, but after many months of indecision IAI was chosen to act as consultant to the Mirage upgrade programme. A joint venture company was set up in Spain by Ceselsa (75 per cent) and CASA (25 per cent), and a contract was finally signed on 28 December 1988. The overall programme—known as C.11M (for modified)—provides for the upgrading of 18 Mirage IIIEE interceptors and five Mirage IIIDE trainers, to be completed by late 1993 or early 1994. The first aircraft (C.11-9) went into the workshops in March 1989, and its 'first flight' is due in early 1991.

Among the improvements planned are: a new AN/APQ-159 fire-control radar; a head-up display and new F/A-18-style cockpit layout with two multi-function displays; compatibility with AIM-9L Sidewinders, AGM-54 Shrike and AGM-65 Maverick missiles; ECM and FLIR pods; a buddy-pack air-to-air refuelling system (with the two-seat aircraft acting as a mini tanker) and possibly canard surfaces to improve combat manoeuvrability. An advanced flight navigator system has also been ordered as part of the contract.

TOP
528 was one of the Ramat David-based Nesher/Mirage squadron, and is seen here after the war of October 1973. Its squadron insignia and yellow and black identification markings are clearly visible, as are those crediting it with two 'kills'. By 1982 most of the surviving Neshers, as well as the Mirages, had been supplied to Argentina as airworthy airframes or broken down for spare parts, and at present the Ramat David squadron operates F-16 Fighting Falcons (IDFAF)

ABOVE
South African Mirage IIID2Z firing a salvo of SNEB rockets from its JL-100 combined fuel tank and rocket pod. 849 was one of 11 Atar 09K-50-powered two-seaters delivered in 1972 (H Potgieter/SAAF)

ABOVE LEFT
Mirage IIIB from EC 2/2 'Cote d'or' before the Armée de l'Air *low-vised its markings*

LEFT
No 89 Combat Flying School at Pietersburg (to which 843 and 852 belong) was one of the first SAAF units to acquire the Cheetah. The Mirage IIID2Z was the first type to be rebuilt to Cheetah standard by Atlas Aircraft with assistance from IAI, and plans are afoot to modify all their surviving first-generation Mirages

ABOVE
A recce-Mirage of ER 33 based at Strasbourg Air Base. Eventually all of the IIIRs and IIIRDs will be replaced by Mirage F.1CRs

ABOVE LEFT
The Spanish Mirage IIIEEs are coded C.11-1 to C.11-24 and the IIIDEs CE.11-25 to CE.11-30 (originally CE.11-1 to CE.11-6). The two-seaters are undergoing a rather modest upgrade mainly of the navigation, communications and RWR systems together with structural modifications. In addition, they may be equipped with a buddy pack system, to enable them to act as tankers, and with externally mounted jamming pods for the electronic escort role

LEFT
A Venezuelan Mirage 5DV (5471) and an Argentine Mirage IIIEA (1-007) during a test flight after leaving Dassault's assembly line at Bordeaux (AMD/BA)

ABOVE
Many ships in the British task force were attacked by Daggers in the South Atlantic; a few were damaged by 30 mm cannon fire or bombs, although in most cases the damage was not telling

TOP
A Mirage IIICJ Interceptor from Grupo 10 de Caza. *Its camouflage is darker than that of* Grupo 4. *The radome contains communications equipment*

ABOVE
Mirage IIIRS R-2115 of Fligerstaffel 10 *leaps into the air thanks to the extra power provided by a set of RATO bottles. The Swiss Mirages are fitted with this system to allow them to operate from dispersed sites* (F + W)

RIGHT
The prototype Swiss ISMA (J-2302) featured canard foreplanes milled from solid light metal, but production canards were of an even lighter sandwich construction. The canard maintains the airflow over almost the entire span of the delta wing which delays flow separation at high angles of attack and improves the effectiveness of the rudder (F + W)

The Mirage IIIC was primarily an interceptor and air superiority fighter, with the air-to-air optimized Cyrano Ibis radar and the Atar 09B engine with its unique, two-nozzled jetpipe. Most Mirage IIICs carried the Matra R530 AAM in its semi-active or IR variants and the AIM-9B Sidewinder, seen here on two IIICs from EC2/10 'Seine'. The aircraft of EC 3/10, however, were modified to carry the Matra R550 Magic (AMD/BA)

Chapter 9
Mirage exports

More than 1500 Mirage III/5s (including Israeli Neshers) were built during the period 1960 to 1985. This chapter is a brief account of all the air arms that have operated the aircraft, with the exception of six nations that are more comprehensively detailed in separate chapters. For convenience, the notes are in alphabetical order.

Abu Dhabi

The Abu Dhabi AF is by far the largest national component of the United Arab Emirates AF, which is jointly funded and managed by the seven Gulf state members of the UAE Federation. Late in 1972, the Abu Dhabi AF ordered 12 Mirage 5ADs and two two-seat Mirage 5DADs, which were all delivered during 1973/74. Two years later a repeat order was signed, comprising an additional two-seat trainer, three Mirage 5RAD tactical reconnaissance aircraft, and 14 radar-equipped Mirage 5EADs—which were basically similar to the Mirage IIIE, but with added electronics. Initially European and Pakistani pilots were hired to fly the aircraft, while a large number of Arab pilots underwent a lengthy training programme in France. Early in 1988, about 27 Mirages remained on the active inventory with *I Shaheen* Sqn at Sharja International Airport, and *II Shaheen* Sqn at Al Dhafra AB: both squadrons are components of Western Air Command. The interceptor variants maintain QRA flights at both locations, as a precaution against the explosive military situation in the Gulf. The UAEAF is due to receive 36 Mirage 2000s by 1989/90.

Belgium

'We are fighter-bombers in the true sense of the word. Our Mirage 5s are bomb haulers, and our principal mission is to get those bombs from point A to point B, destroy the target, and return in one piece. To evade enemy defences we rely on our low-level speed,

effective camouflage, and the Rapport ECM system. Although we practise DACT, we only use it for defensive purposes.' These were the thoughts of a Belgain AF Mirage 5 pilot from *1er Escadrille*, as expressed to the author when a detachment from the squadron visited Manises/Valencia (Spain) early in 1986. Two years later, the once powerful Mirage force was cut in half—replaced by an additional batch of 44 F-16s.

The bilingual Belgian AF (*Force Aérienne Belge/Belgische Luchtmacht*) started to look for a replacement for its ageing F-84F Thunderstreaks and RF-84F Thunderflashes during the second half of the 1960s. After a lengthy evaluation of both the Mirage 5 and the Northrop F-5A, the Government announced in February 1968 that the French aircraft had been selected—albeit with US-made instrumentation and a more advanced (doppler) navigation system.

The original contract included 54 Mirage 5BA fighter-bombers (plus nine options), 22 Mirage 5BR tactical reconnaissance aircraft (plus five), and 12 two-seat Mirage 5BD trainers (plus four). All the options were eventually taken up, making a final acquisition total of 106 airframes. The first of each variant was built in France, and the remainder were assembled in Belgium by SABCA, with a number of subcontractors including Avions Fairey and FN.

The initial French-built fighter-bomber (serial BA.01) was flown for the first time on 6 March 1970, quickly followed by the first trainer (BD.01) on 31 March. The two-seat aircraft was delivered to Florennes AB in Belgium on 29 June, to prepare for the Operational Conversion Unit's formation on 15 July. Courses at the OCU began during October 1970, with eight French-trained senior pilots as the original cadre of instructors. By that time the Belgian assembly line was well under way, having delivered its first attack variant (BA.02) and two-seat trainer

(BD.02) within a few days of each other at the beginning of August. The first photo reconnaissance aircraft (BR.01) was flown by Dassault on 16 October 1970.

Belgian production of Mirage 5s ended in July 1973, with the delivery of the last attack aircraft (BA.63). At that time the operational deployment of the Mirage force was concentrated in two wings, each administering two squadrons. Florennes-based *2e Wing Tactique/2de Tactische Wing*, consisted of *2e Escadrille/Smaldel* with Mirage 5BA fighter-bombers; and *42e Esc/Smd* in the tactical reconnaissance role with Mirage 5BRs. At Bierset AB, *3e Wing Tactique/3de Tactische Wing* administered the fighter-bombers of *1ère Esc/Smd*; and *8e Esc/Smd*, which was the Mirage OCU, equipped with both trainers and attack aircraft. All three operational squadrons also had a small component of two-seat Mirage 5BDs for continuation crew training. This overall disposition of squadrons remained intact until the end of 1987.

During the early 1980s, all Belgian attack and reconnaissance Mirages were fitted with an internal ECM system to make them more able to survive over the modern battlefield. The US-manufactured Loral Rapport II system (Rapid Alert Programmed Power Management of Radar Targets) automatically disrupts hostile radar emissons through active jamming, and analyses the threat to enable the pilot to select chaff or flares as required.

ABOVE
The second Belgian Mirage 5BA (BA 02) and the first two-seat Mirage 5BD (BD 01) in flight together during 1970. The BAF Mirages originally carried a camouflage scheme similar to that developed by the USAF during the Vietnam War. It consisted of two shades of green and one of tan over the top surfaces, with light grey undersides. This was continued until the early 1980s, when most of the aircraft acquired a wrap-around scheme (Belgian AF)

ABOVE RIGHT
A Mirage 5BR from 42e Escadrille/Smaldel *during a navigation training exercise. This squadron moved to Bierset AB in 1988, leaving its place at Florennes to* 1ère Esc/Smd, *which was then in the process of converting to F-16s. The Belgian Mirage 5BRs are unusual in being equipped with a tailhook (just visible) for engaging an arrester cable, rather than relying on the conventional barrier system in an emergency (Belgian AF)*

The vast majority of Mirage 5BA sorties involve the air-to-ground disciplines of interdiction, offensive air support and counter air; while the Mirage 5BR has low-level photo reconnaissance as its primary role, and attack as secondary. Nearly all of these sorties are flown at an IAS of about 475 knots, and at very low level (500 feet in peacetime, and much

lower in wartime). This kind of flying, particularly in marginal northern European weather, is a risky business, and very unforgiving of mistakes. Inevitably the attrition rate has been fairly heavy compared with the high-level interceptor mission, although the Belgian figures are no worse than those of other air forces with a similar mission profile. During 18 years of operations, losses have amounted to 26 attack aircraft, nine reconnaissance and three two-seat trainers.

One of the negative influences on the Belgian AF is the number of hours its combat pilots are allowed to fly each year. During the peak funding period of F-16 procurement, budgetary difficulties forced this figure down to just over 100 hours per year (the NATO proficiency standard is 180 hours). Over the last few years the situation has improved slightly, and the allowance went up to 145 hours in 1985; 160 hours in 1987, and higher still for 1988. The Government is committed to reaching the NATO standard, but in the meantime the pilots' lack of practice is bound to have an impact on operational efficiency and safety— particularly during low-level sorties.

It was originally planned to start replacing the Mirage 5s with another batch of SABCA-built F-16s in 1985, but problems with the defence budget delayed the programme for several years. Re-equipment finally got under way in January 1988, when F-16s began to arrive at Florennes to supplant some of the Mirages of *2e Wing*. The 44

new aircraft will re-equip *2e Esc/Smd* initially, and then *1ère Esc/Smd*, which moved to Florennes from Bierset in 1988. When the programme is completed in 1989, *2e Wing* will be an all-F-16 unit, and the remaining Mirages will be concentrated in *3e Wing* at Bierset. This will consist of the Mirage OCU (part of *8e Esc/Smd*), and the reconnaissance aircraft of *42e Esc/Smd*—which swapped bases with *1ère Esc/Smd* earlier. The Mirages that remain after all the changes, will be upgraded minimally (avionics and airframe strengthening only) to ensure that they are credible as weapons systems in the future. They will then stay in the Belgian AF order of battle until after the turn of the century.

Brazil

Following a trend established by several of its neighbours, the *Fôrca Aérea Brasileira* (FAB) contracted to buy 12 Mirage IIIEBRs (designated F-103E by the FAB), and four two-seat Mirage IIIDBRs (F-103D) in mid 1970. The first aircraft were handed over at Bordeaux during the summer of 1972, and they remained in France for a short period while the initial cadre of pilots underwent training at Dijon. Deliveries were completed to the new air base at Anápolis, 78 km south-west of Brasilia, and the aircraft were integrated into a newly activated *1ª Ala de Defesa Aérea* (later changed to *1º Grupo Defesa Aérea*). The Group comprised two squadrons—*1º and 2º Escuadroes*—and was formed as part of

During 1987 a pair of BAF Mirage 5BAs were specially painted in commemorative colours to honour the seventieth anniversaries of their respective unit insignia. The 'Comet' symbol of 2e Esc/Smd was featured on BA 43, and the Scottish thistle of 1ère Esc/Smd appeared on BA 33. The Mirages were subsequently nicknamed Milky Way *and* Blackbird. *Both aircraft are equipped with the Loral Rapport II ECM system, which can be identified by a bulged area at the base of the fin* (Belgian AF)

LEFT
FAB Mirage IIIEBR coded 4916 in the early style natural metal finish, which was later changed to a blue/grey camouflage scheme. The F-103E designation is the Brazilian AF type number for the aircraft (AMD/BA)

ABOVE
A pair of Mirage 50FC attack aircraft serving with Chile's Grupo de Aviación No 4. *These machines were all ex-Armée de l'Air Mirage 5Fs, re-engined with the Atar 09K-50* (AMD/BA)

Comando Defesa Aérea (Air Defence Command). The squadrons worked in close co-operation with Brazil's air surveillance system called DACTA I, which initially covered the heavily populated areas of Brasilia, Sao Paulo and Rio de Janeiro. The coverage of the system was later extended under the DACTA II programme, and now includes much of the southern part of the country. The radars and computers were manufactured in France by Thomson-CSF and Volex, and the system has a dual military and civilian role.

Brazil has always had a requirement for many more Mirages, and batches of 50 or 60 have been discussed in the past. It was even thought at one time that the aircraft could be built under licence by Embraer, or at least ordered in kit form for final assembly in Brazil. The economic state of the country, however, soon put paid to such plans, and a more realistic repeat order for four interceptors was placed in 1978. A pair of additional trainers was also received in 1984, bringing the overall totals up to 16 interceptors and six two-seaters. During the mid-1980s, the original natural metal finish of the fighter variants was replaced by a more appropriate blue–grey camouflage scheme. The whole fleet was also given a limited mid-life upgrade as part of a refurbishment programme managed by Dassault, and fitted with the locally designed and produced Piranha IR-guided missile.

In spite of the additional aircraft acquired by

Brazil, the established strength of *1° Grupo* had fallen to 12 Mirage IIIEBR and three Mirage IIIDBR trainers by 1987. This was simply due to a heavier than expected loss rate, but it left the FAB without any reserve strength to cope with maintenance or modification programmes. Negotiations therefore began with the French Government to secure a batch of refurbished Mirage IIIEs from the *Armée de l'Air*. On 30 September 1988 the first of four upgraded, canard-equipped Mirage IIIE interceptors was handed over at Istres, and this batch was followed by two ex-*Armée de l'Air* Mirage IIIBE trainers.

Chile

Following the eruption of the 1978 Beagle Channel crisis between Argentina and Chile, the two countries entered a minor arms race, each trying to outdo the other by incorporating new equipment into its armed forces. One of the beneficiaries of this contest was the *Fuerza Aérea de Chile* (Chilean AF). In July 1979, negotiations were completed for the acquisition by Chile of 16 Mirage 50s. The order consisted of eight Mirage 50FC attack aircraft, six Mirage 50C interceptors and two Mirage 50DC two-seat trainers. The interceptors were all equipped with the Cyrano IVM redar, and the attack aircraft were ex *Armée de l'Air* (EC.13) Mirage 5Fs—which had originally been designed as Mirage 5Js for the Israeli Government. Before leaving France, the used aircraft were all refurbished and re-engined with the Atar 09K-50, bringing them up to full Mirage 50 standard.

The initial cadre of Chilean air and ground crews were trained at Dijon and Rochefort respectively, and the first four Mirage 50FCs arrived by sea at Antofagasta in June 1980. They were assigned to *Grupo de Aviación No 4*, and were first seen on 15 September 1980, during a brief commissioning ceremony at the Arturo Merino Benitez International Airport, near Santiago. The four remaining attack aircraft were received before the end of 1980, but the new-build interceptors and trainers were not delivered until 1982–83. In 1984, an ex-*Armée de l'Air* Mirage IIIBE trainer was also supplied. *Grupo No 4* is permanently based at Punta Arenas airfield in Tierra del Fuego. If hostilities were to flare up between Chile and Argentina, this strategically located base would be at the heart of the FACh's air defence network.

Although the Mirage force is still relatively new, the FACh has already opted for an upgrade programme that will make the aircraft even more effective in the future. The project is being managed by ENAER (*Empresa Nacional de Aeronautica*), with conversion kits and technical advice supplied by Israel Aircraft Industries. The aircraft will be fitted with canard surfaces (smaller than those on the Kfir), nose strakes and an AoA sensor, reinforced landing gear, a locally developed Caiquen III RWR, and the

ABOVE
One of the Cyrano-equipped Mirage 50C interceptors (No 511) acquired by the FACh in 1982. The aircraft is seen here over the Andes, demonstrating the effectiveness of the two tone blue/grey camouflage (FACh)

TOP RIGHT
The first Mirage 50C to be modified as part of the current upgrading programme was No 514, photographed here at ENAER's plant after completion of the work. Note the intake mounted canards and small nose strakes. The contoured splitter-plate is characteristic of the Mirage 50 series (ENAER)

ABOVE RIGHT
A pre-delivery shot of 3001, the first of two Mirage 5COD trainers acquired by Colombia. For a variety of reasons, the FAC Mirages have deteriorated badly, and they are now being upgraded and refurbished by IAI (AMD/BA)

Python III and Shafrir 2 air-to-air missile systems. As part of the programme, the single Mirage IIIBE will be re-engined with an Atar 09K-50 to bring it up to the same standard as all the other aircraft. A kit for this conversion is being supplied by Dassault.

The upgrade programme has already been delayed considerably, and by the end of 1988 only one aircraft (514) had been converted fully to the new standard. One single-seater and one trainer are due for conversion in 1989, and the programme will continue at a rate of about four aircraft per year. The fully updated Mirage has been renamed Pantera (Panther), and it bears a marked similarity to the Israeli Kfir C7. The FACh's surviving F-5E/Fs will remain in service for the time being following the collapse of a proposed deal involving the part-exchange of their F-5s for 12 Atar 09K-50-engined Kfir C7s.

Colombia

The *Fuerza Aérea Colombiana* needed a replacement for its small force of Canadair Sabre Mk 6 fighters, which had been withdrawn from use in 1965. Funding was a severe problem, and after several years and a number of evaluations—including Northrop

F-5As and refurbished F-100D Super Sabres—the Colombian Government finally signed a contract with Dassault in 1970. The order called for 14 Mirage 5COA fighters, two Mirage 5COR tactical reconnaissance aircraft and two Mirage 5COD trainers, with deliveries starting in September 1971. The Mirages equipped *1º Grupo de Combate*, which was wholly based on the Palanquero military airfield at German Olano, but detachments are now regularly deployed to Barranquilla and Santa Marta, and to San Andres Island in the Caribbean. Over the years, the fighters have often been used to intercept drug-running aircraft that operate from clandestine airstrips. These are normally forced to land at Government facilities and the crews arrested, but at least two have been shot down after failing to respond to warnings. One at least (believed to have been a DC-3), was destroyed by gunfire during an attack by a 1st Lt Nestor Raminez in 1980.

Colombia found that spares and technical support from Dassault were marginal at best, so backing was obtained from IAI. Over the last few years, the Israelis have supplied both technical advice and parts for the Mirages, and have now been contracted to

carry out a modest upgrade of the surviving aircraft. The programme will concentrate on electronic equipment and minor airframe strengthening, but canards will also be fitted to improve the manoeuvrability of the aircraft. Only two Mirages, both fighters, are known to have been lost, but a number are believed to be non-operational, and these will be refurbished and put back into service as part of the upgrading programme. Colombia has also agreed a US$200 million cash/barter arrangement with IAI for the supply of 13 Kfir C7s and TC7s.

Egypt

The Air Force of the Arab Republic ordered its first fighters of western origin for about 20 years when, in September 1973, a contract was placed with Dassault for the supply of 32 Mirage 5SDEs (basically similar to the Mirage IIIE), and six Mirage 5SDD two-seat trainers. The purchase was funded by Saudi Arabia to cover some of the losses of Soviet-made aircraft during the Yom Kippur War. Due to the urgency of the situation, the first three aircraft of each type were taken from *Armée de l'Air* production slots. After being used for crew training at Dijon, they were delivered to Egypt in Saudi Arabian AF markings, the first batch arriving in October 1974. The Egyptian Government subsequently funded three additional contracts direct from Cairo: 14 Mirage 5SSEs were ordered in December 1975; another eight 5SSEs and six tactical reconnaissance Mirage 5SDRs were ordered towards the end of 1977; and 16 Mirage 5E2s were ordered in 1980. The 5E2 variant was fitted with the more powerful Atar 09K-50 engine,

and equipped with an enhanced nav/attack system which included the Sagem ULISS 81 inertial platform, a head-up display and a laser rangefinder. Egypt therefore received a total of 82 Mirages, all of which were delivered by the end of 1983. The aircraft are all assigned to a single brigade (roughly equivalent to a western-style Group), incorporating three operational squadrons and an OCU, all based at Tanta and Genaclis. Eight of the OCU aircraft formed the national aerobatic team.

Initially the Mirages were used in the air superiority role, and their first operational sorties were as escorts to EAF Su-7s and Su-20s during the July 1977 war with Libya. For an attack on the Libyan air base at El Adem, the Egyptian fighters were painted with large black/yellow identification markings on all the wing and tail surfaces—a ploy originated by the Israelis to avoid air-to-air confusion with Libyan Mirages. In the event, the Libyan AF did not rise to challenge the raiders.

Now that the EAF has F-16s and Mirage 2000s, the main role of the Mirage 5s has been switched to ground-attack. As a result, the aircraft are undergoing a limited upgrade, with technical support from Dassault. Some elements of the attack system will be changed, and all the aircraft will be equipped to launch 'smart' air-to-ground weapons.

Gabon

The *Force Aérienne Gabonaise* ordered three Mirage 5Gs and two Mirage 5DG trainers in mid 1975 (the contract originally included two Mirage 5RG reconnaissance aircraft, but these were subsequently

cancelled). Deliveries were completed in 1978, but all five machines remained in France until 1980 to train FAG pilots and support personnel. When the crews were up to the required standard, the aircraft were ferried to their main operating base at Libreville Airport, close to the country's capital. Just a year after arriving, two of the Mirages were lost in a mid-air collision, and the others began to deteriorate in Gabon's exceptionally hot and rainy climate. A repeat order was announced in 1982, which comprised four Mirage 5G-IIs and two Mirage 5DG-II trainers. The three original FAG aircraft were also refurbished by Dassault, and their reappearance over Libreville in 1985 gave rise to false reports that another three had been ordered.

Lebanon

To supplement the Hunters then in service with the *Force Aérienne Libanaise*, the Defence Ministry in Beirut signed a contract with Dassault for ten Mirage IIIELs and two Mirage IIIBL trainers, plus a small number of R530 air-to-air missiles. Deliveries began in September 1967, and were completed in March 1969. Since then the aircraft have been little used, and are probably stored in an unserviceable condition. Some reports suggest that they are now under Syrian control, but even if this is true, they are almost certainly non-operational due to lack of spares and support.

Libya

Shortly after Mu'ammar el-Gaddafi deposed King Idris in the 1969 coup, oil-rich Libya ordered 110 Mirage 5s for the newly-formed *Al Quwwat Al Jawwiya Al Libiyya* (Libyan AF). This was a major production contract for Dassault, comprising 15 Mirage 5DD trainers, 32 Mirage 5DE radar-equipped fighter-bombers, 10 Mirage 5DR reconnaissance platforms and 53 Mirage 5Ds—which were basically fighter-bombers, but with much simpler avionics than the 5DE variant. The deal also included

ABOVE
With initial deliveries being made in October 1974, the Saudi-funded Mirage 5SDEs were the first western fighters acquired by Egypt for 20 years. In 1977, the aircraft were painted in these yellow and black identification markings to avoid air-to-air confusion with Libyan AF Mirages (AMD/BA)

BELOW
Gabon's small fleet of Mirages was delivered to Libreville in 1980, but they deteriorated quickly in the equatorial African climate and had to be returned to France for refurbishment in late 1984. This Mirage 5G has been fitted with an arrester hook (AMD/BA)

a flight simulator and a substantial amount of ground support.

Delivery of the trainers and radar-equipped fighter-bombers began in 1971, but Mirages had appeared over Tripoli some time before that. Five *Armée de l'Air* two-seaters from ECT 2/2 were painted to represent Libyan aircraft for a display celebrating the first anniversary of the Islamic Republic. They carried their Libyan markings from 28 August to 4 September 1970, and each of them took part in the flypast with a French command pilot and a Libyan student pilot on board. The final batch of Libyan aircraft was delivered in 1974.

At the start of operations, very few local pilots were qualified on the Mirage, and most of the aircraft had to be flown by highly paid foreigners. The main operating base is the ex-RAF airfield at El Adem (subsequently renamed Gemal Abdel Nasser AB), although several outlying airfields have been used as Mirage satellite bases. There were originally four

TOP
This Mirage IIIEL, photographed before delivery in February 1969, is one of ten acquired by the Force Aérienne Libanaise, *together with a pair of two-seat trainers. The internal problems suffered by Lebanon over the past decade or so have resulted in the aircraft being little used, and their present whereabouts and condition are unknown* (AMD/BA)

ABOVE
Libya has been one of the major users of first generation Mirages, with orders totalling 110 aircraft. The November 1969 contract included the acquisition of 53 Mirage 5D attack aircraft (illustrated here), making it by far the most numerous single variant. At least two of these aircraft were shot down over Chad, and the condition of the remaining Mirage force must be in doubt, because the French government has cut off all technical support (AMD/BA)

ABOVE
The first version of the Mirage to enter Pakistan AF service was the Cyrano-equipped IIIEP; these were all delivered between October 1967 and April 1969. The 18 fighter-bombers re-equipped No 5 Sqn, and were used extensively during the 1971 war with India. Aircraft No 67.112 is seen here releasing a cluster of 400 kg bombs from its reinforced RPK-17 tanks (PAF)

operational squadrons, plus an OCU, but this situation may well have changed following aircraft losses and general lack of availability.

During the October 1973 Yom Kippur War, some of the Libyan Mirages were deployed to Egyptian bases, and with EAF markings made a number of raids into Israel: at least five of them were lost to ground and air defences. Libyan Mirages have also been involved in several incidents with USAF and USN Elint aircraft, and with 6th Fleet carrier-borne fighters, although no actual combats have been reported. During the brief war between Libya and Egypt in the summer of 1977, Mirages were rarely used, but their main base was attacked by the Egyptian AF on 22 July, and some of the aircraft were damaged on the ground. During 1987, at least two Mirage 5s were shot down with SA-7 or Stinger missiles in northern Chad, and some of the aircraft may also have been overrun by Chadian forces during the final weeks of the conflict. As many as 30 Libyan aircraft were captured during the final push north, but their types have never been fully detailed.

Libya's intervention in the civil war in Chad was a remarkably short-sighted policy. French troops and aircraft had been supporting Chadian Government forces against guerrillas in the north, and as soon as Libya stepped in to bolster nothern defences, France simply embargoed all further spares and support for nearly 60 Mirage F.1s and about 80 Mirage 5s. A handful of aircraft that were in France for overhaul were also seized. The availability rate of Libyan Mirages has always been poor (some reports suggest that as many as 80 per cent of them are grounded), but it now seems likely that their actual numbers have also declined to about half their original level.

Pakistan

After the 1965 war with India, the Pakistan AF started to look for more fighters, despite giving an excellent account of itself during the year-long hostilities. India had lost 34 combat aircraft to Pakistan's 15, but the IAF still had a substantial numerical advantage. Washington had decreed an arms embargo on both countries, and apart from spares to maintain existing hardware, no further contracts were permitted with US manufacturers. Instead, the PAF acquired an initial batch of 79 Shenyang F-6s (MiG-19SF copies) from China; 90 Canadair Sabre Mk 6s from Germany (via Iran); and a first batch of Mirages to supplement the 12 ex-USAF F-104As that were supplied before the war.

The order placed with Dassault was for 18 Mirage IIIEP interceptors, three Mirage IIIDP two-seat trainers, and three Mirage IIIRP reconnaissance aircraft (these were fitted with British-made Vinten cameras instead of the more usual Omera equipment). The aircraft were initially assigned to No 5 Sqn at Sargodha, with deliveries extending over a period of 18 months, starting in October 1967. In 1970, Pakistan placed a repeat order for 28 Mirage 5PA fighter-bombers and two additional trainers. During the 14-day war with India in 1971, aircraft from the original batch destroyed ten IAF machines without sustaining any losses themselves—although India did make claims to have shot down six.

During 1975 another ten Vinten-equipped reconnaissance aircraft were ordered, and these were followed in 1979 by a second big order for Mirage 5s. This final contract was for 32 aircraft, comprising Mirage 5PA2s with the Cyrano IVM air-to-air radar, Mirage 5PA3s with an Agave surface-attack radar, and two Mirage 5DPA2 trainers. The surface-attack aircraft were configured to fire the AM39 Exocet anti-shipping missile. The last of 96 Mirage III/5s for Pakistan was delivered at the end of December 1982.

Since 1978, all airframe and engine overhauls on the aircraft have been completed by the specialist Mirage Rebuild Factory at the Kamra Aeronautical Centre. A progressive update programme is currently underway, which includes among other items the fitting of a Litton LW-33 inertial nav/attack system. In early 1989 about 70 aircraft remained in service with the following units:

No 5 Squadron	Sargodha AB	Mirage IIIEP and IIIDP
No 8 Squadron	Marsoor AB	Mirage 5PA3
No 20 Squadron	Rafiqui AB	Mirage IIIRP and 5PA
No 22 OCU	Marsoor AB	Mirage IIIDP, 5DPA2 and 5PA
No 33 Squadron	Shorkot AB	Mirage 5PA2

The Combat Command School at Sargodha has a small flight of Mirage 5PAs.

During 1984, No 9 Sqn's Mirage 5PAs were replaced with F-16s. Until the arrival of these American fighters, the Mirage squadrons had flown CAPs over the ill-defined border with Afghanistan, and unconfirmed reports suggest that two or three kills have been claimd against intruding aircraft during the eight years of war.

Peru

The *Fuerza Aérea Peruana* was the first air arm in South America to acquire Mirages. The initial batch of 14 Mirage 5Ps and two Mirage 5DP trainers was ordered early in 1968, and deliveries began on 7 May that year. Follow-up orders were delivered during 1974 (eight Mirage 5DPs); 1976 (one Mirage 5DP) and 1979 (eight Mirage 5Ps and two trainers), making a total of 35 airframes. The aircraft were all assigned to *Grupo 13 de Caza* at Chiclayo AB in northern Peru, where they equipped *Escuadrons* 12 and 14. In May 1982, a batch of ten Mirage 5P ground-attack aircraft was sold to Argentina, and an upgrade programme was initiated on the remaining Peruvian machines. The 5P variant was fitted with the Cyrano IVM radar and Atar 09K-50 engine to become the Mirage 5P3; or with an Agave radar and refuelling probe to become the Mirage 5P4. The corresponding trainers, which were similarly optimized for air-to-air or air-to-ground sorties, became Mirage 5DP1s and 5DP3s. In all cases nav/attack systems were modified to include a Litton inertial platform, a head-up display and a laser rangefinder. The Peruvian aircraft are equipped with Matra Magic air-to-air missiles, and they participated in CAPs and attack sorties during border skirmishes with Ecuador in the early 1980s—

TOP RIGHT
The Pakistan AF received a total of 13 Doppler-equipped Mirage IIIRP reconnaissance platforms, and aircraft 67.213 was the last to be delivered. It is carrying 375 gal (1700 lt) drop tanks, and the speed brakes are partially extended (PAF)

CENTRE RIGHT
Pakistan's 28 Mirage 5PAs were ordered in 1970, and in 1988 they equipped No 20 Sqn and No 22 Operational Conversion Unit. This version does not have the distinctive external doppler housing (AMD/BA)

RIGHT
This Mirage 5DP (No 199) was the last of five two-seat trainers acquired by the Peruvian Air Force. Note the sand and brown camouflage scheme (AMD/BA)

although no losses were incurred on either side. About 18 Mirage 5s remained in Peruvian service at the beginning of 1988.

South Africa

The *Suid Afrikaanse Lugmag* (South African AF) was one of the earliest Mirage customes, with its first order dating back to 1962. Since then a total of 41 single-seat and 17 two-seat aircraft have been supplied in several different variants, all of them delivered between 1962 and 1974. The order batches were as follows:

16 Mirage IIICZ interceptors
3 Mirage IIIBZ trainers
17 Mirage IIIEZ interceptor/attack
4 Mirage IIIRZ tactical reconnaissance
3 Mirage IIIDZ trainers (with doppler)
11 Mirage IIID2Z trainers (with Atar 09K-50)
4 Mirage IIIR2Z tactical reconnaissance (with Atar 09K-50)

The Mirage IIICZ interceptors were all assigned to No 2 Sqn at Waterkloof AB, together with the IIIBZ trainers. When the Mirage IIIEZ interceptor/attack aircraft started to arrive in South Africa, they too were initially assigned to No 2 Sqn, but as their numbers built up, No 3 Sqn was reactivated to receive them and later the Doppler-equipped IIIDZ trainers. The tactical reconnaissance Mirage IIIRZs joined No 2 Sqn from November 1966, and the whole unit was transferred to a new base at Hoedspruit, near the Mozambique border, during the mid 1970s. No 85 Advanced Flying School at Pietersburg AB began to receive the more-powerful Mirage IIID2Z trainers from October 1974, and during the spring of 1975 this unit also took over responsibility for all the Mirage IIIEZ/IIIDZ aircraft, when No 3 Sqn was converted to Mirage F.1s. The Mirage IIIR2Z reconnaissance aircraft were assigned to No 2 Sqn.

Between 1975 and 1988, SAAF Mirage IIIs were frequently deployed to bases inside South West Africa/Namibia, south of the so-called 'operational area' along the 1500 km border with Angola. Most of these deployments were to Ondangwa airfield, close to the centre of the Bush War being fought by South African Defence Forces (SADF), against the South West Africa People's Organisation (SWAPO) and the Angolans—who were extensively backed by Cuban troops and a variety of Eastern Bloc advisers. For its part, the South African Government was providing active support for UNITA (in English, the National Union for the Total Freedom of Angola)—a subversive anti-communist movement within Angola.

Five South African AF Mirage IIICZs in the early paint scheme of No 2 Sqn (AMD/BA)

ABOVE LEFT
Mirage IIIBZ trainer (No 818) shows a slightly developed colour scheme, adding a red fin to the existing red intake surround and cheat line (SAAF)

LEFT
Former Mirage IIID2Z No 845 served as the Cheetah prototype. Photographed here in July 1986, the aircraft shows a marked similarity to the IAI Kfir TC7— particularly around the nose and intake-mounted canards. Eventually all of the SAAF's surviving Mirage IIIs will be converted to a similar standard. The first unit to receive the type was No 5 Sqn, which commissioned on 1 January 1988 (SAAF)

ABOVE
Seen from a similar angle, the transformation of No 845 is clearly visible (AMD/BA)

During this undeclared war, SAAF personnel were rotated through the area for a three-month tour of duty every year. The Mirage IIIs were heavily involved in reconnaissance and attack missions, but many air-to-air sorties were also flown. For these escort or CAP missions, the aircraft carried the locally-developed Kukri IR-guided missile (aerodynamically similar to the Matra Magic). A number of Angolan aircraft were destroyed by Mirage IIIs during strike missions against their bases, particularly during the 1987–88 period of bitter fighting between UNITA and Government forces in SE Angola. The airfield at Wito Wnavale was attacked during this period, and about 20 enemy aircraft were claimed destroyed by the SAAF and many of these were Mirage III kills. Over the years of fighting, Angolan authorities have repeatedly claimed that 'Mirage III-type aircraft' were shot down over its territory, but SAAF HQ denied the claims, and confirmed that no Mirages had been lost in the combat zone.

During 26 years of Mirage III operations, the SAAF has only lost about 8–10 aircraft in accidents, the majority in South Africa, but at least two close to the western operational area. Undoubtedly one of the main reasons for this high safety and combat survival rate is the excellent standard of training provided by No 85 Air Combat School (previously the Advanced Flying School) at Pietersburg. Modelled on RAF lines, the courses at this school produce some of the best low-level fliers in the world.

The United Nations arms embargo against South Africa has forced Pretoria to invest in the formation of an effective aircraft industry. Progress over the last 20 years or so has been fairly good, particularly with Atlas Aircraft Corporation, which assembled the Impala (Macchi MB.326) trainer/light attack aircraft under licence. However, no capacity was available for the complete design and construction of a fast jet in the Mirage III category, and because an imported replacement was out of the question, it was decided to update the existing airframe. Contact was made with Israel Aircraft Industries for 'technical advice', and the final result was the Atlas Cheetah.

The Cheetah is an extensive upgrade of the Mirage III, basically bringing the aircraft up to Kfir standards. About 50 per cent of the airframe is rebuilt during the conversion, which includes strengthening of the major structural components, new landing gear, additional stores stations, canard surfaces, strakes under the nose and an extended dog-tooth wing. All these external changes make the Cheetah look very similar to a Kfir, but the continued use of the Atar 09K-50 engine instead of the embargoed J79, has done little to improve the aircraft's overall performance. The avionics suite is also similar to the latest Kfir C7, with the Elbit WDNS82 Weapons Delivery and Navigation System, an Elbit armament control and display panel, and the Elta EL/M2001B dual-purpose lightweight radar. The two-seat aircraft are known as Cheetah Ds and the single-seaters as Cheetah Es.

The first prototype aircraft (Mirage IIID2Z, serial 845) was converted by Atlas with IAI assistance, and shown for the first time in July 1986. After testing and a few minor changes, the design was fixed and a programme established to modify all surviving Mirage IIIs to the new standard. Following the conversion of the 48 or so existing airframes, there is a possibility that the line could be extended into building completely new aircraft, but this would almost certainly lead to some degree of 'sanctions busting' by component manufacturers, or an Israeli-style unlicenced copying operation.

The first Cheetah unit to be activated was No 5 Sqn, which was re-equipped from Impalas and commissioned on 1 January 1988 at the new Louis Trenchardt AB in Northern Transvaal. This base was opened in October 1987, and constructed very much along Israeli lines—with widely dispersed and camouflaged facilities, hardened aircraft shelters, and broad parallel taxiways that can serve as standby runways.

Venezuela

The *Fuerza Aérea Venezolana* received its initial order for 15 Mirages in three batches, starting with four Mirage 5V attack aircraft during November 1972. These were followed by two Mirage 5DV two-seat trainers in February 1973, and then nine Mirage IIIEV interceptors, which began to arrive in May 1973. They were all originally assigned to *Grupo Aéreo de Caza 11* at El Libertador AB, Palo Alto, where they equipped *Escuadron No 34* (Mirage 5Vs and 5DVs—which included the OCU task) and *Escuadron No 33* (Mirage IIIEVs). The Group's primary role was air defence of the country and its coastline, and all the Mirages were configured to carry the old AIM-9B Sidewinder missile. The air defence task was switched to *Grupo 16 de Caza* during 1984–85, when the first squadron of General Dynamics F-16A/Bs was activated. The new aircraft moved into El Libertador, close to the capital Caracas, and the Mirages were transferred to Barquisimeto AB, about 200 km west of Caracas.

A single attrition replacement Mirage IIIEV was acquired in 1977, but losses overall have been very

high, and by December 1987 only eight Mirages remained in service. Three of the fighter variants were lost in a single mid-air collision during 1986. The surviving aircraft are reported to be two Mirage 5Vs, five Mirage IIIEV interceptors and one 5DV trainer, all of which now form *Escuadron 36* of *Grupo de Caza 12*.

In March 1988, Venezuela signed a contract with Dassault for 12 Mirage 50s. These aircraft will be taken from *Armée de l'Air* stocks, and modified up to Mirage 50 standard during an extensive refurbishment programme. As a follow-on to the acquisition of these aircraft, all the existing Venezuelan Mirages will be updated to Mirage 50 standard. The whole programme will be completed by the end of 1991.

Zaire

The *Force Aérienne Zairoise* ordered 14 Mirage 5Ms and three dual-control Mirage 5DMs in late 1973. Deliveries began in 1975, and the aircraft equipped *211 Escadrille* at Kamina, which is part of *21 Wing de Chasse et d'Assaut*, administered by *2 Groupement Aérienne Tactique*. The conversion of FAZ air and ground crews was initiated with ECT 2/2 at Dijon, and completed in Zaire by Belgian and French instructors. The Mirages and MB.326s of 21 Wing form the primary interception and attack elements of Zaire's small but effective air force.

During 1983/4, a flight of four Mirages from 211 *Escadrille* were deployed to Djamena International Airport in Chad to support the French and Chadian

A beautiful study of Mirage 5V No 2473 of the Fuerza Aérea Venezolana, *taken during an acceptance flight near Bordeaux* (AMD/BA)

forces during Operation 'Manta'. The serviceability and loss rate for the Mirage in Zaire has been poor, due almost entirely to lack of resources and maintenance capability. At the end of 1988, the squadron's strength was reported to be down to seven Mirage 5Ms and only one trainer.

Chapter 10
Falklands combat – the Dagger

In 1978, as tension between Argentina and Chile over the Beagle Channel affair began to build up, it looked as though open warfare between the two could break out at any time. As a precaution, the *Fuerza Aérea Argentina* (FAA) entered a mad scramble to buy some more fast combat jets. The new aircraft were needed to complement the existing fleet of Douglas A-4B/C Skyhawks, and a small number of Dassault Mirage IIIEA/DAs. It was originally intended that they replace the old F-86F Sabres serving with *Grupo 4 de Caza*, but in the event, the Sabres were not finally retired until 1986.

The threat of a full-scale war developing in South America, coupled with the obvious human rights abuses of Argentina's military *junta*, made most of the 'traditional' sources reluctant to supply any further combat aircraft. Contact was therefore made with Israel, and almost immediately the supply problems disappeared. At that time the IDFAF had just established the Kfir in squadron service, and the 40 or so surviving Neshers were being withdrawn from use and sent to reserve parks for storage. The opportunity to get rid of most of them in one block was just too good to miss.

For the FAA, one of the biggest advantages of acquiring this copy of the Mirage 5 was the quick delivery offered by the supplier and 39 airframes (including four trainers) were obtained in 'fly away' condition. The aircraft were renamed 'Dagger' in Argentinian service, and on 28 August 1978 the first group of pilots for the temporarily named *'Escuadrón Dagger'* were selected. These early crews received

Grupo 6 de Caza was formally commissioned as the operational element of VI Brigada Aérea during December 1979. In the foreground is Lt Col Villar, who was to take part in dive bombing attacks on British troop concentrations on 4 June 1982 (FAA)

their initial training in Israel, then went on to fly the Mirage 5 with *Grupo 13* in Peru, before finally completing their conversions with *Grupo 8 de Caza* in Argentina. In November 1978, the first six Daggers arrived at Buenos Aires by sea. They were dispatched by road to *Aérea Material Rio IV* (the FAA's central air depot), where, with Israeli help, they were completely overhauled, assembled, and finally test flown. There were a few initial problems with engine bay overheating and small fires as a result of corroded fuel pumps, but these were quickly resolved as experience built up.

The Dagger's first public appearance was at the *Escuela de Aviación Militar* (Military Air School) in January 1979, during a display to celebrate Brig Gen Garaffigna's succession to the post of Chief of the Air Staff. After a six-month period of testing, training and generally working up to operational status, the first Dagger was delivered to Tandil AB on 8 August 1979. The base itself (which has an 8500 foot runway)

takes its name from the nearby city, about 300 km south of the capital. During the following weeks all the available aircraft at *Rio IV* were ferried to Tandil, and on 3 December the *VI Brigade Aérea* was commissioned, with the temporary '*Escuadrón Dagger*' becoming *Grupo 6 de Caza*.

Delivery of the first batch of aircraft, which comprised 24 Dagger A single-seat fighter-bombers and two Dagger B trainers, was completed in 1980. The second batch (11 Dagger As and two Bs) was received between May 1981 and February 1982. The majority of these aircraft had been used by the IDFAF as interceptors or air superiority fighters during the Yom Kippur War, and the FAA received a terrific operational boost from their early delivery. On arrival, most of them had less than 1000 hours airframe flight-time, and some were even as low as 500 hours. This represented, on average, only about 25 per cent of their anticipated fatigue lives. The equipment fit was fairly basic, with VOR, DME, ILS

and an Israeli-developed RWR, but the Dagger was a rugged aircraft, capable of absorbing a lot of combat damage without becoming unflyable. In the air-to-air role it carried two IR homing Shafrir 2 missiles. At the beginning of 1982, the FAA was working with the Israelis on a plan to update and modernize its Daggers, but the whole scheme was brought to an abrupt halt by the Argentinian occupation of a little-known group of islands in the South Atlantic.

April 1982—Preparing for the Inevitable

On 31 March 1982, *Grupo 6 de Caza* was under the command of Comodoro (Colonel) Thomas Rodriguez. His two flying squadrons were commanded by Maj Carlos Napolean 'Napo' Martinez (*1 Escuadrón*) and Maj Juan Sapolski (*2 Escuadrón*), both of whom had taken the Dagger conversion courses that began in Israel four years earlier.

The Argentinian occupation of the Falkland Islands on 2 April 1982 came as a big surprise to the majority of *Grupo 6* personnel—a pleasant surprise to some, but worrying for most of them. First Lieutenant Cesar Roman, an FAA Dagger pilot, explains his mixed feelings at the time:

As a Flight Commander, I was given some hours' notice by my superiors of the Argentine landings close to Stanley. I was made very nervous and tense by these events, but as a member of a fighter outfit I had a great desire to participate in any hostilities, because it would be our baptism of fire— putting all the daily training to good use . . .

Dagger B (C-426) seen at Tandil AB in October 1984. This was one of four two-seat trainers delivered to Argentina before the Falklands conflict. It has a Grupo 6 de Caza *badge on the tail* (Roman)

On the day of the occupation, *Grupo 6* had a total strength of 37 Daggers (a single-seat aircraft and a trainer had already been lost in separate accidents), of which 60/70 per cent were serviceable. Most of the ordinary pilots had very little experience on the type because the two squadrons had only recently been activated, but a small cadre within each squadron was very experienced in overall fast jet operations—these were the pilots who had already done tours of duty on the Sabre, Skyhawk or Mirage III. Summing up, the group's level of readiness for combat in the Dagger was a good deal lower than its commanders would have wished. One of the pilots, Jose Luis Gabari Zoco, said:

I had only just been posted to *Grupo 6 de Caza*, after a tour flying the A-4C Skyhawk at Mendoza. During early April 1982 I was instructed in the theoretical side of flying the Dagger, and I made my first actual flight on 20 April, together with other newcomers such as Capt Demierre and 1st Lt Antonietti. After that I flew as much as possible, even ferrying replacement aircraft to San Julian and Rio Grande . . .

Cesar Roman, a pilot with *2 Escuadrón*, was also very aware of his lack of readiness for combat against the force that he would soon encounter:

LEFT
The Argentine Dagger acquisition included a quantity of Shafrir 2 AAMs, seen here being checked by a Grupo 6 *armourer* (FAA)

ABOVE
Capt Carlos A Maffeis (left) and Maj Carlos N Martinez walk towards their Daggers for a training sortie before the invasion of the Falklands. The control tower at Tandil AB can be seen in the background (FAA)

BELOW
Four of the Grupo 6 de Caza *pilots deployed to San Julian pose together in front of Dagger C-412 on 2 May 1982. They are (left to right) Capt Dimeglio, 1st Lt Roman, 1st Lt Callejo and Lt Aguirre Faget* (Grupo 6)

During most of April I was involved in intensive training at Comodoro Rivadavia, learning as much as I could about anti-shipping operations against target vessels provided by our own navy. One thing certainly became very clear: attacking a moving target such as a ship at speed was a much more difficult task than I ever imagined before . . .

When the occupation of the islands was announced, *Grupo 6* as a whole immediately commenced an intensive training schedule, concentrating on maritime strike and air combat missions. On 25 April, most of the unit's strength was deployed to bases in southern Argentina, and thus two 'mobile squadrons' were activated. The first of these—*Escuadrón Aeromovil No 1*—took nine aircraft down to Rio Grande NAS in Tierra del Fuego, under the command of 'Napo' Martinez. At the same time Juan Sapolski deployed his unit—*Escuadrón Aeromovil No 2*, with ten aircraft—to the small civilian airfield at San Julian in the province of Santa Cruz. Both 'squadrons' were declared operational that afternoon, and began the uneasy wait for the British Task Force's arrival in the area.

In the air-to-air arena, the Dagger's main misson would be that of providing fighter cover for the Argentinian strike aircraft. One of the early worries during the long wait for the Task Force, was the risk of a night raid by the RAF on these remote and lightly

ABOVE
*Capt Horacio Mir Gonzalez from the Rio Grande-based
'Escuadrón Aeromovil No 1'. Note the silhouettes of a
warship and a cargo vessel on the nose of Dagger C-418*
(Gabari)

defended temporary bases. It was already known that
Vulcans and Victors had deployed to Ascension
Island, and the next logical step in a purely military
campaign would have been the destruction of any
runway within reasonable flying range of the
Falklands. These concerns are hinted at in Cesar
Roman's details of the deployment:

The distance from Tandil to San Julian was covered in
90 minutes, at a cruise speed of 500 knots at 35,000 feet.
During the last week of April, the tension among us reached
a high level as the British Task Force continued south, and
we became increasingly sure that a confrontation was
unavoidable. At 19:30 hrs on 29 April, the radar detected
some 'blips' far out into the ocean, and approaching San
Julian. (These were later thought to have been caused by

British electronic countermeasures.) The order was given
for the Daggers to redeploy immediately to Comodoro
Rivadavia, and the first aircraft were launched 30 minutes
later. Within ten minutes everyone was in the air, including
an A-4C Skyhawk squadron, but the whole thing proved to
be a false alarm and by mid-morning of the next day we
were all back at San Julian . . .

The Early Missions

The *Fuerza Aérea del Sur* (Southern Air Command)
launched the first Dagger mission towards the
Falklands at 07:45 hrs on 1 May. It was a section from
the Rio Grande-based No 1 Sqn, operating under the
callsign 'Toro' and crewed by Capt Moreno as leader,
and Lt Volponi as wingman. The aircraft were
conducting an air cover sortie, and each of them
carried two Shafrir 2 AAMs, 250 rounds of HEI
cannon ammunition and three 285 gal (1300 lt) drop
tanks. When they were about 50 nm west of Port
Stanley at 22,000 feet, the FAA radar controller
(using a Westinghouse AN/TPS-43E portable surveillance set) advised them about the presence of a
number of Royal Navy Sea Harriers that had just
raided the airfield. Almost before the message had
finished, two Sea Harriers, piloted by Lt Cdr Kent
and Lt Haigh from No 801 Sqn, came head-on for the
Grupo 6 Daggers. The two sections crossed over each
other, with the Daggers about 4000 feet above Kent
and Haigh. The four fighters started to fly in circles,
trying (unsuccessfully) to detect each other visually.
Diminishing fuel levels began to worry the Argentinian pilots seriously, and after some rapid mental
calculations they decided to abandon the search and
turn for home. Pushing the throttles into full
afterburner, Mareno and Volponi climbed towards
their best economical cruise altitude as quickly as
possible. Despite bad weather on their return to Rio
Grande, both aircraft acquired the ILS successfully
and landed without incident.

It was interesting to note afterwards that in this first
(bloodless) air engagement of the war, both Argentinian and British pilots believed that the others had
made use of air-to-air missiles. In fact this was not
true of either side. The impression of a smoking
missile was almost certainly caused by their fleeting
glances at drop tanks, which had been released to
improve dogfight manoeuvrability. These tumble
earthwards trailing a plume of vapourized fuel, and
their slender shape simply adds to the optical illusion.

At about 09:00 hrs on the same day, two more
Daggers were launched from Rio Grande, this time
with the callsign 'Foco'. Crewed by Capt Mir
Gonzalez and Lt Bernhardt, the aircraft provided
cover for several formations of Skyhawks from
Grupos 4 and 5. They met and engaged the Sea
Harriers in a similar way to 'Toro' section, but once
more they were forced by lack of fuel to break contact
and return home. By noon, a third air cover sortie had
been assigned to 'Ciclon' section, but after reaching

the Falklands, the pair failed to make contact with any Sea Harriers.

During the early hours of the afternoon, Brig Gen Crespo—the then commander of *Fuerza Aérea del Sur*—received information that several Royal Navy ships had been detected south-east of Port Stanley, probably getting ready for a shore bombardment session. He immediately issued a fragmentary order to the air bases under his command, to launch a new wave of strike and escort aircraft (those launched in the morning had not found any naval targets). At 15:30 and 15:40 hrs, two Dagger sections under the callsigns '*Dardo*' and '*Fierro*' were launched from San Julian, to provide cover for the fighter-bombers. '*Torno*' section followed immediately afterwards, composed of three Daggers, each armed with two 500 lb bombs and carrying the normal load of three 285 gal drop tanks: this section was led by Capt Dimeglio, with Lt Aguirre Faget in the number two slot and 1st Lt Roman as number three. Five minutes later '*Fortin*' section was launched in the escort role, with Capt Donadille and Lt Senn as pilots.

At 15:55 hrs '*Rubio*' section was due to depart from Rio Grande, but one of the pair developed a technical problem and was forced to abandon the take-off. The section leader, 1st Lt Jose 'Pepe' Ardiles (the cousin of a famous soccer star, who was then playing in England), decided to carry on with the mission, despite being fully justified in aborting when he lost his wingman. The decision was courageous but ill advised, and it would turn out to be a bad omen for the young Argentinian pilot. Capt Guillermo Posadas, the maintenance officer for *Escuadrón Aeromovil No 1* at San Julian, describes his feelings during the afternoon of 1 May:

ABOVE
Lt Aguirre Faget took part in the attack on three British warships on 1 May 1982. The Dagger in the background (C-432) was assigned to Capt Dimeglio during the same action, and the half-painted 'kill' marking denotes a damaged ship (FAA)

RIGHT
At the end of every mission, all aircraft that had been in the combat zone were carefully inspected for this kind of damage. The VHF antenna on this Dagger has been hit by shrapnel from British AA fire (Posadas)

At around 3.45 p.m. we launched a total of nine Daggers, which out of the ten available at San Julian was a pretty good effort. From our safe position on the ground, watching our friends depart into the dangerous eastern skies was very moving. On the runway threshold, with the Atars at maximum power and engaging afterburner, the noise level was overwhelming. The ground crews waved before take-off, and the pilots, like knights from a futuristic epic with their sun visors down and oxygen masks fitted, returned the salute.

After the noisy take-off, each one of us remaining on the field at San Julian was left with the same unanswered questions. Will they all come back? Will the engines work OK for the long over-water transits? Will they all be able to release their bombs or fire the guns when needed? And perhaps the most agonizing question of all, will the ejection seat work instantly on demand? These feelings probably haunt every combat aircraft engineer, and the anguish is only really dissipated by sight of the returning aircraft.

About 90 minutes later we received a message stating that our aircraft had engaged the enemy, and confirming that several British ships had been hit. A short time later, over the sea, we began to discern the landing lights of the first returning Daggers. We were very happy, mainly because all the aircraft were apparently coming home without damage.

At dusk, just after the last aircraft had landed, all the ground crews raced to meet the excited pilots, who gave us a first-hand account of the attack. Then we all went into the squadron's ready-room for an extensive post-mission debrief, which allowed the engineers to note any discrepancies in the aircraft and prepare them for the next sortie. The war had started in earnest . . .

While the Daggers from San Julian were still approaching the combat zone, the solitary aircraft from Rio Grande was unwittingly flying into trouble. Arriving over East Falkland, C-433 flown by Ardiles was vectored by the Argentine GCI onto a Sea Harrier CAP approaching from the north-east. A few seconds later, he 'tally-hoed' the Fleet Air Arm pair, and was visually detected by the British pilots at the same time. The Dagger was at 33,000 feet and the Harriers at 20,000 feet, and all three aircraft were closing head on. Ardiles began a shallow dive and launched a Shafrir missile against the Sea Harrier flown by Lt Martin Hale from No 800 Sqn. Despite being fired apparently outside its normal parameters, the missile successfully locked onto its potential victim, who immediately turned away and dived at high speed in an attempt to evade it. The Shafrir pursued the Sea Harrier down to 5000 feet, until finally losing its lock and veering off, either because its propellant was exhausted, or because one of Hale's flares had seduced it away. It did, however, pass uncomfortably close to the Sea Harrier.

Meanwhile Ardiles had started a hard, climbing turn with full afterburner, in order to maintain his altitude advantage over the British aircraft. Flt Lt Bernie Penfold, in Sea Harrier XZ455, made good use of the temporary tactical disadvantage in which Ardiles had placed himself, and with the Dagger providing a high IR signature against the clear, cold sky, he locked an AIM-9L and fired. The Sidewinder's running time between the two aircraft was only a matter of seconds, and it went right into the Dagger's tail pipe before exploding. The fireball that followed totally disintegrated the Argentinian fighter, with pieces falling all over Lively Island: the unfortunate pilot had no time to eject. It was the first air-to-air kill of the war, timed at approximately 16:40 hrs.

Thousands of feet below, at Port Stanley airfield, the GCI controller heard the anguished cry of Ardiles as he spotted the Sidewinder smoke trail approaching his aircraft. At the last moment he entered a violent turn in an attempt to shake it off, but the missile was far too close, and slammed into the Dagger with considerable force. Ardiles disappeared from the radio frequency at the same time as his aircraft vanished from the radar screen. It had been an almost suicidal mission to fly without a wingman, and the price paid was a heavy one.

At the time that C-433 exploded, 'Torno' flight from San Julian was approaching the Falklands. Cesar Roman unfolds the progress of his mission:

About 100 miles west of the Falklands we descended to 30 feet above the sea to avoid enemy radars and the Sea Harrier CAPs. We were coasting the nothern shores when 'Torno 1' (Dimeglio) saw an object in the sea. We changed our heading to attack, and then found to our embarrassment that the 'ship' was actually a solitary rock that protrudes from the sea in the northern mouth of Falkland Sound. After arriving in the area where the enemy ships were supposed to be, we found nothing. Dimeglio decided to follow the coast for several minutes, and near Stanley we could see artillery fire from shore positions being directed out to sea. Changing our heading, we spotted three big warships in arrow formation, engaging shore targets with their guns. The leader assigned a target to each of us, and we accelerated, descending still more to avoid detection. I did not fire my guns during the run for fear of being discovered. Over the target AA fire was very light, so I think we caught them off guard. I dropped the two 500 lb parachute-retarded bombs onto my target, and after some low-level evasive manoeuvres, I started to climb over Isla Soledad (East Falkland) and set course for home. Checking each other on the radio, we were all very happy to be alive and in one piece.

We were still climbing at about 15,000 feet, when I saw an aircraft in my two o'clock. I alerted the leader, informing him that it did not pose any threat because it was in a diving turn, going away from us. After an uneventful landing back at San Julian, I was surprised to learn that the aircraft I had detected was Dimeglio himself. He had been obeying a GCI alert—which I did not hear—to go low level in order to avoid a Sea Harrier CAP that was getting dangerously close. 'Torno 1 and 2' had therefore descended as advised, but I continued up to my optimum cruise altitude, completely unaware of any excitement below me. The low-level pair were forced to dump their centreline tanks to create less drag, and during the landing circuit I gave priority to Dimeglio because he declared a fuel emergency. This was one of the few missions on which the Sea Harriers actually gave chase during our escape, and it seems certain that they were going after Aguirre in 'Torno 2'. We were

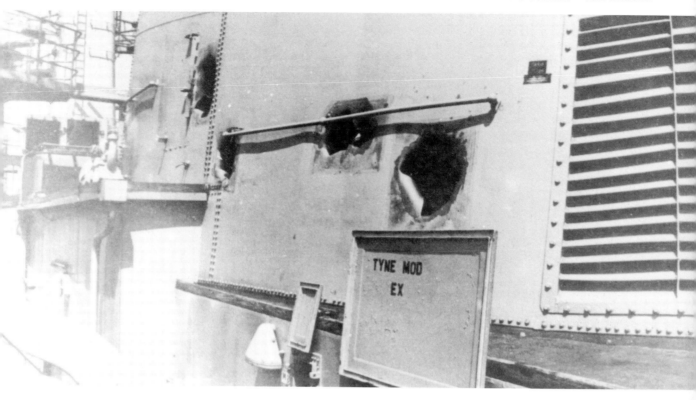

Four of the eleven 30 mm hits sustained by HMS Arrow *during the attack by* 'Torno' *flight on the afternoon of 1 May 1982* (UK MoD)

well supported by 'Fortin' section, who distracted their attention long enough for us all to get home unscathed . . .

The Royal Navy Type 21 frigates, HMS *Alacrity* (F 174) and HMS *Arrow* (F 173), and the 'County' class destroyer, HMS *Glamorgan* (D 19), were indeed caught by surprise as Cesar Roman suggested, although fortunately for them the six bombs all fell into the water. Two or three of them exploded fairly close, causing some structural damage to *Glamorgan* and *Alacrity*, while *Arrow* received 11 hits from 30 mm guns on her superstructure, near the funnel area. During 'Torno' section's escape, they were pursued for about 80 miles by a pair of Sea Harriers. The Shafrir-armed 'Fortin' section was nearby, and it was directed to intercept the British fighters. Already low on fuel, and with 'bogeys' approaching from the rear, the two Harriers co-ordinated a split S manoeuvre and abandoned the chase.

These were the last sorties flown by *Grupo 6* on 1 May. The day's events had clearly shown the Dagger pilots that they had insufficient fuel capacity to establish a CAP over East Falkland Island for more than 3–5 minutes—and even that allowed no reserves for mistakes in computing the best approach and egress profiles. Another significant element was the obvious difference between the Shafrir 2 missile and the Lima model Sidewinder. Although the Shafrir was very good, the AIM-9L offered so much more flexibility in achieving a firing solution that any contest between the two would always be unequal. Perhaps the biggest difference of all was the degree of tactical training and awareness of the Sea Harrier

pilots. They were then (and indeed still are) among the best in the realms of modern air combat, and were never lured into the trap of engaging the Daggers at high altitude, where the natural advantages of the Sea Harrier configuration are slightly diminished.

A Dagger and its pilot had been lost in the courageous but foolhardy act of engaging in air-to-air combat without the support of a wingman—a vital lesson for today's combat arena. After 1 May the Daggers were tasked almost exclusively on strike missions, mainly against the British shipping.

On 4 May, two Dagger sections from *Escuadrón Aeromovil No 1* were launched from Rio Grande at 10:20 and 15:00 hrs respectively. Their task was to provide a fighter escort for *Grupo 1 de Transporte* KC-130H tankers, which in turn were refuelling two sections of *Aviacion Naval* Super Etendards. These missions were designed to confirm the position of, and then attack, the British Type 42 destroyer, HMS *Sheffield* (D 80), which was acting as a radar picket ship for the Task Force. The Dagger sections were operating under the callsigns 'Tango' (Robles/Cimatti) and 'Mate' (Dimeglio/Mir Gonzalez). For them, the day was uneventful, but HMS *Sheffield* was struck by an Exocet missile which caused an uncontrollable fire on board, and she finally sank on 10 May.

During the following few days weather conditions in the area were very bad and no missions were flown, but on 9 May the skies cleared a little and frag orders were issued to both San Julian and Rio Grande. These indicated 'possible' naval targets near Port Stanley, and two four-aircraft Dagger formations were organized to investigate. 'Puma' flight launched at 13:46 hrs, followed by 'Jaguar' flight at 15:09 hrs. Unfortunately, a few minutes before arriving at Jason Islands (NNW of the Falklands) both flights were forced to turn back by very low cloud, and gusting winds with rain and snow showers.

Three days later, on 12 May, a combined attack was planned, with two flights of A-4Bs from *Grupo 5 de Caza*, and two flights of *Grupo 6* Daggers. They were due to attack Royal Navy warships that were bombarding Argentinian positions on the islands, but due to technical and communications problems, it was impossible for the Daggers to take part in the mission. The Skyhawks mounted the attack without escorts, and suffered heavy losses as a result.

The following few days passed fairly quietly, with a few alerts and some unproductive local air defence scrambles. Most of this activity was caused by radar contacts coming from Chilean territory in Tierra del Fuego. At that time the FAA staff was concerned that Chile might use the Falklands situation to conduct pre-emptive strikes against Argentina, and thereby resolve the Beagle Channel dispute by force. Other evidence suggests that a pair of RAF elint/photo-reconnaissance Canberras were secretly deployed to Punta Arenas, and it was missions conducted by these aircraft that were causing the FAA to react.

The evening of 20 May was very tense for all the *Grupo 6* personnel stationed at San Julian and Rio Grande. Rumours about British landings on the Falklands had reached them, and it was feared that an SAS/SBS commando raid would be mounted against the Super Etendards based at Rio Grande. Most of the pilots had a hard time trying to sleep that night, and it would prove to be the eve of dramatic events for all of them.

Capt Janett was one of the three pilots of 'Nandu' flight on 21 May 1982. HMS Broadsword was damaged by 30 mm gunfire during their attack, but one of the Daggers—flown by Lt Bean—was destroyed by a Sea Wolf missile fired from the ship (FAA)

Battle of San Carlos

The morning of 21 May dawned cold and damp, but with clear skies. The weather on the Falkland Islands was similar, although an ominous front was approaching. At Comodoro Rivadavia AB, in the headquarters complex for the *Fuerza Aérea del Sur*, Brig Gen Ernesto Horacio Crespo was nervous and impatient. As the Command's CO, he had been awake since 05:00 hrs, and in the War Room all morning. He was trying to get some reliable information from the islands, because the last thing he wanted to do was send his crews into a dangerous area against phantom targets. At about 08:30 hrs, some sketchy information began to arrive about the supposed British landings at the nothern end of Falkland Sound, but there were few details, and no positive confirmation. Two hours later confirmation was received. The British landings were not a feint, they had established a beachhead at San Carlos, and were coming ashore in their thousands.

A short time before this message came through, Crespo had taken the decision to send some of his aircraft on armed reconnaissance missions to find and attack the British ships. At 09:44 hrs 'Nandu' flight (Capt Rodhe, Lt Bean and Capt Janett) was launched from Rio Grande, followed one minute later by 'Perro' (Capt Moreno, Lt Volponi and Maj Martinez). San Julian launched 'Zorro' (Capt Diez, Lt Aguirre and Capt Dellepiane) and 'Leon' (Capt Dimeglio and Lt Castillo), both sections departing at 09:53 hrs. The aircraft were all armed to the same standard, with a single Mk 17 1000 lb bomb and a full load of 30 mm cannon ammunition.

By 10:25 hrs the first Daggers had arrived in the San Carlos area. 'Nandu' flight attacked the Type 22 frigate, HMS *Broadsword* (F 88), and the 'Leander' class frigate, HMS *Argonaut* (F 56). The old Leander vessel escaped damage, but *Broadsword* took several 30 mm hits from both Bean and Janett before launching a Sea Wolf missile. This scored a direct hit on Bean's aircraft, and he was killed instantly as C-428 disintegrated just above the water.

'Perro' flight was next into the attack, and all three aircraft went for the 'County' class destroyer, HMS *Antrim* (D 18). The ship was hit by a number of 30 mm rounds, but also received a direct hit from one of the Mk 17s. This bomb went through several compartments without exploding, before finally coming to rest in the Sea Slug missile storage room. Because of this damage, *Antrim* was taken out of action, seeking refuge in San Carlos Water to make emergency repairs and deactivate the bomb. The three Daggers escaped unscathed from an inferno of AA and missile fire, overflying the Sound on a southerly heading. One of them in particular was extremely lucky: a Sidewinder missile launched at extreme range by Lt Martin Hale from No 800 Sqn, just failed to reach the Dagger before it fell away with its propellant exhausted. Hale and his section leader tried to get within range, but without drop tanks the Argentinian aircraft were too fast, and the Harriers were forced to abandon the pursuit because of shortage of fuel.

At 10:51 hrs 'Zorro' flight made its appearance, and immediately attacked the Type 22 frigate, HMS *Brilliant* (F 90). A curious electrical fault affected all three aircraft and prevented them dropping their bombs, so the pilots emptied the 30 mm gun magazines in the general direction of the ship. *Brilliant* took at least 20 hits, many of them penetrating into the operations centre and wardroom, injuring several members of the crew. Two minutes later 'Leon' section attacked two ships with bombs and cannon fire, but without causing damage to either vessel.

The second wave of Argentinian aircraft was exclusively composed of A-4B/C Skyhawks, but the third wave involved the *Grupo 6* Daggers again. They began taking off during the early afternoon, with 'Cueca' flight (Capt Mir Gonzales, Lt Bernhardt, Capt Robles and 1st Lt Luna) departing from Rio Grande at 13:55 hrs. Five minutes later, 'Laucha' (1st Lt Roman, Maj Puga and 1st Lt Callejo) took off from San Julian, followed by the ill-fated 'Raton' flight (Capt Donadille, Maj Piuma and 1st Lt Senn).

The four Daggers from 'Cueca' flight went in 'feet dry' (over land, rather than water), heading east at very low level, through a valley formed between Mt Maria and Mt Robinson of the Horandy chain. The weather conditions forced them to fly much lower than the surrounding hills, and with some of the rising ground covered in a deep blanket of cloud, they adopted trail formation as the only survivable way through the valley. The leader saw something resembling a hole between the mountains, the cloud cover and the valley floor below, and all four Daggers went through it, rather than face the dangers of the unseen hillsides. They were slightly north of Chartres Settlement when they were detected by radar, and a Sea Harrier CAP from No 800 Sqn lost no time in getting after them. Robles and Luna ('Cueca' 3 and 4 respectively) were seen by Lt Cdr Frederiksen aboard Sea Harrier XZ455, and the Royal Navy pilots firewalled their throttles and approached to within launching range of the AIM-9L. With the Sidewinder 'growl' growing in his headset, Frederiksen pressed the button and a missile came off the left pylon and headed straight for 'Cueca 4'. Seconds before the impact, Luna saw one of the Sea Harriers out of the corner of his eye. It was the aircraft flown by Frederiksen's wingman, Sub Lt George, and Luna quickly tried to alert his comrades. The events that followed are narrated first-hand by Hector Luna:

A few seconds after seeing the Harrier, just as I was trying to alert the other members of my flight, I saw a fireball in the cockpit rear-view mirrors, and immediately felt the missile hit my aircraft. The Dagger went out of control, with the stick completely useless in my right hand. I tried to gain height, but to no avail, and when the aircraft rolled inverted I thought I was a dead man. Releasing the stick, I searched frantically for the face-blind ejection handle. When I reached it the aircraft must have been upright because the ejection was normal. I felt the cartridge explode with a great noise, then a jolt as the 'chute opened just as I hit the ground very hard, breaking my left shoulder and dislocating a knee with the impact . . .

Luna's Dagger (C-409) crashed uncomfortably close to him, some 20 km west of Port Howard. The next day he was found by a group of Kelpers, who helped him to contact the Argentinian HQ at Port Stanley by radio. He was then recovered by a *Grupo 7* Bell 212 helicopter and flown to Goose Green, and eventually on to Port Stanley. On 25 May he was evacuated to Comodoro Rivadavia in an FAA C-130.

Robles in 'Cueca 3' was unaware of what had happened. He was also unaware that Frederiksen had followed him through the valley and fired about 200 rounds of 30 mm ammunition at him (air-to-air gunnery at very low level is a difficult art). Mir Gonzalez and Bernhardt also failed to realize that George had been following them in the second Harrier, using his guns at every opportunity. All three Argentinian pilots had been far too busy trying not to crash into the hillsides while flying through the valley. Once they found the exit, Robles broke radio silence to report that Luna had disappeared from behind him. It was assumed that he had crashed into the mountains during the last phase of the dangerous low-level navigation.

The diminished 'Cueca' flight crossed the eastern shores of West Falkland to emerge over the waters of the Sound. They saw the Type 21 frigate, HMS *Ardent* (F 184) at Grantham Sound, south of San

Carlos, and after a small course correction, they were ready to attack across her stern. The Daggers began to receive light AA fire, but as soon as they were within effective range they opened up with their own guns and released the Mk 17s. Mir Gonzalez's bomb fell about 12 metres short, creating a huge plume of spray as it somersaulted towards the ship and embedded itself in the stern without exploding. Bernhardt's bomb also struck the stern, but it fell cleanly and detonated on impact, destroying the Lynx helicopter and its hangar, and wrecking the Sea Cat missile launcher. The bomb from Robles fell harmlessly into the sea, but as he passed over the frigate he saw debris from the earlier explosion gyrating wildly through the air. He glanced at the clock on his instrument panel: it was 14:47 hrs.

The three surviving aircraft from 'Cueca' flight egressed on a southerly heading through Falkland Sound, and after almost an hour arrived back at Rio Grande without further trouble. HMS *Ardent* was badly damaged, and although she still had some power left and set course towards San Carlos Water to make repairs, she finally succumbed to her wounds and sank not long after the attack. Of her crew, 22 were killed in the action, and 30 were injured.

Of the six Daggers to take off from San Julian that afternoon, 'Laucha' flight was the first to reach the combat zone. The attack is described here by Cesar Roman:

The last phase of the flight was completed over land, bordering the northern coast of Gran Malvina Island (West Falkland). Once Rosalie Mountain was passed, we located the waters of Falkland Sound and pushed on towards them. After flying very low over the island, we found ourselves higher than expected over the water because the eastern coast at that point was high, and plunged abruptly downwards. I pushed the stick forwards to 'scrape' the waves and avoid detection by radar. Ahead of me I could see a warship near San Carlos Water, with flames and a long column of smoke pouring from it as a result of earlier attacks. With No 3 (Maj Puga), I attacked a frigate, which raised a huge plume of water with her AA armament. I had to fly straight through one of these geysers, which considerably reduced my vision and aiming effectiveness. We both fired our cannons and dropped the bombs, and then egressed at full bore on an easterly heading, while No 2 attacked another warship situated to the north of us. We had to change course just one minute after dropping the bombs in order to follow an escape corridor prepared beforehand, during the mission's navigation planning. As I flew over the frigate I could no longer see No 2, so I triggered the chronometer and said over the radio: '40 seconds to go', so that he would know the time remaining before our turn.

During the attack, Maj Puga noted that something had hit his aircraft. While we were climbing to cruise height on the return leg, I closed in to inspect his Dagger from several angles, but could see nothing abnormal. After landing a hit was observed, on the central armoured panel of the windscreen, at the same level as the pilot's helmet. Fortunately for Puga the bullet (or piece of shrapnel) only dented the glass, and did not penetrate all the way through.

After quite properly feeling happy to be home in one piece, we were immediately saddened by the news that 'Raton' flight was overdue. During the next day we learned that all three aircraft had been brought down by Sea Harriers, but luckily all the pilots were recovered ...

Roman and Puga had both attacked the Type 22 frigate, HMS *Brilliant* (F 90), but their bombs missed the target—although the ship did collect

LEFT
The British Type 21 frigate, HMS Ardent *(F 184) was badly damaged by* 'Cueca' *flight on 21 May 1982, and was later hit again by an Argentine Navy A-4Q formation. She is seen here at anchor, burning fiercely at the stern, and developing the list to starboard that would eventually sink her (UK MoD)*

ABOVE
1st Lt Cesar Roman poses alongside Dagger C-401. The picture was taken at Tandil AB some time after the war, but the aircraft still carries a full 'kill' marking to record its participation in the attack on HMS Plymouth *(which was not sunk as the marking implies). Painted on the intake lip are the 'battle honours' in the form of a small outline map of the Falklands (Roman)*

several 30 mm rounds, which caused slight damage and some casualties. Callejo also attacked a vessel later described as a frigate, but again the bombs exploded harmlessly in the water. All three aircraft escaped in a hail of tracer fire and missiles, and eventually made it back to San Julian. 'Raton' flight followed one minute behind the 'Laucha' attack, but

its misfortunes have been described in detail elsewhere. Suffice it to say that the aircraft were visually detected by Lt Cdr Ward (CO of No 801 Sqn) in Sea Harrier ZA195, and after a crossover and some other manoeuvring, Piuma in Dagger C-404 was downed by Thomas (Ward's wingman), who then went after Donadille in C-403, bringing him down with his second Sidewinder. After a brief pursuit, Senn was shot out of the sky with an AIM-9L fired by Ward:

The Dagger changed to a westerly heading. I was at 300 feet over the local terrain, and dived after him. I got a lock on the Sidewinder and fired—it couldn't fail! Seconds later it hit the target, and then, as if in slow motion, I saw the Dagger disintegrate and hit the ground, with its right wing and intake cartwheeling among the smoke, flames and debris. I did not observe an ejection, but later I learned that the pilot had escaped ...

All three pilots from 'Raton' flight were eventually rescued by their own forces. They assembled one by one at Port Howard, before being transferred to Port Stanley by helicopter, and then on to the mainland by C-130.

The 'Raton' engagement signalled the end of missions for *Grupo 6 de Caza* during that dramatic

21 May. The FAA had launched an overall total of 54 sorties from mainland bases (out of 63 originally planned), and lost seven aircraft—an alarming 13 per cent. In isolation, the *Grupo 6* losses were even heavier. The two Dagger squadrons had launched 23 escort or attack sorties during the day, and five aircraft failed to return. This represented a staggering loss rate of 23.5 per cent. The fate of the five pilots was not immediately known, but by mid-afternoon of the following day, news had come through that at least four of them had been recovered.

A number of factors contributed to these high losses, not least of which was the limited experience most pilots had of the Dagger itself (this was especially true when compared to the Skyhawk pilots). Another shortcoming was the obvious lack of a sound tactical background, both in anti-shipping operations, and in mutual support when 'bounced' by opposing fighters. In retrospect, perhaps the most important tactical error was the constant targetting of heavily armed warships, rather than concentrating on the transport elements of the Task Force. This would become clear after the war, but it was not at all obvious while the fighting was in progress. On the positive side, *Grupo 6* pilots had completely disabled HMS *Ardent*, caused moderate damage to HMS *Antrim*, and inflicted light damage on a number of other vessels. Several tactical and defensive measures were studied during the night, especially the possibility of changing the flight profiles over the islands in

LEFT

Three Daggers from 'Escuadrón Aeromóvil No 2' on the alert ramp at San Julian on 22 May 1982. There were no combat missions on that day because bad weather covered the islands. Yellow identification markings are just visible on the aircraft tails and wing leading edges, and in some cases on the undersides of drop tanks (Posadas)

BELOW LEFT

The logistic landing ship, RFA Sir Bedivere *(L 3004), seen here through the gunsight of Capt Maffeis' Dagger, over San Carlos Water on 24 May 1982. The plumes of spray are from exploding cannon shells* (FAA)

RIGHT

Capt Carlos Maffeis in 'Azul-3' (C-431) overflies RFA Sir Bedivere *during the attack on 24 May 1982. The bright identification panel on the tail of the aircraft stands out clearly against the dark hillside* (UK MoD)

an effort to avoid Sea Harrier CAPs.

During the following day there were no Dagger sorties due to bad weather, but on 23 May conditions improved slightly and two flights were launched at 08:43 hrs from Rio Grande. Both were forced to turn back later because low cloud had settled over and around the islands. During the afternoon, San Julian launched '*Coral*' (Capt Dimeglio, Lt Aguirre and 1st Lt Roman) and '*Daga*' (Capt Rodhe and 1st Lt Ratti), while '*Punal*' section (Maj Martinez and Lt Volponi) departed from Rio Grande. They were over the Falklands at about 15:00 hrs, when the FAA radar controller warned them that there were Sea Harrier CAPs nearby. '*Punal*' jettisoned its bombs and turned for home at low level. The two Daggers were detected north of Pebble Island by Lt Cdr Auld (CO of No 800 Sqn), and his wingman, Lt Hale. Martinez was going too fast to be caught, but Volponi in C-437 had slightly delayed firewalling the throttle, and was some way behind. Hale, in ZA194, was about two miles behind Volponi when he first spotted the Dagger, and when this distance had been reduced to about half a mile, he launched a Sidewinder. The unfortunate *Grupo 6* pilot seemed unaware of the danger, and took no evasive action. The missile flew into the Dagger's tailpipe and exploded with a brilliant flash, the doomed fighter disintegrating and cartwheeling into the ground, west of Elephant Bay on Pebble Island. Volponi was killed instantly.

On 24 May, the FAS issued 12 fragmentary orders for attacks on British shipping in San Carlos Water, and by 11:20 hrs the first Daggers had arrived over the anchorage. They were '*Azul*' flight, launched about an hour earlier by *Escuadrón Aeromovil No 1* at Rio Grande. Each aircraft carried two 375 gal

(1700 lt) drop tanks, and a single Mk 17 1000 lb bomb on the centreline weapons station. Capt Carlos A Maffeis flew as No 3 in the formation, and he recalls the action that developed:

The flight consisted of four Daggers, and we were briefed to attack any naval targets within San Carlos Water. As I remember, '*Azul*' was the first to arrive in the area, and in some way we surprised the British—perhaps that is why all four of us escaped without being hit by anything worse than small-arms fire. On that day, I was flying aircraft C-431 as section leader (No 3), with Capt Robles as my wingman. The flight leader was Capt Mir Gonzalez, and his wingman was Lt Bernhardt. As usual we ingressed at very low level, crossing Bahia Ruiz Puente (Grantham Sound) and the nearby hills on a south to north radial, before entering San Carlos itself. Contrary to my three buddies, I went over the eastern shore, where there was a major accumulation of British ships. On the western side there was a big transport, but I was forced to attack only the smaller vessels, because a few minutes earlier the generator on my Dagger had failed and without its power the bomb would not release. This was one of the limitations of the aircraft's electrical system, and it left me with just the 30 mm guns. I pulled the trigger three times in all. The first rounds fell short and raised big plumes of water, but I feel certain that the following bursts

ABOVE
HMS Fearless *had a lucky escape with this near-miss by a
500 lb parachute-retarded bomb released from 'Plata-1'.
Despite having four quad-launchers for Seacat missiles, the
ship is reported to have fired only one round at 'Plata'
flight, and even that failed to find its target* (UK MoD)

RIGHT
*San Carlos Water was known as 'bomb alley' to the British
forces. This picture was taken on 24 May 1982, and it
shows the requisitioned P & O cargo ship,* Norland, *being
straddled by the bombs from 'Plata' flight. The density
of shipping in the area during the landings is evident*
(UK MoD)

impacted on the target. Everything happened very fast, but
it still remains firmly recorded in my mind—and of course
on the gun-camera films. When these were developed, apart
from the technical details (350 degree attack heading, etc),
six ships could be seen, which represented about 50 per cent
of all British vessels inside San Carlos water . . .

'*Azul*' flight caused only light damage to some of the
amphibious ships, but the four Daggers were
profusely recorded by British photographers, and
some of their pictures illustrate this book.

Fifty minutes later '*Plata*' flight, again from Rio
Grande, arrived over San Carlos Water. The pilots

were Capt Dellepiane, 1st Lt Musso and Lt Callejo, and this time the aircraft were armed with two 500 lb parachute-retarded bombs each. As soon as these had been released over the target area (without any real effect), the three Daggers egressed on a northerly heading. At about ten miles from Pebble Island, they were detected by two British warships, one of which launched a pair of surface-to-air missiles from a considerable distance. Because of their evident size, these are thought to have been Sea Darts (or 'white telephone poles' as they were nicknamed by the Argentinians). The extreme engagement range, and some clever evasive manoeuvring by the *Grupo 6* pilots, caused both missiles to fall away harmlessly.

Some time later, 'Oro' flight (Maj Puga, Capt Diaz and Lt Castillo) from San Julian, was following the northern coast of West Falkland, towards San Carlos. Before passing Pebble Island, the Daggers were detected by the frigate, HMS *Broadsword* (F 88), which was acting as radar picket and forward air defence ship, together with the Type 42 destroyer, HMS *Coventry* (D 118). A Sea Harrier CAP from No 800 Sqn, flown by Lt Cdr Auld in XZ457 and Lt Smith in ZA193, was quickly vectored onto the Dagger formation by *Broadsword's* operations room. The Harriers climbed to get a better overall view, and in order to dive onto their targets as a way of cancelling out the Dagger's speed advantage. The Argentinian pilots dropped all their external stores and tried to escape, but the 'bounce' had been too well

planned by the Royal Navy pair. Auld launched his two Sidewinders one after the other. The first missile hit Puga's Dagger (C-419), which started to break up, then exploded and went into the water. Puga recalls his last-second ejection:

We were flying very low over the waves, and saw the two Harriers when they were almost upon us. We all jettisoned the stores and tried to escape, but to no avail. I saw Castillo's Dagger blow up, and at the same time felt the missile slam into my aircraft. Pulling back the stick I tried to gain some height, but the aircraft began to roll, with flames pouring from the cockpit area backwards. Then a wing folded, and I ejected with a 90 degree bank angle, parallel to the water surface. I never lost consciousness, and remember perfectly the jerk as my parachute started to open. I was amazed to feel that I was still alive, and thanked God for it, because the canopy was not fully deployed when I hit the water ...

Puga's ordeal was not yet over. Although injured, he had to spend several hours in the cold ocean, struggling to keep his head above water as he slowly swam towards Pebble Island. He spent the night on a rocky beach, and was found next day by an Argentinian patrol, which was led by a Marine Lieutenant. Puga's wristwatch had stopped at 11:08 hrs—the time of his ejection—and to this day he keeps it as a reminder of those dramatic few seconds.

Auld's second Sidewinder got Capt Diaz in C-430. He also ejected, and the Dagger fell in the water to the north of Pebble Island, close to where Puga's aircraft

ABOVE LEFT
'Plata-1', flown by Capt Dellepiane, is seen passing the amphibious assault ship, HMS Fearless *(L 10), in spectacular fashion. British anti-aircraft defences—particularly the Sea Wolf missile—forced the Argentinian pilots to adopt these extremely low approach techniques, often resulting in their bombs failing to fuse and explode. HMS* Fearless *appears to have been surprised by this attack—certainly the forward Seacat launcher is nowhere near being trained on such an obvious target (UK MoD)*

ABOVE
Sea Harrier XZ457/14 from No 800 Sqn was flown by Lt Cdr Andy Auld during the engagement with 'Oro' flight (it has two Dagger 'kills' stencilled below the cockpit). The same aircraft was used by Lt Morrell a few days earlier, to shoot down a pair of A-4Q Skyhawks. Only one A-4 victory is recorded here, but with four confirmed, XZ457 became the top-scoring Sea Harrier of the whole campaign (RNAS Yeovilton)

LEFT
Daggers C-430 and C-419 were both part of 'Oro' flight, which was completely wiped out by a Sea Harrier section on 24 May 1982. By chance they were photographed together on the morning of the raid, but a few hours later they both fell victim to Sidewinder missiles fired by Lt Cdr Andy Auld, RN. The fin and leading edge of the wing have faded identification markings (Posadas)

had crashed. Smith fired an AIM-9L against Castillo in C-410. In a textbook engagement, the missile scored a direct hit on the Dagger, which was immediately enveloped in flames and fell to the ground on the western side of Elephant Bay. The unfortunate Castillo was killed. The two Sea Harriers then pursued a fourth Dagger for a few seconds, believing it to be part of the same flight. In fact it was No 3 of the earlier 'Plata' flight, and he managed to escape without damage.

On 29 May, Puga and Diaz, together with a number of other personnel and the body of Lt Volponi, were picked up from Pebble Island in a daring rescue operation led by Capt Uriona of *Grupo 6 de Transporte Aéreo*, in a DHC-6 Twin Otter. Yet again *Grupo 6 de Caza* had suffered grievous losses of men and equipment at the hands of the deadly Sea Harrier/AIM-9L combination. 'Oro' flight was the second Dagger trio to be completely wiped out, all for minimal positive results against the Task Force. It was clear that this loss rate could not be sustained for long without the entire Group running out of aircraft. Six out of the eight Dagger pilots downed by Sea Harriers during the Battle of San Carlos (21–27 May) had been saved, but even this would not have been possible without the brilliance of the Martin-Baker JM6 zero–zero ejection seat.

During the following few days, partly because of bad weather, but also because the strategy followed by *Grupo 6* needed to change, the Daggers made very few sorties. On 25 May, two sections ('Nandu' and 'Fuego') were launched on an offensive reconnaissance mission, departing from Rio Grande at 11:00 and 11:02 hrs respectively. After passing over the southern side of Falkland Sound, both flights returned unscathed, having found no sign of the Task Force ships.

On 26 May a single Dagger flight ('Llama') dive-bombed the British troop concentrations near Port San Carlos. The formation attacked through the cloud cover with parachute-retarded bombs, and although no AA fire was observed, it was also impossible to judge the effectiveness of the raid.

By 27 May the beachhead was fully established, and British troops had begun to advance on Argentinian positions throughout the islands. The Battle of San Carlos was conceded as a victory for the forces of the United Kingdom, despite the courageous efforts of the *Fuerza Aérea del Sur* pilots. *Grupo 6* had contributed 47 escort/cover or attack sorties (21 from San Julian and 26 from Rio Grande), for the loss of nine aircraft and three pilots. Many of the Daggers had also been hit by small arms fire or shrapnel, and although they made it back to their bases, some had to be taken out of service temporarily while repairs were completed. The result of all this effort was originally seen as comparitively meagre, but the extent of the damage to HMS *Antrim*, and the sinking of HMS *Ardent*, were both unknown to the Argentinians at that time.

Protecting the Army

On 28 May, the Argentine garrisons at Goose Green and Darwin were being hard pressed by the advancing British Paras, and in order to support them the FAS planned ten fragmentary orders, including one Dagger flight. The missions were designed to attack British troops on East Falkland, as well as the ships engaged on shore bombardment duties, but weather conditions at the time were hardly suitable for conducting air operations. The Daggers were launched without any problem, but the islands were affected by an intense low pressure area, producing rain and snow and very poor visibility. None of the aircraft were able to penetrate the weather safely, and they all returned home with their weapon loads intact.

Next day the conditions improved a little, and the FAS ordered the launch of several more flights. First to reach the operational area was 'Limon' section (Capt Mir Gonzalez and Lt Bernhardt) from Rio Grande. They were tasked with an offensive reconnaissance mission, and each aircraft carried three parachute-retarded 500 lb bombs and a full load of 30 mm cannon ammunition. The pair arrived over San Carlos Water at 12:25 hrs, but found no ships there, or in Falkland Sound. Mir Gonzales thought it better to return home, saving the bombs for another misson, but then he spotted the silhouette of a large ship on the northern horizon. As they turned to engage the ship, Bernhardt, who was in C-436 and some distance behind his leader, was shot out of the sky by a Rapier missile. The pilot had no chance to eject as the Dagger broke up and crashed into San Carlos Water.

Almost two hours later, the remaining aircraft of 'Puma' flight (one had aborted on take-off) were approaching Falkland Sound by the northern route around Pebble Island, when they visually detected a Sea Harrier CAP some way to the south of them. Believing that they were about to be intercepted, the two pilots jettisoned their stores and returned to San Julian. In fact, the Harriers were part of a No 800 Sqn raid on the small airfield at Pebble Island, and the Daggers had not been seen by the British pilots.

The aircraft shot down earlier in the day was the last Dagger lost by *Grupo 6 de Caza* during the conflict, and Lt Bernhardt was the fifth and last fatality among its pilots. Most of these losses occurred during about nine days of effective fighting, and the accumulation of setbacks over such a short period had a dramatic effect on the unit's morale— especially in view of the appalling overall results obtained. The Group was also seriously short of aircraft, making operations even more difficult.

In a rare act of South American solidarity, Peru came to the rescue and sold the FAA ten Mirage 5Ps for US 14 million dollars. This acquisition covered the Dagger losses, but although the aircraft were delivered almost immediately, they came just too late to participate in the war. They were however, active and on standby alert at Rio Gallegos, during the uneasy truce that followed the 14 June surrender. Shortly after the war, the aircraft were rotated through *Rio IV* to bring them up to FAA standards, which involved the fitting of VHF radios, VOR, ILS, different instruments and a revised starting system. The 'new' aircraft all took the serials of Daggers lost in the conflict.

After the loss of Lt Bernardt, *Grupo 6* had several days of comparative calm, while weather conditions continued to hinder normal taskings. By 4 June, the situation of the Argentine garrison on the Falklands was beginning to get difficult, and the FAS decided to launch several close support missions in an attempt to relieve the pressure. The weather was still causing problems, because low cloud (ceiling varying between 150–500 feet) and rain squalls made low level attacks impossible. Instead it was decided to try medium height conventional attacks, or use dive bombing techniques.

A sortie was planned for *Escuadrón Aeromovil No 2* at San Julian. The pilots assigned to the mission were Comodoro Villar, Capt Demierre, and 1st Lts Musso and Roman, and each Dagger carried two 500 lb retarded bombs. By 16:30 hrs the flight was over the target area near Mt Kent, and the bombs were dropped from 60 degree dives through the cloud cover. No results were observed, but all the aircraft returned safely.

At 14:46 hrs on 5 June, 'Fierro' section arrived over the islands for an armed reconnaissance mission. Each aircraft carried only its full 250-round load of 30 mm HEI ammunition, and despite making a sweep along the entire length of Falkland Sound, they could find no trace of the British ships. By 15:30 hrs, the three aircraft of 'Nene' flight were over West Falkland, tasked with finding a Type 42 destroyer that was presumed to be in the area on radar picket duties. Starting from the south, they searched every inlet and creek of King George Bay, before fuel problems forced them to return home without finding their objective. The ship was apparently on station, but several miles south of West Falkland.

The cloud and misty weather of the previous few days relented on 8 June, and the day dawned with crystal clear skies, dotted around with a few light clouds. In the FAS war room at Comodoro Rivadavia, messages started to pour in during the early morning about a new beachhead being established by British forces at Port Pleasant, some 18 miles south-west of Port Stanley. Two amphibious landing ships—later identified as RFA *Sir Galahad* (L3005) and RFA *Sir Tristram* (L3505)—were within the bay area, apparently unloading men and supplies without any hurry, almost as though it were a peacetime exercise. The reports also noted that there were no visible signs of defensive measures against air attack.

Brig Gen Crespo wanted to go for the targets, but he was well aware of the carnage that Sea Harrier CAPs could inflict on his fighter-bombers, unless they could be kept clear of the area. The fragmentary order was relatively simple. The mission was planned to include an attack element of *Grupo 5* Skyhawks and *Grupo 6* Daggers, and a decoy element consisting mainly of Mirage IIIs from *Grupo 8*, but including a Dagger section from *Grupo 6*. The decoys would simulate fighter-bomber profiles heading into the San Carlos area, hopefully drawing the Sea Harriers away from Port Pleasant.

The *Grupo 6* attack element was formed by six Daggers, each carrying two 375 gal (1700 lt) drop tanks, two 500 lb Mk 82 bombs and 250 rounds of 30 mm ammunition. The mission was divided into two flights: 'Perro' (Capt Rodhe, 1st Lt Gabari and 1st Lt Ratti) and 'Gato' (Capt Cimatti, Maj Martinez and 1st Lt Antonietti), both of which launched from Rio Grande at about 13:00 hrs. Just after take-off, Cimatti's aircraft suffered a major bird stike, which caused some cracking around the windshield and forced him to abort the mission. The five remaining aircraft were joined by Learjet TC-23 from *Grupo 1 Aerofotografico*, which would act as pathfinder, using its state of the art navigation system to guide the formation towards the south-west coast of West Falkland. From there, the Daggers would establish a north-east heading towards Falkland Sound,

The Daggers of Maj Martinez and Lt Antonietti formate on the Learjet pathfinder during the raid on 8 June. Although this picture is generally poor, it does show the value of the yellow identification patches on FAA Daggers (FAA)

LEFT
Dagger C-414 inside a hardened aircraft shelter at Rio Gallegos in October 1982. Although the war had finished some months earlier, Grupo 6 *remained on alert throughout this period, as evidenced by the loaded bomb trolley beneath the aircraft. The ship silhouette on the port intake was applied because the FAA thought that HMS* Plymouth *had been sunk during the 8 June attack: C-414 had been part of that raid* (Romero)

intending later to turn east, crossing southern East Falkland to make the attack from the west. The weather began to deteriorate, and in order to avoid the worst of the low cloud, rain and snow squalls, the formation deviated slightly from the planned route. Crossing Falkland Sound on their north-easterly heading, the pilots were amazed to find the Type 12 frigate, HMS *Plymouth* (F 126), all alone and making for the relative security of San Carlos Water after a night spent on shore bombardment duties. It was about 14:00 hrs, and as the formation had clearly been detected by *Plymouth* (and therefore lost the vital element of surprise for the Port Pleasant raid), the leader changed the original plan and decided to attack the frigate instead.

The Daggers began a wide turn to position for the attack, while the ship speeded up in an attempt to reach the defences of San Carlos. All five aircraft ran in across the port side at an IAS of 550 knots. Rodhe was on the right of the formation, Ratti in the centre and Gabari on the left; behind them, in line abreast, were Antonietti and Martinez. The ship opened up with 20 mm AA fire, and launched a Sea Cat missile, but the aircraft pressed home the attack, hitting *Plymouth* with a number of 30 mm cannon shells and five out of the eight bombs dropped (Ratti's bombs would not release due to generator failure). Miraculously for the ship's crew none of the Mk 82s exploded, but a fierce fire was started at the stern

when one of the 30 mm rounds set off a depth charge, and the flooding caused a 6 degree list. Only one of the Daggers was slightly damaged by shrapnel.

After the attack, the fighters turned for home on a south-westerly heading, and were pursued during the early part of their flight by a Sea Harrier CAP. This had presumably been called into the area by *Plymouth*'s operations room, but it arrived too late to catch the Daggers. On their return to Rio Grande, the five pilots were acclaimed as heroes, because the Argentinians firmly believed that the frigate had been sunk. In fact this was not the case. Although certainly damaged, *Plymouth* remained operational until the end of the conflict, and eventually returned to UK under her own power. The real focus of the day's missions, the RFAs *Sir Galahad* and *Sir Tristram*, were not so lucky. The formation of *Grupo 5* Skyhawks did get through the British defences to inflict heavy damage on both vessels. Of the two, the *Sir Galahad* was by far the most seriously affected, taking several direct hits from Argentinian bombs, which caused major fires on board, and many secondary explosions as the cargo of fuel and ammunition was engulfed. British casualties during that single raid amounted to 57 dead and over 60 injured.

On 13 June the situation was becoming critical for the Argentine forces on the Falklands, as British troops advanced inexorably towards Port Stanley. In what amounted to the last combat missions of the war for the FAS, it was decided to launch the maximum number of attack sorties against UK ground forces, in order to buy some time for the Argentine Army. Relatively few of the Command's aircraft were 100 per cent combat-ready at that stage, due primarily to technical discrepancies caused by the harsh winter climate with its high humidity factor. Combat damage had also taken its toll, and some aircraft were also tied up on normal routine maintenance.

LEFT
A gun camera frame from Lt Gabari's 'Perro' flight Dagger during the 8 June 1982 attack on the Type 12 Frigate, HMS Plymouth. *The ship was caught alone on the open sea, and suffered much damage as the result of the raid, including multiple cannon hits from Gabari's aircraft* (FAA via Gabari)

The staff of *Grupo 6 de Caza* scheduled four missions for 13 June, all of which originally included three Daggers. Of the 12 planned departures, four aircraft were forced to abort or turn back because of technical malfunctions, and none of the others actually got through to attack the British ground forces. The final missions developed as follows (it should be noted that *Escuadrón Aeromovil No 2* had moved to Rio Gallegos AB by this time):

Frag Order 1317

Three Daggers were launched at 11:10 hrs, tasked with the bombing of British troop concentrations on the slopes of Mt Longdon. The No 3 aircraft was forced to abort the mission because the landing gear would not retract after take-off. The two remaining aircraft reached the target area, but were confronted with heavy cloud cover and rain. Through holes in the blanket of cloud the Argentinian pilots visually detected a Sea King helicopter and a pair of Sea Harriers. The GCI controller advised them that two 'blips' were approaching at high speed, and believing they were in grave danger of being intercepted, the Daggers abandoned the mission and made good their escape. They were not engaged by the Harriers.

Frag Order 1318

Crewed by Capt Dimeglio, Lt Aguirre Faget and 1st Lt Roman. Before take-off from Rio Gallegos, Aguirre had to abandon the mission due to brake failure. The remaining pilots wandered away from their planned route while approaching the islands, and were seen by a British helicopter some 45 nm south of Falkland Sound. This machine was a Lynx HAS.2 (XZ233) from No 815 Sqn, operating from the Type 42 destroyer, HMS *Cardiff* (D108). Realizing that the helicopter would have alerted all the AA defences on the islands, the two Dagger pilots decided to abandon the main mission and attack the Lynx instead. Dimeglio and Roman made several gunnery runs each, but the helicopter crew had obviously been well briefed on fighter evasion tactics, and successfully dodged all efforts to shoot them down. Low on fuel, the frustrated *Grupo 6* pilots were forced to give up the chase and return home to Rio Gallegos.

Frag Order 1323

A three-Dagger attack mission with the callsign 'Zeus'. One of the aircraft had to abort before departure for technical reasons, and a second turned back when it was only 60 nm from the target due to severe engine surging. The pilot of this aircraft later said that he hardly dared to breathe during the long trip home: flying more than 400 nm over a freezing ocean, with an engine that could seize up at any time, is not a situation that encourages peace of mind. The third aircraft pressed on alone for a short time, but wisely turned back when Sea Harrier CAPs were reported in the target area.

Frag Order 1324

The three aircraft of 'Vulcano' flight ran into problems with the weather, and then a Sea Harrier CAP was vectored towards them. The Daggers were not configured for any air-to-air fighting, so they were forced to abandon the mission and turn for home. The last aircraft landed back at Rio Gallegos at 16:42 hrs, bringing to an end *Grupo 6 de Caza*'s part in the Falklands conflict. By late afternoon of the following day, the occupying forces had surrendered and the hostilities were over.

It must be said that the Dagger was not spectacularly successful during the war. Despite the sinking of HMS *Ardent* and the damage inflicted on *Antrim* and *Plymouth*, the aircraft was not really suited to long range anti-shipping sorties. The A-4 Skyhawk, although an older design, was far better equipped for these operations because it had air-to-air refuelling capability. Another influence on the Dagger's comparative lack of success was the inexperience of its pilots. First Lieutenant Jose Luis Gabari Zoco recalls his part in the war:

I was new to the Dagger and to *Grupo 6*, so at the height of the battle I was still training or ferrying replacement aircraft between Tandil, San Julian and Rio Grande. Having achieved 50 hours of Dagger time, I reported to Rio Grande on 1 June 1982, for a tour of duty with *Escuadrón Aeromovil No 1*. Once there, I was given a number of briefings on the war situation, on Sea Harrier tactics, and on bombing profiles and ship recognition. The small Rio Grande base was overcrowded, with a large Navy contingent of A-4Qs, Super Etendards and ancilliary types, plus our own Daggers. The runway also had to be shared with civilian users. The cold was intense, and frozen mud seemed to be everywhere. The aircraft were dispersed in order to minimize the effects of a commando raid or air attack, and a pair of Shafrir-armed Daggers were kept on dawn to dusk alert, with the pilots and groundcrew sheltered in a nearby hut. Crew quarters generally were clean and warm, although some pilots had to sleep in hotels in the town. There was a certain 'atmosphere' about the place, not unlike the stuff you see in old WW2 movies. In the briefing room and officers' mess you could meet Army, Navy and Air Force personnel, Coast Guard officers and deeply-impressed civilian aircrew, all swapping stories about flying or women (very typical!). In spite of the high loss rate, our morale was good. Most of the pilots thought the war would continue for a month or two, and it seemed likely that most of us would get killed eventually. There was also the constant possibility of conflict with the Chileans, because it was clear that they had helped the British in some way. None of us really thought too much about tomorrow.

I only flew a couple of combat missions. On 8 June I took part in the attack on HMS *Plymouth*, and on 13 June we were forced to return by bad weather and the probability of being intercepted. On 14 June we could not fly because the weather over the mainland and the islands was very bad, and during the evening we received the news that Gen Menendez had surrendered. That message shocked and demoralized us, but because he'd only surrendered the Argentinian forces on the islands, we were kept on a high state of readiness for several days, just in case higher authority requested an all out attack on the British forces. This did not happen, and by the end of June we were all back at Tandil. The war was over, and we had lost five good friends . . .

Between 1 May and 13 June, *Grupo 6 de Caza* had flown 133 combat sorties out of a planned total of 160. The enemy was actually engaged in one form or another on 88 of these sorties, and of those that did not make contact, the majority were turned back by bad weather or the risk of interception by Sea Harrier CAPs. Eleven Daggers were lost during the conflict—more than any other mainland-based type—and five pilots were killed. Some of the pilots who managed to eject were injured by ground impact, but none of them were seriously hurt.

The remaining Daggers (24 were in service at the beginning of 1988) are being updated with technical support from Israel Aircraft Industries. The programme is being completed in several phases, but will ultimately include a digital RWR, compatibility with 'new weapons', air-to-air refuelling probes, and the *Sistema Integrado de Navegacion y Tiro* (SINTA). This is basically the integrated weapons and attack system fitted to the Kfir C7, combining a HUD, an inertial platform and a weapons computer. The nose cone of the Argentinian aircraft will also be changed to that of the Kfir, with its small Elta radome and aerodynamic strakes. The FAA Mirage 5Ps are also receiving a limited upgrade.

The Israelis have also supplied a modern mission/instrument simulator to the FAA, which is expected to significantly improve the readiness standards of Dagger pilots by giving them more 'air time' at minimum cost. This equipment has been operational at Tandil since 1984.

LEFT
Taken at Rio Grande five days after the cessation of hostilities, this picture shows many of the Grupo 6 *personnel involved. From left to right they are: 1st Lt Ratti, Majo Monesca, Maj Martinez, Capt Cimatti, unknown, Maj Lupieñez, Comodoro Corino (now promoted to Commanding Officer of Rio Grande Air Defence Sector), 1st Lt Antonietti, Capt Mir Gonzalez, 1st Lt Gabari and Capt Moreno (via Gabari)*

LEFT
A postwar picture of Dagger C-415, equipped with supersonic tanks and armed with dummy Shafrir 2s and 12 125 kg 'slicks'. All FAA Daggers are now undergoing a modernization programme, which is centred on the fitting of a new nav/attack system (FAA)

Chapter 11
Falklands combat –
the Mirage III

During the late 1960s the senior staff of the FAA was acutely aware of the inadequacy of Argentina's air defences. At that time the task was undertaken by the already obsolete F-86F Sabre, and a few even older Gloster Meteors. After evaluation of several aircraft, the F-4E Phantom II was selected as the new fighter/interceptor, but the US State Department vetoed the sale because the political regime in the country was considered to be unstable. At that point the FAA turned towards its second choice, the Mirage III.

It was originally thought that FMA at Cordoba could build about 100 Mirages under licence, but this was later cut back to 50. Finally, due to the perennial economic problems of Argentina, this ambitious licence-production idea was abandoned, and ten Mirage IIIEA interceptors were ordered direct from Dassault. This aircraft was a simplified variant of the Mirage IIIE, without the Doppler radar and a number of other expensive systems, but incorporat-

ing specific FAA requirements, such as VOR, and all cockpit lettering in English. The order also included two dual-control Mirage IIIDA trainers. The serials chosen for the interceptors were in the range I-003/I-012, while the trainers were I-001 and I-002.

A number of experienced fast jet pilots were sent to Dijon for conversion to the aircraft with ECT 2/2, and they returned to act as instructors to other Argentine pilots. The aircraft were delivered between June and December 1972, and assigned to the temporarily named 'Escuadrón Mirage', located at Base Aerea Militar (BAM) Dr Marianno Moreno. This facility has a 7900 foot runway, and is positioned some 25 miles south of the capital, Buenos Aires.

To follow the normal squadron designation system used by the FAA, the Mirage unit was provided with a more formal context when VIII Brigada Aérea was activated on 9 December 1975. Shortly afterwards, Grupo 8 de Caza, Grupo 8 Base and Grupo Tecnico 8 were formed around the Mirage fleet. The main

LEFT
The Mirage IIIEA was a simplified version of the Mirage IIIE. Some of the more expensive options (such as the Doppler system) were omitted, but VOR was a firm requirement. Ten interceptors were finally ordered in October 1970 (Romero)

ABOVE
Two Mirage IIIDA trainers were also ordered in October 1970. This machine (I-002) was the only two-seater with Grupo 8 de Caza during the 1982 Falklands conflict. Apart from its continuing training commitment, it also flew several armed surveillance sorties from Comodoro Rivadavia AB (Romero)

RIGHT
The Grupo 8 de Caza badge depicts a plan view of the Mirage itself, in afterburner, and obviously towing a stylized shock wave, above an outline map of Argentina (Bosich)

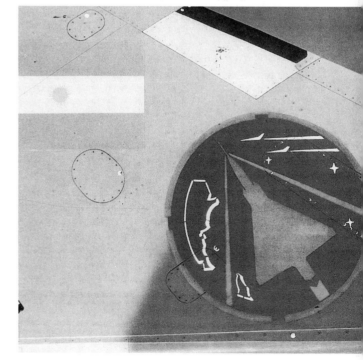

operational role of the aircraft at that time was the air defence of the capital.

Between June 1972 and the Falklands conflict in April 1982, only two Mirages were lost in accidents. The first was a single-seat aircraft (I-009), which crashed as the result of a flat spin during 1976. Its pilot, 1st Lt Garcia, managed to eject safely. Three years later in March 1979, the same thing happened to a two-seat trainer (I-001), and again the pilots escaped. The two men involved were Comodoro Viola, and Capt Huck—who was of Scottish origin! Seven new Mirage IIIEAs (I-013/019) were acquired in 1979; and in November 1981, two ex-*Armée de l'Air* Mirage IIIBEs (I-020/021) were ordered for delivery in December 1982.

The Falklands

On 2 April 1982, the Mirages of *Grupo 8 de Caza*— together with the Daggers of *Grupo 6*—formed part of *Comando Aérea de Defensa* (Air Defence Command). With FAA mobilization, the unit was initially put on a high state of readiness, but this was relaxed soon afterwards. As the Task Force got steadily closer to the Falkland Islands however, the FAA began to accept that the British were not joking, and the pressure for instant readiness was reapplied. The most immediate danger was the possibility of attack by Royal Air Force Vulcans, so the Mirage IIIs were configured for their primary interceptor role, rather than being used as fighter-bombers. *Grupo Tecnico 8*

worked overtime to prepare the maximum number of operational aircraft, and of the 16 Mirage IIIEAs potentially available, 12 were finally cleared as fully combat-ready.

Meanwhile the pilots were receiving instruction on the firing parameters of the new (to them) Matra Magic IR guided missile, and studying all the available information about the Harrier. The FAA had even acquired a copy of the pilot's manual for the AV-8S—either from a sympathetic Spanish naval officer or from an Argentine Military Attaché who knew his job. Whether it was a gift, or had to be paid for, will probably never be known, but in the long run it served little purpose because it said nothing about the radar-equipped Sea Harrier, or about the tactical skill of the British pilots.

The possibility of basing the Mirages at Port Stanley airfield was studied, but this option was discarded because the runway, at only 4100 feet, was simply too short to operate safely with external loads. After FAS was given overall responsibility for co-ordinating FAA operations in the war theatre, *Grupo 8 de Caza* deployed eight Mirage IIIEAs to Comodoro Rivadavia AB. A few days later, four of these were transferred to Rio Gallegos—still in the provence of Santa Cruz, but located some 400 miles south of Comodoro Rivadavia, and about the same distance from the Falklands. The other four serviceable aircraft remained at Dr Mariano Moreno as reserves, and to protect the capital.

The eight aircraft deployed to the southern bases were administered by the temporary *Escuadrón Caza Interceptor*, commanded by Comodoro Carlos Corino, who was the regular CO of *Grupo 8 de Caza*. For surveillance of the airspace around the Patagonia and Tierra del Fuego bases and installations, the FAA had AN/TPS-43E radars at Comodoro Rivadavia, Rio Gallegos and Rio Grande.

LEFT
Of 16 Mirage IIIEAs potentially available at the start of the Falklands conflict, 12 were finally cleared to combat-ready status by Grupo Technico 8 (Romero)

BELOW
Seen here on 21 April 1982, Mirage IIIEA (I-016) is in long-range configuration, taxiing towards the active runway at Dr Mariano Moreno AB before departing to Comodoro Rivadavia. During the conflict, this particular Mirage flew seven top cover sorties over the Falklands, without once making contact with a Sea Harrier patrol. On 8 October 1983, the aircraft was badly damaged at Rio Gallegos by Capt Gonzalez, but it was later re-built and put back into service (FAA)

The distance between the Falklands and the nearest practical bases for the Mirage was a significant handicap. The Daggers, with their extra 110 gal (500 lt) upper tank aft of the cockpit, could at least remain on station for about five minutes, but the Mirage was restricted to arriving over the Falklands at very high level, and remaining there throughout its (short) patrol. It was just not possible for the aircraft to get into a low altitude fight with Sea Harriers, and then make it back to the mainland on its limited fuel reserves. Thus, even before the start of hostilities, the Mirage III had lost any chance of gaining air superiority over the islands.

Engaging the Enemy

On 30 April, after the long wait as the Task Force made its way south, everything seemed to happen at once. The British were suddenly very close to the islands, and the mainland-based Mirages were put on QRA, while the radars probed continuously for hostile contacts. At 04:45 hrs on 1 May, the airfield at Port Stanley (which had become BAM Malvinas to the Argentinians) was hit by 21 1000 lb bombs from Royal Air Force Vulcan XM607. As a result of this raid, the FAS issued Frag Order No 1090, and two Mirage IIIEAs with the callsign 'Fiera' were launched from Rio Gallegos. The section leader was Maj Sanchez, and the purpose of the mission was to provide top cover for the airfield in case another Vulcan raid was planned. At 07:30 hrs, after having been on station for only a few minutes, the flight returned to Rio Gallegos without incident. This mission, in common with all the others over and around the islands, was controlled by a mobile

ABOVE
Four Mirage IIIEAs on their deployment flight to Comodoro Rivadavia in late April 1982. The picture was taken from a two-seat Mirage IIIDA flown by 1st Lt Horacio Bosich (FAA via Bosich)

BELOW
Mirage IIIEA I-014 departing Rio Gallegos for a top cover mission over the Falklands. The interceptor is in 'heavy' configuration, with two 375 gal (1700 lt) drop tanks, two Matra R550 Magic missiles and a single R530 missile (FAA)

AN/TPS-43E radar located close to Stanley, operating through a Command Post installed in the town itself.

Later in the morning 'Tablon' and 'Limon' sections were launched, taking off just two minutes apart. At 20,000 feet over the islands they were vectored onto a Sea Harrier CAP that was preparing to 'bounce' a section of A-4B attack aircraft. The Royal Navy fighters broke off the engagement, but seconds later 'Limon' section (Capt Garcia-Cuerva and 1st Lt Perona) received instructions to intercept yet another Sea Harrier CAP. This was a section from No 801 Sqn, flown by Lt Cdr Ward and Lt Watson. Garcia-Cuerva and Perona pursued the British fighters until they got to within 15 miles of them, then the Harriers suddenly made a 180 degree turn to confront the Mirages head-on. The aircraft was closing rapidly, when the British pilots disengaged because they thought one of the Mirages had launched missiles. In fact, only a single Matra R530 had been fired during the chase, and even that was launched by mistake, without securing a radar lock on its target. The 'missiles' spotted by the Royal Navy pair were actually big drop-tanks, released by the Mirages to improve their dogfighting agility. This illusion— often seen only fleetingly—was to become a common error in the combat reports of both sides during the conflict. After the initial descending chase, both Mirages were critically short of fuel, and were forced to break off completely and return to Rio Gallegos. They landed safely with very little fuel to spare, and found that 'Tablon' section had returned some minutes earlier.

The next Grupo 8 missions were again designed to provide CAPs over the islands. 'Dardo' section was launched at 15:30 hrs, and 'Buitre' followed at 15:53 hrs. By 16:10 hrs, 'Buitre' (Garcia-Cuerva and Perona—their second sortie of the day) had reached the nothern edge of Pebble Island, when they engaged a Sea Harrier CAP flown by Lt Thomas and Flt Lt Barton. The Argentinian pilots approached head-on and with an altitude advantage, trying to entice the enemy into a vertical scissors manoeuvre. During the initial approach they could only see Thomas, because he and Barton were in the standard, widely separated, line abreast battle formation. This enabled Barton to split off into a pincer movement without being seen, moving away to the north-west to approach the Mirages from the rear. At about four miles separation, Thomas again mistook the jettisoning of drop tanks for missile launches, and in his efforts to evade them, he passed immediately above and very close to Perona's Mirage. The Argentinian pilot remembers seeing every detail of the Sea Harrier's dark grey undersurfaces, complete with drop tanks and Sidewinders. They were at 12,000 feet, and as Perona initiated a left turn to keep track of Thomas visually, his Mirage (I-015) was hit by an AIM-9L fired by Barton in Sea Harrier XZ453. The two Argentinian fighters seemed to be in a smooth 2.5 G turn at the time, but the British pilot had been forced to execute a hard turn of about 6 G in order to position behind them, finally getting the lock with his left-hand Sidewinder at a range of about one mile. It was the Sea Harrier's first kill of the war.

For Perona the missile came as something of a surprise, because he was not really sure about Barton's position. Fortunately he managed to eject from his disintegrating aircraft, and he now recalls the encounter:

The original tactical idea was that each of us would engage one of the 'bandits' by locking into a 1 v 1 combat. At that moment our aircraft and one of the Sea Harriers crossed over each other, so I started what is known as a scissors manoeuvre, which involves climbing to gain as much height as possible, turning and banking to port and starboard in order to seize the advantage from the enemy and put your aircraft in his 6 o'clock. The Sea Harrier's characteristics allow it to slow down in the air much more rapidly, and besides, I was having trouble controlling my Mirage due to a drop tank hang-up. When I took a glance sideways I was surprised to see that we were only 100–200 feet apart, so I closely followed him until he disappeared from my field of view through the top aft section of the cockpit canopy. I was just starting a manoeuvre to 'eyeball' the Harrier again, when I felt a big jolt. My aircraft started to shudder badly and I lost control, and all the warning lights on the Caution and Advisory Panel snapped on in quick succession, like an illuminating Christmas tree. My efforts to regain control of the Mirage were futile, so I ejected before it disintegrated completely. I succeeded in steering my parachute towards land—which was lucky, because falling into the water at those latitudes can be a dramatic shock to the system. When I was still some metres above the ground however, a gust of wind caught the parachute and drove me hard into some rocky terrain. My final contact was 'unorthodox' to say the least, and I suffered considerable wounds to both legs . . .

Perona was rescued by his own forces some time later, and taken to Port Stanley. From there, he was evacuated in an FAA C-130 to Comodoro Rivadavia, where he spent most of the remaining days of the war in a military hospital, recovering from his injuries.

Moments after Perona was shot down, Thomas in Sea Harrier XZ452 launched a Sidewinder towards Garcia-Cuerva in Mirage IIIEA I-019. Thomas recalls the incident:

I got a visual at about eight miles, and saw it was a Mirage. I also saw his wingman, just behind the leader, and to the right. I could not believe that a pair of fighter pilots would approach like that. Their formation was poor; what the Americans would call 'welded wing' because they were so close. I was trying to lock a Sidewinder onto the leader, but the missile would not acquire because the solution was wrong. At five miles the leader launched a missile, but I saw it diverge and go down to my left. At the same time something came off the second aircraft and began tumbling. I started to turn hard to the right, and passed about 100 feet above the top of their leader. I could make out every detail of the aircraft's camouflage pattern, and even see the pilot in his cockpit. I continued to turn towards the wingman, who by now was about 500 yards in trail, on the leader's left.

While I was in the turn, I passed over the top of Paul (Barton) as he moved in to attack. I could see his guns firing. Then the rear man rolled off the bank and started a gentle climb, seemingly unaware that Paul was sitting right behind him. My opinion was that these pilots were not very good tactically—they didn't seem to know what was going on. They both seemed to know that I was there, but I do not think they knew where Paul was, or what he was up to.

I saw the Sidewinder launched by Paul streak towards the wingman. It exploded, and the rear end of the Mirage became a bright yellow torch. The front half of the aircraft remained more or less intact, but shedding pieces it continued on and on upwards in a ballistic trajectory.

Meanwhile I was continuing my turn, and the enemy leader was doing quite a fast descending turn to the left, going down towards the top of solid cloud cover at 4000 feet. I rolled into a vertical descent behind him, locked one of my missiles, and fired. The 'Lima' streaked after him, and just before he reached the cloud I saw it pass close to his tail—then the aircraft and the Sidewinder disappeared . . .

It seems that the missile exploded close to the aft underside of the Mirage, puncturing the fuel tanks and damaging some of the control runs. In an effort to save the valuable aircraft, Garcia-Cuerva decided to attempt a landing at Port Stanley's airfield, less than five minutes' flying time away. The GCI controller advised him to eject, but he stayed with the crippled machine despite the risks of a bomb-damaged runway. The AA defences were told about his approach and then, on short finals, he jettisoned his two Magic missiles on inert mode (by pulling an emergency handle in the cockpit). This would have made the aircraft much safer to land, but the nervous crew of an Army 35 mm gun saw the missiles fall away and thought it was a British aircraft attacking the airfield. They opened fire on the slow-moving Mirage, hitting it almost immediately. Garcia-Cuerva was heard by the controller to shout, 'Hell, they hit me . . .' as the aircraft was enveloped in flames, rolled inverted and crashed into the water just south of Freycinet Peninsula. He was the only Grupo 8 pilot to be killed during the conflict.

Shortly after the dramatic end to 'Dardo' section, 'Buitre' landed back at Rio Gallegos without engaging the Sea Harriers.

At the end of the first day of real combat with the Task Force, Grupo 8 de Caza had notched up 12 sorties over the Falklands. During the first few missions the Mirage IIIEAs carried two 375 gal (1700 lt) drop tanks and a single R530 radar-guided air-to-air missile, but for later sorties the armourers added two R550 Magic IR guided missiles. This configuration was strongly discouraged in the pilot's notes for the aircraft, but it added considerable flexibility of operation, and as the safety margins were not eroded too much, the theoretical advice was ignored.

This first day of fighting shocked the Mirage pilots. Apart from losing one of their colleagues—an experienced flight commander—two virtually brand new interceptors had been shot down with compara-

tive ease by the Sea Harrier pilots. After assessing the day's activities, it was obvious that the negative aspects were very similar to those experienced by the Dagger squadrons. Clearly the most important limitation was the range at which the Mirages were operating. They had almost no freedom of manoeuvre, and without high-level loiter time they were unable to dictate the terms of an engagement. This passed the initiative over to the Sea Harrier, which was equipped to a far higher standard (RWR, chaff/flare defences, etc), and armed with the frontal-aspect AIM-9L Sidewinder. The 'Lima' Sidewinder was probably the most advanced short-range missile in the world at that time, and certainly far exceeded the capabilities of the R530 and R550 carried by the Mirage. The interceptor pilots had also discovered weaknesses in their own tactical appreciation of an air-to-air battle, which made life comparatively easy for the supremely well trained British pilots. For all these reasons the evening of 1 May was a time of extreme frustration for Grupo 8 personnel. They had been bettered by an enemy that they had underestimated—a fact that had to be considered for the remainder of the conflict.

There was obviously no point in risking the few available Mirage III interceptors in further engagements with the Sea Harrier, which had so many clearcut advantages. The FAS staff were also worried (quite logically) that the next Vulcan raids could be against mainland air bases in southern Argentina—particularly Rio Grande and Comodoro Rivadavia. Accordingly Grupo 8, with its 24-hour QRA mission at Rio Gallegos and Comodoro Rivadavia, was held in readiness against any threat detected by the early warning radars. These alert duties—which were maintained throughout the war and for several weeks afterwards—were terribly boring, with pilots inside the Mirage's narrow cockpit, enduring intense cold and not really knowing what kind of mission they would be scrambled for, or even if they would be scrambled at all. Maintaining this long, cold vigil, led fellow airmen from more active FAA units to call the Mirage people (somewhat unfairly) the 'trench foot pilots'. Maj Sanchez, the Operations Officer of Grupo 8 de Caza during the conflict, relates some of his experiences while on readiness duty at Rio Gallegos:

I made a couple of alert scrambles, searching for low-speed targets (probably helicopters) flying very close to the Argentina/Chile border in the Tierra del Fuego region. The 'bogey' would enter Argentina briefly, we would scramble, and then they would return to Chilean territory and were lost to radar, but we would remain on patrol until 'bingo' fuel. On other nights we patrolled over Tierra del Fuego, near Rio Grande, looking for bogeys we could fix. Although we did not have RWR on the Mirage at that time, we could always tell if the Chilean radar at Punta Arenas was 'painting' us by monitoring the IFF.

We were held on permanent readiness, and had the capability to cover any type of mission. Thanks to the operational training exercises that we did regularly, we

BELOW
During the first few missions, the Mirage interceptors were armed with their two cannon, and a single Matra R530 radar-guided AAM. Every sortie over the islands needed two 375 gal (1700 lt) external tanks (FAA)

LEFT
Later sorties were flown with the addition of two IR-guided Matra R550 Magic AAMs. This extra armament was very much against 'the book', but it added considerable operational flexibility (FAA)

knew the interception role perfectly, and could handle any air defence sortie in all kinds of weather.

I'd like to emphasize that all our personnel were trained to endure intense pressure. During some of our time at Rio Gallegos we were reduced to only one pilot per aircraft. Despite this lack of aircrew, all the Mirages remained on 24-hour instant readiness throughout the period.

Our alert covered all the FAS bases, and the naval air station at Rio Grande. We also occasionally made top cover or decoy flights over the Malvinas (Falklands), and after returning from these, we had to turn the aircraft around very quickly, and then go back on standby alert—perhaps to scramble again almost immediately. In one instance, I returned from an escort sortie which had lasted for more than two hours, and as my aircraft was being refuelled on the ramp, I received an urgent scramble order, so the refuelling was cut short and I launched with only internal fuel . . .

The period 2–20 May was relatively quiet for the Mirage pilots, although, like every other unit in the Argentine forces, they were constantly working under the stress of not knowing the future course of events.

Battle of San Carlos

The British landings around San Carlos and adjacent areas caught the FAA by surprise, because the beachhead was not expected to be so far away from Port Stanley. A week before the main landings, the SAS had raided the small airstrip on Pebble Island, and this should have given the Argentinians a strong hint about the Task Force commander's intentions—but the point was obviously missed. This tactical blunder allowed the British troops to come ashore virtually unhindered by Argentine ground forces, and air strikes became the only practical means of slowing down their advance. The strike missions began almost immediately, and some of these were provided with top cover by *Grupo 8*.

During the Battle of San Carlos (21–27 May), the small detachment of Mirages at Comodoro Rivadavia was flown south to join the others at Rio Gallegos, and *Grupo 8* flew a total of 18 sorties in support of strike missions against the British landings. The Mirage III's availability rate was very high during this period (close to 100 per cent), and every sortie was dispatched on time and arrived over the operational area without any problems. Unfortunately the missions were all of doubtful value, because the interceptors needed to stay at high altitude to conserve fuel, and the Sea Harriers found all their most profitable 'trade' at low level. The British pilots were fully aware of these limitations, and were

certainly not interested in climbing to engage the Mirages, because they represented no real danger to the Task Force while they remained at high altitude. During those six days of hectic fighting, none of the Mirage III sorties engaged Sea Harrier CAPs. Comodoro Carlos E Corino, the CO of *Grupo 8 de Caza*, explains the problems faced by the interceptor pilots:

Basically, our aircraft operated only at high level because they would lose the advantage by going lower to engage. We were fully conscious of our advantages and disadvantages, and naturally the British pilots were also aware of our problems. To exploit the Mirage convincingly, we should have had a better guidance (GCI) capability. Although the aircraft is equipped with a search and fire-control radar, its target tracking range is limited to 25 miles. This meant that guidance had to be provided from ground-based radar if we were to position favourably in relation to the enemy—that is, within range of the onboard Cyrano radar. Our interceptors were operating at the extreme edge of their radius of action, and at the best of times they could only remain on patrol over the islands for a very few minutes—even at high level. The Sea Harrier pilots had a far better guidance capability from a respectable quantity of destroyers and frigates, all with highly experienced fighter controllers on board. After the 1 May combat, there were only a few skirmishes, and none of these had any real consequence. Whenever the Mirages were in a favourable position the Sea Harriers disengaged, and vice versa as soon as the Mirages lost the advantage of altitude ...

During the final phase of the conflict *Grupo 8* made a total of 15 air cover sorties over the islands, without once engaging the Sea Harriers. It is worth pointing out that the four cover/decoy sorties flown by the Mirages on 8 June, attracted Sea Harrier CAPs away from the Port Pleasant area, allowing the first Skyhawk and Dagger sections to have a relatively undisturbed run to their targets.

Perhaps the most dramatic escort mission involving the Mirages took place on 13 June. It was to be the FAA's last combat mission of the war, and because of the drama involved, it is perhaps worth describing in detail.

At about 19:00 hrs on Sunday 13 June, the hated black telephone rang in the Command Centre of Rio Gallegos AB. A pair of Frag Orders (1326 and 1327) were transmitted, requiring the station to prepare for a strike mission by a section of Canberras from *Grupo 2 de Bombardeo*, against British positions on East Falkland. The Canberras were to be accompanied by an escort section of Mirages from *Grupo 8 de Caza*. The two bombers had repositioned from Trelew NAS to Rio Gallegos earlier in the day, in order to cut their transit times to and from the target.

The mission planning for the escort fighters was very complicated because of the range problem. It was necessary to compute routes, rendezvous points and schedules exactly, to enable the Mirages to protect the bombers during the dangerous approach and attack phases of the mission. The crews attended

a joint briefing to establish all the procedures to be followed, and shortly afterwards the Canberra section, under the callsign '*Baco*', was launched. The lead aircraft was crewed by Capt Pastran (pilot) and Capt Casado (nav/bombardier), and No 2 by Lt Rivollier (pilot) and 1st Lt Anino.

Fourteen minutes later the Mirage III escort section ('*Pluton*') was launched, led by Maj Sanchez, and with Capt Gonzalez as wingman. It was an extremely dark night with no moon, and at 5000 feet there was dense cloud cover that extended almost all the way to the islands. As soon as the two aircraft reached their pre-established cruise altitude, they switched off all external lights, and began the long transit towards the Falklands in complete radio silence. They were using an open trail type formation, with the wingman keeping station on the leader by using the Cyrano radar.

It was important that both Mirage pilots were very experienced, because the mission was fraught with difficulty for any single-seat aircraft. The long night crossing of a vast expanse of ocean without any external references or visibility; the deep sense of loneliness caused by radio silence and complete darkness; and the monotonous drone of the engine, which can cause instant panic with even the slightest change in noise level or fluctuation of the RPM indicator. These conditions can easily create complete spatial disorientation, which leads the pilot to disregard or mistrust the indications of his softly lit instruments and radar display.

When the Mirages were at 30,000 feet and close to the southern coast of West Falkland, the cloud cover began to break up a little, and through one of the holes both pilots noted some bright flashes of variable intensity. They assumed it was some kind of storm, but it seemed to be restricted to one part of East Falkland, and the flashes had a very regular rhythm. The Canberra section was now directly ahead of them, within range of the Cyrano radar, and flying at 40,000 feet on final approach to the target area. Breaking radio silence, the formation established contact with Falklands radar, and the controller confirmed that the flashes were artillery shells exploding in the area. British naval and field artillery units were both bombarding Argentinian positions around Port Stanley, but so far the radar's operational capability had not been affected. No Sea Harrier CAPs were reported, so the Mirage pilots eased their search.

The ground-based radar guided the Canberras towards their objective, which was a British troop concentration and HQ area near Mt Kent. From the relative security of his fighter cockpit, Maj Sanchez shadowed the bombers as they passed the IP (initial point) virtually together, and then released their bombs over the signalled co-ordinates. Through some holes in the cloud cover, Sanchez had a perfect view of the brilliant flashes caused by the exploding bombs.

The Mirage interceptors were always operating at the extreme edge of their radius of action, and were forced to carry a heavy fuel load just to reach the combat area. Here Capt Testa rotates in I-017 just before the end of the Rio Gallegos runway (FAA)

Nearby he noted a missile being launched, which was probably defective because it started gyrating wildly. This certainly did not happen with subsequent launches, and Sanchez suddenly realized the danger as four or five more SAMs started climbing almost vertically towards them. He alerted Capt Gonzalez, but the missiles seemed to be locked onto the Canberra section—probably 'Baco-2'. Lt Rivollier was warned of the situation by radio, and he launched several flares and chaff bundles while initiating a series of evasive high G turns. The missiles eventually passed behind him and were lost in the darkness.

The observation of these events had distracted the attention of Sanchez for a while, and he almost missed a new volley of missiles. He saw them first with his peripheral vision, much lower, but climbing very fast in his 12 o'clock position. He could distinguish the cluster of bright red exhaust trails perfectly, as the weapons scorched up towards the formation. One of them in particular grew much bigger, seemingly

locked on to his Mirage. At that time he was at 30,000 feet, in a wide turn at Mach 0.92. The missile was inside his turn, but somewhat lower. Reducing his engine power, he tightened the turn and began a deep, spiral descent. He kept his eyes glued on the rapidly closing light, which was now in the centre of an imaginary circle drawn by the Mirage.

The flashes coming from Port Stanley and Mt Kent had stopped, so the sky and earth were confused in a frightening, velvety, never ending blackness. It was difficult to tell which way was up and which way down, but it was vital to watch for the missile, and forget about the instruments for the time being. Sanchez began to feel the first signs of disorientation, but the descending spiral had to continue. Then the missile exploded in a brilliant flash and fireball, sending shrapnel from its warhead to trace an angry porcupine of red lines in the night sky. The Argentine pilot sighed with relief as he realized the Mirage had not been hit, but then a new and even bigger missile—probably a Sea Dart—could be seen climbing rapidly towards him. He barely had time to register any fear of this new threat before the missile had passed by on the starboard side, still ascending and seeking its target elsewhere.

Temporarily out of danger, Sanchez took a quick look at his instruments. He had lost over 15,000 feet during those frantic few seconds, and was well to the west of his planned course. Establishing contact with

After the cessation of hostilities, Grupo 8 interceptors remained at Rio Gallegos, but the squadron returned to its normal peacetime routine. This picture was taken during 1983, and the aircraft are preparing for a practice air-to-ground sortie. Note the small 'supersonic' external tanks, rather than the 375 gal variety used for long range missions over the islands (FAA)

contact his leader. A request to ground radar soon confirmed that all contact with 'Baco-1' had been lost. Canberra B-108 had been downed by a Sea Dart missile launched from the Type 42 destroyer, HMS *Exeter* (D 89). Its pilot, Capt Pastran, ejected safely and was subsequently captured by British troops, but the navigator, Capt Casado, fell to his death in the spinning aircraft, which finally crashed into Mt Kent. The three remaining aircraft all returned safely, landing at Rio Grande at 23:55 hrs.

This was the last mission flown by *Grupo 8 de Caza* during the Falklands conflict. The squadron completed a total of 45 air cover and decoy sorties over the islands, losing two aircraft and one pilot in the process. In addition, 46 alert scrambles and patrols were completed over the mainland or over territorial waters. The apparently poor results of the squadron were heavily criticised in some FAA circles, although it must be understood that the aircraft was never really designed for a Falklands style operation—and geography was certainly against it, which is why it never seriously challenged the Sea Harrier's air superiority. Despite its lack of effectiveness over the islands, its important contribution to the air defence of the mainland bases should not be overlooked.

Post-war Changes

After the conflict, *Grupo 8* returned to peacetime routine, but due to the galloping economic crisis in Argentina, the number of flying hours allocated to each pilot was constantly being cut back. It finally reached an all-time low of only five hours per month in 1984. Detachments were (and indeed still are) periodically stationed at Rio Gallegos to conduct exercises and provide supplementary air defence assets in the south. During one of these deployments, on 8 October 1983, Mirage IIIEA I-016 was badly damaged when Capt Gonzalez—a combat veteran and one of the squadron's most experienced pilots—attempted a slow roll on finals, with the wheels down and carrying large drop tanks and two Magic missiles! Not surprisingly, the aircraft rapidly lost lift and crash-landed beside the runway. The impact tore off the landing gear and much of the belly, and a post-crash fire consumed the aft fuselage and fin. For this 'macho' gesture, Capt Gonzalez was grounded for over a year. The Mirage itself was eventually rebuilt by the highly professional *Talleres Rio IV* overhaul unit, but not before many hundreds of man hours had been devoted to its resurrection. In another incident just after the war, Carlos Perona was forced to land at Dr Mariano Moreno AB in extremely bad weather. He had no chance to divert to another airfield, and the resulting touch-down in almost nil visibility was hard enough to collapse the undercarriage and start a fire in the aft fuselage. The fire was extinguished very rapidly, and the valuable Mirage was again repaired by *Rio IV*.

Over the last 10–15 years, the residential areas of

the FAA radar at Port Stanley, the controller confirmed that he had both Mirages on the screen. They were virtually overflying Goose Green, with Capt Gonzalez much lower, and almost within range of AA artillery and Blowpipe or Stinger missiles.

The Mirage section quickly regained its cruise altitude, and tried to establish radio contact with the Canberras. 'Baco-2' replied, and told the Mirage pilots that he had been trying unsuccessfully to

LEFT

After the war the FAA was determined to make good its combat losses, and to this effect acquired 19 Mirage IIICJs and three Mirage IIIBJ trainers from Israel, together with a large quantity of spares. By late 1983, the first of them had been modified to FAA standards, and were delivered to Mendoza-based Grupo 4 de Caza *(FAA)*

BELOW LEFT

In May 1982 Peru sold the FAA ten Mirage 5Ps as attrition replacements. The aircraft were initially assigned to Grupo 6 de Caza, *but some time after the war they were completely overhauled and reassigned to* Grupo 10 de Caza *at Rio Gallegos. The squadron now provides a permanent air-defence presence in southern Patagonia. This aircraft carries lighter (Peruvian) camouflage scheme, and the serial C-409—from a Dagger that was shot down during the war (Romero)*

ABOVE

An ex-Israeli Mirage IIICJ undergoing some open air maintenance. It has the darker camouflage scheme, and the badge of Grupo 10 de Caza *on the fin (FAA)*

greater Buenos Aires have spread out towards Dr Mariano Moreno AB, and continuous flying from the airfield became both a nuisance and a safety hazard to the civilian population. The FAA therefore decided to close the base, and move *Grupo 8 de Caza* and all the assets of *VIII Brigada Aérea* to Tandil. The move also made good economic sense, because Tandil is the main operating base of the *VI Brigada Aérea* Daggers. The transfer of personnel and equipment was progressively completed during 1988.

Mirage IIICJ/BJ

Shortly after the Falklands conflict, the FAA acquired 19 Mirage IIICJ interceptors and three Mirage IIIBJ trainers. These were purchased from surplus Israeli stocks for US 70 million dollars. They arrived in Argentina by sea between December 1982 and February 1983, and were all delivered to *Rio IV* for overhaul and adaption to FAA standards. Israel had re-engined the Mirages with Atar O9Cs during the mid 1970s, and they had all been put through an IAI update programme, which included new spars and wing skins. The technicians at *Rio IV* found them all to be in remarkably good condition, despite the fact that many of them had been involved in combat flying for about 20 years.

By late 1983, the first adapted Mirage IIICJ/BJs were delivered to Mendoza-based *Grupo 4 de Caza* of *IV Brigada Aérea*. This former Skyhawk squadron has a regular operational commitment, but it also acts as the OCU for all young pilots posted to the other Mirage/Dagger squadrons. Only seven of its A-4Cs survived the war, and these were transferred to *Grupo 5 de Caza* of *V Brigada Aérea*, which had also suffered heavy losses in the fighting.

For a time, one of the Mirage IIICJs (C-701) remained at *Rio IV* to conduct air-to-air refuelling trials with a domestically developed probe. These trials were initially unsuccessful, but later reports indicate that modifications have been made—possibly with IAI assistance—and soon all the Mirage/Dagger fleet will have this capability, which will increase their range dramatically.

Appendices

Appendix 1
Mirage III/5/50 Production and Serials

Abu Dhabi	12 Mirage 5AD	401 to 412
	14 Mirage 5EAD	501 to 514
	3 Mirage 5RAD	601 to 603
	3 Mirage 5DAD	201 to 203
Argentina	2 Mirage IIIDA	I-001 and I-002
	17 Mirage IIIEA	I-003 to I-019
	2 Mirage IIIBE	I-020 and I-021 (ex *Armée de l'Air* No 271 and 272)
	24 Dagger A	C-401 to C-424
	2 Dagger B	C-425 and C-426
	11 Dagger A	C-427 to C-437
	2 Dagger B	C-438 and C-439
	10 Mirage 5P	C-403, C-404, C-407, C-409, C-410, C-419, C-428, C-430, C-433, C-436 (ex Peruvian, all using serials of lost Dagger As)
	19 Mirage IIICJ	C-701 to C-719
	3 Mirage IIIBJ	C-720 to C-722
Australia—*see Appendix 6*		
Belgium	16 Mirage 5BD	BD01 to BD16 (first three were originally MD01 to MD03)
	63 Mirage 5BA	BA01 to BA63 (first three were originally MA01 to MA03)
	27 Mirage 5BR	BR01 to BR27
Brazil	6 Mirage IIIDBR	4900 to 4905
	16 Mirage IIIEBR	4910 to 4925
Chile	8 Mirage 50FC	501 to 508
	6 Mirage 50C	509 to 514
	2 Mirage 50DC	515 to 516
	1 Mirage IIIBE	517
Colombia	2 Mirage 5COD	3001 to 3002
	2 Mirage 5COR	3011 and 3012
	14 Mirage 5COA	3021 to 3034
Egypt	6 Mirage 5SDD	2011 to 2016 (first three ex *Armée de l'Air*)
	32 Mirage 5SDE	9101 to 9132 (first three ex *Armée de l'Air*)
	22 Mirage 5SSE	9133 to 9154
	6 Mirage 5SDR	9155 to 9160
	16 Mirage 5E2	9161 to 9176

France	1 Mirage I	01
	1 Mirage III	001 (later modified to Balzac V 001)
	10 Mirage IIIA	01 to 010
	28 Mirage IIIB	01 (prototype) then 201 to 227
	5 Mirage IIIB-1	231 to 235
	10 Mirage IIIB-2(RV)	241 to 250
	20 Mirage IIIBE	257 to 276, (257, 258 and 265 to Egypt. 271 and 272 to Argentina. One to Chile)
	95 Mirage IIIC	1 to 95
	192 Mirage IIIE	01 to 03 (prototypes) 401 to 408, 410, 412, 414, 415, 417 to 419, 421 to 440, 443, 445, 447, 449, 451 to 458, 460 to 463, 465 to 531, 533 to 535, 537 to 539, 541, 545 to 579, 583 to 590, 605 to 625 (589 converted to Milan S-01, then to Mirage 50 01, then to Mirage IIING. 406 converted to Mirage IIIC2. 557 to 559 transferred to Egypt with Saudi funding)
	52 Mirage IIIR	01 and 02 (prototypes) then 301 to 350 (344 to Milan 01)
	20 Mirage IIIRD	351 to 370
	58 Mirage 5F	1 to 58 (1, 3, 5, 8, 16, 23, 28, 30 converted to Mirage 50FC standard for Chile)
	1 Mirage 5	01 (prototype)
	1 Mirage IIIT	01 (prototype—engine test bed)
	2 Mirage IIIV	01 and 02 (prototypes—VTOL trainers)
Gabon	4 Mirage 5DG	201 to 204
	3 Mirage 5G	401 to 403
	4 Mirage 5G-II	501 to 504

Israel—*see Appendix 3*

Lebanon	10 Mirage IIIEL	L501 to L510
	2 Mirage IIIBL	L511 and L512
Libya	53 Mirage 5D	401 to 453
	15 Mirage 5DD	201 to 215
	32 Mirage 5DE	101 to 132
	10 Mirage 5DR	301 to 310
Pakistan	18 Mirage IIIEP	67.101 to 67.118
	13 Mirage IIIRP	67.201 to 67.213
	5 Mirage IIIDP	67.301 to 67.305
	28 Mirage 5PA	70.401 to 70.428
	30 Mirage 5PA2/3	79.429 to 79.458
Peru	32 Mirage 5P	101 to 114 and 181 to 196
	5 Mirage 5DP	197 to 199
		(in both cases the 'extra' aircraft have re-used the serials of crashed machines)
South Africa	16 Mirage IIICZ	800 to 185
	3 Mirage IIIBZ	816 to 818
	17 Mirage IIIEZ	819 to 834 and 842
	4 Mirage IIIRZ	835 to 838
	3 Mirage IIIDZ	839 to 841
	11 Mirage IIID2Z	843 to 853
	4 Mirage R2Z	854 to 857
		(all now being converted to Cheetah standard, first was Mirage IIID2Z 845)

Spain—*see Appendix 2*

Switzerland	1 Mirage IIIC	J-2201
	36 Mirage IIIS	J-2301 to J-2336
	18 Mirage IIIRS	R-2101 to R-2118
	4 Mirage IIIBS	U-2001 to U-2004
	2 Mirage IIIDS	U-2011 to U-2012
Venezuela	10 Mirage IIIEV	0624, 1207, 2483, 7163, 7381, 8940 (others not known)
	4 Mirage 5V	1297, 2473, 7162 and 9510
	2 Mirage 5DV	5471 and 5472
Zaire	3 Mirage 5DM	M201 to M203
	14 Mirage 5M	M401 to M414

Appendix 2

Spanish *Ejército del Aire* Mirage IIIEE/DE serials (*Ala No 11*)

	Full serial	Orig code	New code	Remarks
Trainers	CE.11-1	101-16		Crashed 1971 after flat spin: both pilots ejected
(Mirage IIIDE)	CE.11-25	111-13	11-70	
	CE.11-26	112-13	11-71	
	CE.11-27	111-14	11-72	
	CE.11-28	112-14	11-73	
	CE.11-29	111-15	11-74	
	CE.11-30	112-15	11-75	Crashed in Med on 12 May 1988 during ACM ten nm off Gandia (Valencia) after stalling and entering an irrecoverable flat spin. Capts Espresati and Terol ejected safely
Interceptors	C.11-1	111-01	11-01	
(Mirage IIIEE)	C.11-2	112-01	11-02	
	C.11-3	111-02	11-03	
	C.11-4	112-02	11-04	
	C.11-5	111-03	11-05	
	C.11-6	112-03	11-06	
	C.11-7	111-04		Written off 2 May 1977 during take-off. Caught leader's jetwash and skidded off runway. Capt Sevilla escaped, but the aircraft caught fire. Airframe now Manises gate guardian
	C.11-8	112-04	11-08	
	C.11-9	111-05	11-09	
	C.11-10	112-05	11-10	
	C.11-11	111-06		Written off 14 September 1979. Skidded off runway during landing and badly damaged. Lt Col Laporta unharmed
	C.11-12	112-06		Written off 7 August 1979. Hit by ricochet during practice strafing mission. One of its own 30 mm shells entered under left intake and destroyed the compressor. Maj Poyo ejected
	C.11-13	111-07	11-13	
	C.11-14	112-07		Crashed in Albacete province on 19 November 1974. Capt Barcala killed
	C.11-15	111-08	11-15	
	C.11-16	112-08	11-16	
	C.11-17	111-09	11-17	
	C.11-18	112-09	11-18	
	C.11-19	111-10		Crashed in Albacete province on 8 May 1978. Irrecoverable flat spin. Maj Sacanell ejected safely
	C.11-20	112-10		Crashed into sea 14 nm off Denia (Alicante) on 14 July 1978. Lt Cembranos killed
	C.11-21	111-11	11-21	
	C.11-22	112-11	11-22	
	C.11-23	111-12	11-23	
	C.11-24	112-12	11-24	

Appendix 3

IDFAF Mirage IIICJ and IIBJ serials

In 1961 the IDFAF ordered 72 single-seat Mirage IIICJs and four Mirage IIIBJ trainers. For the first few years of operation they were all allocated two-digit serial numbers, but in 1966 this policy was changed, and three-digit numbers began to appear on most of the aircraft (with a few exceptions). The numbers were allocated on a completely random basis, in a deliberate attempt to confuse the enemy. Unfortunately, it also confused aircraft buffs and, as a result, no definitive list has ever been issued.

The information provided below is based on known sightings of Mirage serials over the years. At least one reliable source gives two numbers (458/758) to the same airframe, and this is believed to have happened on a number of other occasions—159/259/459 and 287/787 are two reported examples.

The first batch shows single-seat Mirage IIICJs, powered by an Atar 09B engine. They have all been seen or photographed in their original uncamouflaged condition. The figure in parentheses alongside some of the serials indicates the number of 'kill' markings seen on that particular airframe:

02, 08, 11, 12, 14, 15, 33, 34, 44, 52, 27, 67, 109, 259 (10), 729, 732, 743, 745, 753, 778 (2), 779 (1), 780, 833, 915, 941 (1), 942, 948 (3), 951 (1), 952.

Aircraft No 11 has been seen with a large, non-standard black radome, and No 259 was displayed at the IDFAF Day in July 1970.

The second batch consists of 09B-powered Mirage IIICJs, but

these have all been seen in a multi-role camouflage scheme based on green, brown and sand upper surfaces which was adopted during the War of Attrition. The 'kill' markings are indicated in the same way, and a 'T' alongside the serial denotes that the aircraft has been seen carrying the big, yellow identification triangles:

82 (6), 83 (7), 148, 151, 158, 159 (13), 178, 180, 296, 406, 409, 459 (13), 522, 524, 534, 620, 649, 733 (T), 748, 749, 758 (8), 764, 768, 771, 776 (3).

507, 755, 756 and 775 have been seen in both the natural metal finish and the green, brown and sand camouflage.

Aircraft No 159 was equipped with a large radome for display on IDFAF Day in July 1975.

The third batch of serials shows Mirage IIICJs that have been re-engined with the more powerful Atar 09C:

103, 107 (T), 111 (1), 144 (6), 147, 150, 153 (5, T), 171 (5), 176 (3, T), 177 (5, T), 287, 458 (13, T), 720, 741 (3).

Aircraft Nos 103, 144 and 153 were seen with air superiority grey camouflage, but the others were all in the green, brown and sand scheme. Aircraft No 111 is now displayed at the IDFAF

Museum, with 13 'kill' markings.

The final batch of Mirage serials is for the Mirage IIIBJ trainers:

287 (T), 787 (the same as 287?), 789 and 988.

Aircraft no 988 was the test bed for the J79 engine and canards and is now preserved at the IDFAF Museum. Nos 287 and 988 were seen in the standard multi-role camouflage and 787 in the natural metal finish. 789 has been seen in both.

Only a small number of pictures of the Nesher were released—all single-seaters.

The aircraft were all painted in the multi-role camouflage scheme, and most of them carried combat identification triangles. The following list has been compiled from photographs and sightings:

501 (1), 524 (4), 525, 526, 527, 528, 533, 536, 537, 538, 539, 541, 543, 549, 562, 563, 565, 566, 568, 569, 574, 598, 599, 701, 705, 707, 709, 710, 712, 714, 716, 720.

Nesher No 524 took the serial of a lost Mirage IIICJ, and No 712 became the prototype Kfir.

Appendix 4

IDFAF Mirage III and Nesher losses

The first IDFAF Mirage IIIs entered service in April 1962, and the last Neshers were withdrawn from use in 1983. During the intervening period about 40 of the aircraft were lost in accidents or combat, and this unique list records 28 of those losses in as much detail as possible. Israeli military security is highly restrictive, and of necessity the information shown below cannot be complete:

Date	Unit	Location	Remarks
63/64 (?)	'RD' Sqn	Ramat David AB	Engine stopped. Pilot 'R' ejected. First IDFAF Mirage lost
?	?	Israel	Engine stopped. Pilot Ran Peker ejected at low level. Aircraft crash-landed with minimal damage and eventually rebuilt
64/65 (?)	101 Sqn	?	Fuel starvation after combat with RJAF Hunters. Pilot ejected
1967	?	?	Crashed during some sort of experimental work. Details unknown. Pilot Ben Barak killed
5 June 67	101 Sqn	Zagazic	Lost in combat with MiG-21. Pilot Y Noyman ejected, but murdered by civilians
5 June 67	119 Sqn	?	Fuel starvation after chasing and shooting down an EAF MiG-21 over Abu Suer. Israeli pilot ejected safely
5 June 67	'RD' Sqn	Damascus	Hit by AA fire. Pilot (Amihai) wounded, finally ejecting over Golani Junction in Israel
5 June 67	'RD' Sqn	Damascus	Hit by AA fire. Pilot (M Sahar) killed. Was Amihai's No 4
6/7 June 67	101 Sqn	Mitla Pass	Night mission. Hit by SA-2 missile. Pilot B David killed
7 June 67	'RD' Sqn	'H3'	Shot down by Iraqi AF Hunter. Pilot G Dror ejected, but taken PoW in Iraq
7 June 67	101 Sqn	Tel El Kabir	Hit by SA-2 missile. Pilot B Rommach killed
10 June 67	119 Sqn	Sheik Maskir	Hit by AA fire. Pilot S Sheffer wounded, but managed to eject. Rescued by helicopter
15 July 67	?	Suez Canal	Hit by AA fire. Pilot's name and fate unknown
1968 (?)	?	?	Landing accident. Pilot 'S' badly injured. Aircraft (755) later rebuilt
20 July 69	?	Suez Canal	Hit by AA-2 missile from EAF MiG-21. Pilot ejected over Sinai
9 Sept 69	119 Sqn	Nile Delta	Hit by AA-2 missile from EAF MiG-21. Pilot wounded, but ejected and taken PoW in Egypt
?	101 Sqn	?	Mid-air collision. Pilot S Hetz ejected
2 Feb 70	'RD' Sqn	Syrian border	Hit by AA fire. Pilot S Weintraub killed
9 Feb 70	?	?	Hit by AA-2 missile. Pilot A Keldes ejected and taken PoW in Egypt. Missile launched by MiG-21
March 71	?	El Arish AB	Engine stopped and aircraft crashed on landing. Pilot (Irmi) badly injured. Aircraft 755 written off
13 Sept 73	?	Mediterranean	Shot down by Syrian AF MiG-21. Pilot ejected over the sea, and rescued by CH-53 helicopter
6 Oct 73	?	Lebanon	Technical malfunction after shooting down a Syrian AF MiG-21. Pilot 'A' landed on Lebanese beach after ejection, and was rescued by IDF Navy missile boat
7 Oct 73	101 Sqn	Port Said	Hit by AA fire after shooting down two EAF aircraft. Pilot E Carmi ejected over Sinai

7 Oct 73	101 Sqn	?	Take-off accident. Pilot injured, and aircraft (159) eventually rebuilt
8 Oct 73	?	Nile Delta	Shot down during combat with MiG-21. Pilot 'A' ejected
? Oct 73	?	Port Said	Hit by AA fire after shooting down an EAF MiG-17. Pilot 'S' ejected over Sinai
13 Oct 73	101 Sqn	Syria	Shot down by MiG-21. Pilot A Lanir ejected safely, but taken PoW in Syria. Tortured to death
? Oct 73	101 Sqn	Syria	Hit by unknown surface-to-air missile while on recce flight shortly after the war. Pilot E Carmi ejected over the sea near Akko Beach. Rescued by IDF Navy patrol boat

Appendix 5

IDFAF Mirage Aces

This section deals with the personal accounts of three IDFAF Mirage pilots who were involved in air-to-air combat during the Six Day and Yom Kippur wars. At the time of writing two of them were still on reserve with the IDFAF, and so their names cannot be revealed.

Six Day War

At 09:00 hrs on the first day of the Six Day War (5 June 1967), I was scrambled to take part in a Mirage formation that had been briefed to attack the Egyptian airfield at Abu Sueir, west of Ismailia. As a 22-year-old lieutenant, I was one of the youngest pilots on the squadron, and this was to be my first sortie over enemy territory.

We had earlier flown a local air defence mission, and were given no time to change to long-range external tanks for this new sortie, so fuel would be a little tight. We climbed to gain the briefed altitude, and set course for Egypt. As we reached the target area, it was obvious that the base had already been visited, because the main runway was a shambles, and some parked Il-28s were burning fiercely. Suddenly, as we came in for the attack, an Egyptian AF MiG-21 started its take-off run on the parallel runway, so I went in low and manoeuvred into a firing position behind him. My No 1 stopped me: 'Don't touch him! He's mine!' I moved aside and the leader went in. That was that. It was the first time I had ever seen an enemy aircraft explode.

As if by magic, the whole sky filled with aircraft and all hell broke loose! There were explosions everywhere, and dogfights all around me. The entire area was filled with smoke and fire. Through the haze I saw two MiGs chasing a pair of our Mirages. I went into afterburner and closed in on one of the Egyptian aircraft. I opened fire on him at 200 metres range—and missed. I felt terrible. What a rookie! All my self-confidence seemed to fade away. For three years I had prepared myself for this moment, and when it finally came, I failed to live up to my own expectations. I tried again. Closing to 150 metres this time, I fired another short burst. The MiG exploded in a searing ball of fire right before my eyes. I felt nothing. On my way home I caught another MiG-21, and after a short chase I shot him down as well! I was now drunk with elation, but also very short of fuel. During the return flight I heard my leader report that he was bailing out due to fuel starvation, and I only reached base on my last few drops. My first combat sortie was over, and I had two 'kills' to my credit.

During the afternoon we were briefed to attack Cairo International. I was already strapped into the cockpit, when a messenger came up and handed me a map with revised instructions. The new target was 'H4', one of the most distant air bases in Syria. We took off as a four-ship formation, following our leader, Eitan. The flight was a long one for the Mirage—about 30 minutes in each direction.

When we reached the target area, we saw two MiGs patrolling over their base. Sitting ducks. But our orders were strictly to attack the airfield, and there could be no deviation from plan.

As we circled the base, Asher was engaged by one of the MiGs, and he managed to shoot it down while the rest of us went in for our straffing runs. As I came out after my first run, I saw another MiG about 1000 metres away. Warning the others, I dropped my external tanks and turned into him. He began to take evasive action, and as we tangled with each other, several other Mirages arrived over the field. One of them pulled up to fire on 'my' MiG, and promptly stalled. The Syrian pilot stopped worrying about me and turned his attention towards the helpless Mirage. I saw what was happening and set off after him, with calls from the stricken Mirage pilot filling my headset. The MiG launched two missiles, but missed with both of them, presumably because the Mirage's engine had flamed out in the stall. I then took my chance, aimed and fired, and watched as the MiG caught fire over the desert airfield and crashed in flames. Suddenly I was alone. Climbing rapidly up to 35,000 feet, I crossed the Syrian border very short of fuel, and only began to relax a little when I saw Lake Galilee below me. At least then I new I could make it back to base.

Next day I flew with a formation attacking the Golan Heights. We were tasked to strafe a Syrian tank position overlooking the River Jordan bridge, and when we arrived the entire Hula Valley below seemed to be on fire or covered with thick smoke. We went in low to strafe the tanks, and encountered heavy flak. During my third pass I felt a tremendous crash below my seat, and remember thinking: 'That's it!' Checking the instrument panel I noticed that none of the lamps were lit. All systems were dead. I knew that I would have to eject, and turned sharply to cross over to the western side of the Jordan.

One of the gauges showed the engine at 10,000 rpm, and up until then I had always understood that 8700 rpm was the maximum before total siezure! In theory, my engine had gone, but I was still flying. There was no electrical power to the controls, so the stick became rigid and stone heavy. I grabbed it with both hands, but its tendency to push forward all on its own was very difficult to stop. I tried frantically to climb, but the systems failed to respond. I was on course for Ramat Davis AB throughout this struggle, and suddenly found myself directly above it. Making my approach with a virtually dead aircraft, I hopefully lowered the undercarriage, but as the indicators were not working, I had no way of knowing whether it was down or locked. Guiding the aircraft away from the sun, I looked at its shadow to confirm that the wheels were at least deployed, but I could not line up on the runway because the aircraft was hardly functioning. Flying off to the west, I got into a very wide turn until I was roughly aligned, and then just let the aircraft sink as slowly as possible, hanging on to the shaking stick with both hands and praying. I just made it on to the runway, and luckily managed to stop without any further problems—but then I found I could hardly move. Afterwards a check revealed that a 37 mm round had hit the aircraft immediately under my seat, damaging the left-hand side of the cockpit and destroying the control wires. There was even some shrapnel in my leg, which I'd not noticed during the flight! I spent that night in hospital, but could not rest properly. I kept on thinking that here I was, laying on my back, while the war was getting away from me, so I talked my way out of there and back into action.

I was back on the flying roster of my squadron the following day, assigned to attack an Egyptian armoured column near Sharm El-Sheikh. While we were in transit, the controller ordered ut to jettison our bombs and change to a new heading at 20,000 feet. I caught a glimpse of a MiG flying close to the ground, and the lost it again almost immediately. I dropped my fuel tanks and dived, calling on the others to follow me down. As we closed, I saw two MiG-17s dogfighting with a pair of Super Mystères. I joined the battle, flipping upside down momentarily to mark where one of our aircraft was going down. The two MiGs were virtually on the deck by now, racing for home. I closed in fast, leaving my two wingmen behind—those two MiGs were going to be mine alone! I reduced range on the first and let fly with my guns, and watched part of his aircraft fly off as he steered away and climbed for his life. The other aircraft broke contact and disappeared. I stayed on the first MiG, and was so close at times that I could easily make out the pilot and his instrument panel. Suddenly he ejected, and the aircraft smashed into the ground below me. I rolled out and started to chase his wingman. Flying very low to silhouette him against the horizon, I was blinded by the setting sun. I finally caught up with him over the swamps north of Ismailia, and we started an incredible dogfight over the Canal. The man was stubborn, and he tried every trick in the book. I was hard at it, trying to hold on to him, when I received an urgent call from the formation leader asking me to break contact and return east. Disappointed, I turned for home.

Yom Kippur War

Col Marom, a retired IDFAF fighter pilot, recalls a determined chase over the Golan Heights:

During a combat air patrol over the Golan Heights, my wingman spotted two Syrian AF Su-7B strike fighters coming in at 12 o'clock high. A quick warning shout alerted me to the danger, and we prepared to engage them. They barrelled on downwards towards our troop positions, sweeping low over the area, followed closely by a trail of smoke puffs as their rockets exploded on the ground below them. At the end of their run, the two intruders pulled up sharply to gain the altitude for another attack. We hit the afterburners and rolled into position behind the Syrian leader, just as he started a straffing run. As soon as he saw us he pulled up and broke hard to starboard, and then turned to meet us head on with his 30 mm cannon. Realizing the danger, I tried to get inside his turn.

We were now down to hilltop level, and the Su-7 vanished momentarily as we rounded some high ground. He was turning incredibly tightly, and the brown earth and blue skies seemed to mingle together as we followed the low-level chase. My Mirage closed in on the Sukhoi's tail, but the

G forces were too high for a clear shot. The enemy pilot was either an ace or a madman. By now the fight was down to virtually zero altitude, twisting and turning among the wadis around Mount Hermon. The Syrian pulled some crazy tricks, throwing his aircraft into even sharper angles. He was certainly a good pilot, and I was sweating hard trying to keep up with him.

Suddenly I got my chance. Only for a moment, but I managed to fire a quick burst. The Syrian broke hard, with a small fire blossoming bright red below his wing root. Still he flew on. By now the fight was on again, over the ceasefire line as the Sukhoi frantically tried to shake me off and make a dash for home. I noticed the fire had begun to spread, and drew closer, watching the pilot struggling in his cockpit. Suddenly his aircraft blew up, engulfing my Mirage in a cloud of fire and smoke. I was temporarily blinded by the force of the explosion, and felt the stick jerk in my hands as the blast hit my elevons. It was like hitting a brick wall in a racing car. The aircraft kicked back like a mule as I tried to roll and turn at low speed. Struggling to keep my fighter on an even keel, I managed to get clear of the fireball and flying debris. The fight was over . . .

Lt Col 'G' was a top-scoring IDFAF ace during the Yom Kippur War. He describes some of his 17 confirmed kills:

We flew a CAP sortie towards the northern Bitter Lake, because the Egyptians were attacking in masses. They would arrive in large waves of aircraft, and climb while turning to attack our positions parallel to the Canal strip, then head for home as quickly as possible. We had little time to catch them. As we reached the Israeli bridgehead near Deversoir, we watched a flight of five Su-7s pulling hard left in order to pounce on our forces below. We came in from behind them, and I launched a missile against the last man, and saw his aircraft explode almost immediately. The leading pair of Sukhois both managed to drop their bombs, but the leader of the second section failed to do so, and turned for home with me in hot pursuit. I chased him for some way at low level, with my Mirage shaking from the speed. This buffeting made it difficult to keep him in the gunsight, but just before entering the Egyptian SAM zone I managed to hit him.

Back at Refidim we were soon scrambled again, and I shot down two Su-20s [sic] over the Canal. During this engagement some of our F-4E Phantoms arrived on the scene, and a four-ship formation got in behind the first wave of Sukhois—without realizing that a second Egyptian section was diving down behind them. Sandwiched between two enemy formations, one of the F-4Es was in immediate danger of being shot down. My wingman jockeyed into position, but we were afraid that the Egyptian pilot would hit the Phantom before we could do anything about it. It tried to warn the driver, but not knowing his callsign I simply yelled: 'Phantom—break!' He did so . . . instantly, and my wingman equally quickly shot down the pursuing Sukhoi. Returning to Refidim that day, morale was high. We had downed 11 enemy aircraft during the morning.

Next day we were directed to Jebel Oubeid, near Suez. At 10,000 feet we detected a pair of MiG-21s heading north in a wide turn. We dropped our external tanks and immediately gave chase. I manoeuvred into position on one of the MiGs, and at 1000 metres range I launched one of my Shafrirs. The missile ran true, and the enemy aircraft exploded instantly—then I realized we had fallen into a trap. Slightly pre-occupied by the exploding MiG, I only just saw out of the corner of my eye, scores of MiGs as they climbed to challenge us. They looked like mushrooms in the sky. We split into two pairs and dived to engage, and the mêlée started almost immediately. My wingman closed in on one of the MiGs and launched a missile towards him, but then had to break off the engagement after reporting mechanical problems. The two other Mirages were forced to disengage due to low fuel, but another MiG was downed before they left the area.

I was chasing one MiG all this time, and its pilot was good. He did all sorts of crazy things at incredibly low level, including a series of split S manoeuvres that were so low that he was throwing sand every time he pulled out of his dive. I was right behind him, virtually glued to his tail. Some of the other MiGs tried to get in behind me to shoot me off, but I

figured that if I couldn't get him in my sights, what chance would they have against me? At last, when the MiG in front pulled up, I got my break and managed to put some rounds into him. He dived into the ground and exploded. As I pulled round I saw—only just in time—that two of my pursuers had launched missiles at me, but they both missed as I continued to turn. I broke sharply in the opposite direction, and watched as two more MiGs launched their missiles straight ahead of me! This time I had no chance to react, and instinctively ducked in my seat as both weapons passed directly over the top of me. My luck continued to hold. Instantly I turned, only to find yet another pair closing in behind. By this time everything was getting far too hectic, so I broke away sharply and made for home ...

Appendix 6

A3 GAF (Dassault) Mirage IIIo(A)/(F)/IIID

1	IIIO(F)	c/n 100 (?); F/F 13/2/61 (14/3/63 France?); H/O 9/4/63 (*City of Hobart*); Del to Australia abroad RAAF C-130E; GAF Avalon received 27/11/63; F/F in Australia 11/1/64; Despatched 17/1/64; H/O Avalon 29/1/64; ARDU. W/O Avalon 7/12/64
2	IIIO(F)	Retained in France initially, for trials (Including IIIO(A) conversion?); ARDU (1971, 1972, 3/84, 10/84, 3/1/85, 18/6/85, 2/86, 8/10/86, 16/11/86, 20/8/87, 15/11/87, 21/2/88). C/S VM-HJA
3	IIIO(F) IIIO(A)	GAF Avalon Received 28/5/63, F/F 16/11/63, Despatched 20/12/63 RAAF T.O.C. 29/1/64; 2 OCU (20/9/64) (Tropical Trials Darwin); 77 Sqn (2/71); 76 Sqn; Stored Avalon 1973-77; 77 Sqn Del (after storage) 1/77; 2 OCU (Damaged Townsville 1/11/82, R/H MLG collapsed. Repaired); 2 OCU (16/11/84, 10/84); 77 Sqn (6/85, 22/8/85, 10/85); ARDU (7/4/86); Display Centre Williamtown; (TT. Approx. 3200 hours, 4300 landings), restored in 76 Sqn c/s. C/S VM-HJB
4	IIIO(F) IIIO(A)	GAF Avalon Received 2/7/63, F/F 2/1/64, Despatched 13/3/64 (H/O 29/1/64?); 2 OCU (Cr Williamtown, F/F after repair 6/10/66); 77 Sqn (+ 18/4/71); ARDU. W/O 3/8.72 Avalon
5	IIIO(F) IIIO(A)	GAF Avalon Received 26/4/64, Flight Shed Received 2/6/64, F/F 27/7/64, Despatched 31/8/64; 77 Sqn (12/80); 3 Sqn (1985, 29/1/85); 77 Sqn (8/10/86), 'B' Flt (8/11/87); 75 Sqn (?)
6	IIIO(F) IIIO(A)	GAF Avalon Received 20/4/64, Flight Shed Received 27/6/64, F/F 20/8/64, Despatched 16/9/64; Stored Avalon 1972-78; 2 OCU (1979, 1/1980); 3 Sqn (29/1/85, 2/85, 4/85); 75 Sqn (6/87, 6/10/87)
7	IIIO(F) IIIO(A)	GAF Avalon Received 19/12/63, Flight Shed Received 10/3/64, Despatched 24/6/64; 77 Sqn; 2 OCU (4/74, 4/2/80, 9/82); 3 Sqn (1985, 29/1/85); 75 Sqn. WFS 1986, Reduced to Spares Darwin (Fuselage only noted 19/6/87)
8	IIIO(F)	GAF Avalon Received 26/2/64, Flight Shed

	IIIO(A)	Received 11/5/64, F/F 17/7/64, Despatched 10/8/64; 2 OCU (+ 20/9/64, 2/65); 76 Sqn (18/4/71), WFU 22/8/73 (76 Sqn Disbanded); Stored Avalon 1973-78; 77 Sqn. W/O 17/2/78 (17/1/78) East Sale; salvaged and used for Ground Test Instrument Fits (R/H wing to Wagga Wagga for fitment to A3-41). Destroyed by fire during road transportation 2/2/81 (12/2/81?)
9	IIIO(F) IIIO(A)	GAF Avalon Received 19/6/64, Flight Shed Received 17/7/64, F/F 15.10.64, Despatched 10/10/64; 75 Sqn 'Heckle' (2/65); 76 Sqn; (+ 7/72), WFU 22/8/73 (76 Sqn Disbanded); 77 Sqn; Despatched to Avalon for Storage 2/74; 75 Sqn (3.9.86, 9/87, 12/9/87, 6/10/87)
10	IIIO(F) IIIO(A)	GAF Avalon Received 24/7/64, Flight Shed Received 8/64; F/F 13/10/64, Despatched 26/11/64; 2 OCU (+ 1980); 3 Sqn (1981, 1985, 29/1/85, 7/4/86) 77 Sqn (10/12/86, 11/3/87); 75 Sqn (17/10/87)
11	IIIO(F) IIIO(A)	GAF Avalon Received 12/9/64, Flight Shed Received 10/10/64, F/F 24/11/64, Despatched 11/1/65; 2 OCU (12/4/75, 1977, 4/2/80, 4/9/80, 9/82); ARDU (Loan, 2 OCU C/S) (10/84); 77 Sqn (25/8/85, 28/8/86, 8/10/86, 11/3/87, 11/4/87), 'B' Flt (20/8/87, 8/11/87)
12	IIIO(F) IIIO(A)	GAF Avalon Received 16/10/64, Flight Shed Received 10/11/64, F/F 7/1/65, Despatched 8/2/65; 75 Sqn (2/65); 76 Sqn (1967, 18/4/71); 77 Sqn (+ 1980, 25/8/85, 8/10/86, 11/3/87, 4/87), 'B' Flt (20/8/87, 8/11/87)
13	IIIO(F) IIIO(A)	GAF Avalon Received 14/11/64, Flight Shed Received 4/2/65, F/F 8/2/65, Despatched 23/2/65; 75 Sqn (3/65); 2 OCU; 76 Sqn (+ 18/4/71, 4/72), WFU 22/8/73 (76 Sqn Disbanded); 2 OCU (1979-80, 9/82); 3 Sqn; 77 Sqn (8/85, 28/8/86, 8/10/86, 11/3/87); To RAAF Museum Pt Cook, Del by CH-47C 7/8/77, Held for National Aviation Museum
14	IIIO(F) IIIO(A)?	GAF Avalon Received 17/12/64, Flight Shed Received 4/2/65, F/F 16/3/65, Despatched 12/4/65; 76 Sqn; 77 Sqn 'Deltas' (18/4/71, 21/5/75). W/O 16/3/76 3 km west of Williamtown

15	IIIO(F) IIIO(A)	GAF Avalon Received 4/2/65, Flight Shed Received 2/3/65, F/F 26/4/65, Despatched 4/5/76; 75 Sqn (1965); 76 Sqn; 77 Sqn 'Deltas' (4/71, 18/4/71) (1981—Diamond Jubilee of RAAF C/S) (3/4/81, 10/8/81, 9/82); 75 Sqn (8/84, 23/1/85, 1986, 9/6/87, 7/10/87)
16	IIIO(F) IIIO(A)?	GAF Avalon Received 9/3/65, Flight Shed Received 2/4/65, F/F 27/5/65, Despatched 18/6/65; 76 Sqn (4/73); ARDU. W/O 27/10/74 (24/10/74?) Tullamarine. Fuselage only tendered for disposal by GAF Avalon (Lot No 279.6), purchased by N Mason and noted in outdoor storage Braybrook Vic. 8/5/86/. Sold to J McDonald
17	IIIO(F) IIIO(A)	GAF Avalon Received 29/3/65, Flight Shed Received 26/4/65, F/F 27/5/65, Despatched 14/7/65; 76 Sqn (4/73); 77 Sqn (+ Mid 1971, 5/72); 75 Sqn (1980, 10/83). No longer with 75 Sqn 1/85; 77 Sqn (25/8/85, 10/85); Noted Butterworth 7/86 (?); 77 Sqn (28/8/86, 8/10/86). 'B' Flt (20/8/87, 8/11/87)
18	IIIO(F) IIIO(A)?	GAF Avalon Received 14/4/65, Flight Shed Received 19/5/65, F/F 9/7/65, Despatched 5/8/65; 77 Sqn (4/73); 75 Sqn. W/O 1/4/74 Butterworth
19	IIIO(F) IIIO(A)	GAF Avalon Received 29/4/65, Flight Shed Received 10/6/65, F/F 26/7/65, Despatched 10/8/65; 77 Sqn 'Deltas' (4/71, 18/4/71, + 1974), Despatched to Avalon for Storage 2/74; 77 Sqn (17/11/80, 12/80, 31/10/81, 18/1/83, 1983, 10/83); ARDU (Loan) (3/1/85); 77 Sqn (25/8/85, 10/85)
20	IIIO(F) IIIO(A)	GAF Avalon Received 13/5/65, Flight Shed Received 10/7/65, F/F 13/8/65, Despatched 2/9/65; 75 Sqn (1968); 76 Sqn (18/4/71), WFU 22/8/73 (76 Sqn Disbanded); 2 OCU (+ 12/4/75, 10/76, 1979, 1980, 3/80); 75 Sqn (8/82); 77 Sqn (17/5/85, 25/8/85, 10/85, 24/1/86, 28/8/86, 8/10/86), WFU To No. 1 Central Ammunition Depot (CAMD), Orchard Hills (Villawood) NSW 11/86 as INST A/F. (Del by RAAF CH-47C)
21	IIIO(F) IIIO(A)	GAF Avalon Received 28/5/65, Flight Shed Received 7/65, F/F 26/8/65, Despatched 20/9/65; 2 OCU (3/79, 1980, 1981); 3 Sqn (8/82, 1985, 29/1/1985); 79 Sqn (31/3/86); 77 Sqn (28/8/86, 8/10/86); Wings noted at RSTT Wagga Wagga 21/9/87?); 75 Sqn (6/10/87)
22	IIIO(F) IIIO(A)	GAF Avalon Received 19/6/65, Flight Shed Received 9/8/65, F/F 8/10/65; 77 Sqn (1975, 10/79, 1/80, 12/80, 3/81, 3/4/81, 4/84, 10/84, 10/85, 28/8/86, 1987, 11/3/87, 11/4/87), 'B' Flt (20/8/87, 8/11/87)
23	IIIO(F) IIIO(A)	GAF Avalon Received 26/6/65, Flight Shed Received 20/8/65, F/F 23/9/65, Despatched 8/10/65; 75 Sqn; 76 Sqn (+ 18/4/71), WFU 22/8/73 (76 Sqn Disbanded); 2 OCU; 75 Sqn (10/79, 1981, 10/83); 77 Sqn (10/81?); 75 Sqn (5/84, 23/1/85, 6/10/87)
24	IIIO(F) IIIO(A)	GAF Avalon Received 15/7/65, Flight Shed Received 31/8/65, F/F 6/10/65, Despatched 14/10/65; 75 Sqn; 76 Sqn, WFU 22/8/73 (76 Sqn Disbanded); 2 OCU (+ 12/4/75, 12/80); 3 Sqn, (8/82); 75 Sqn (11/83, 11/84, 23/1/85, 3/9/86); 77 Sqn (4/87); 75 Sqn (19/6/87, 7/10/87)
25	IIIO(F) IIIO(A)	GAF Avalon Received 30/7/65, Flight Shed Received 9/9/65, F/F 19/10/65, Despatched 29/10/65; 75 Sqn (+ 1970); 76 Sqn (+ 18/4/71), WFU 22/8/73 (76 Sqn Disbanded); 75 Sqn (8/82); 3 Sqn (+ 1983); 79 Sqn 22/1/88
26	IIIO(A)	Retained in France until near completion of trials; GAF Avalon Received 18/4/68, Flight Shed Received 5/8/68, F/F 15/10/68, Despatched 4/11/68; 75 Sqn (1970); 3 Sqn (1/11/71). W/O 6/7/76 Butterworth, collided with A3-64 on runway
27	IIIO(F) IIIO(A)	GAF Avalon Received 9/8/65, Flight Shed Received 23/9/65, F/F 1/11/65, Despatched 29/11/65; 77 Sqn (18/4/71, 8/71, 1972); 75 Sqn; 3 Sqn (1983); 75 Sqn (11/84, 23/1/85, 3/9/86, 1987, 19/6/87, 6/10/87)
28	IIIO(F)	GAF Avalon Received 20/8/65, Flight Shed Received 10/10/65, F/F 18/11/65, Despatched 7/12/65; 75 Sqn; 76 Sqn; 75 Sqn. W/O 29/7/66 Queenstown (Queanbeyan?)
29	IIIO(F) IIIO(A)	GAF Avalon Received 2/9/65, Flight Shed Received 19/10/65, F/F 18/11/65, Despatched 8/12/65; 75 Sqn; 3 Sqn (1/11/71); 76 Sqn; 77 Sqn (18/4/71, 1971, 4/73, 8/4/79, 16/11/82). W/O 9/4/84 (8/4/84?) Bluff Downs Homestead (150 km south-west Townsville), Collided with A3-30
30	IIIO(F) IIIO(A)	GAF Avalon Received 17/9/65, Flight Shed Received 27/10/65, F/F 9/12/65, Despatched 18/1/66; 76 Sqn (+ 1971), WFU 22/8/73 (76 Sqn Disbanded); 77 Sqn (8/74, 12/80, 1981, 9/82, 1983, 10/83). W/O 9/4/84 (8/4/84?) Bluff Downs Homestead (150 km south-west Townsville), collided with A3-29
31	IIIO(F) IIIO(A)	GAF Avalon Received 28/9/65, Flight Shed Received 9/11/65, F/F 9/12/65, Despatched 2/2/66; 76 Sqn, WFU 22/8/73 (76 Sqn Disbanded); 77 Sqn (8/4/79, 3/81); 3 Sqn (8/82); 77 Sqn (1985, 25/8/85, 10/85, 1986, 11/3/87), 'B' Flt (20/8/87)
32	IIIO(F) IIIO(A)	GAF Avalon Received 11/10/65, Flight Shed Received 18/11/65, F/F 21/12/65, Despatched 23/2/66; 75 Sqn; 2 OCU (+ 12/4/75, 27/3/77, 1981); 75 Sqn (1981). W/O 29/10/81 into sea off Butterworth. (27/5/85 Muka Head Penang?)
33	IIIO(F) IIIO(A)	GAF Avalon Received 20/10/65, Flight Shed Received 2/12/65, F/F 3/2/66, Despatched 22/2/66; 75 Sqn; 76 Sqn; 77 Sqn. Despatched to Avalon for Storage 2/74; 2 OCU (12/80, 1981, 8/82); 77 Sqn (1986, 8/10/86, 11/3/87, 11/4/87); 75 Sqn (7/10/87)
34	IIIO(F) IIIO(A)	GAF Avalon Received 1/11/65, Flight Shed Received 15/12/65, F/F 22/2/66, Despatched 18/3/66; 75 Sqn (1967-68); 2 OCU (+ 12/73, 4/75, 3/80, 12/80); 77 Sqn (25/8/85, 10/11/85, 1986); 79 Sqn (31/3/86, 22/1/88, 16/4/88)
35	IIIO(F) IIIO(A)	GAF Avalon Received 12/11/65, Flight Shed Received 23/12/65, F/F 3/3/66, Despatched 6/4/66; 2 OCU (4/74); 75 Sqn (+ 1981)—no longer with 75 Sqn 1/85; 77 Sqn (17/5/85, 16/6/85); ARDU (21/8/85); 77 Sqn (10/85, 1986); 75 Sqn (19/6/87, 6/10/87)
36	IIIO(F) IIIO(A)	GAF Avalon Received 24/11/65, Flight Shed Received 2/2/66, F/F 25/3/66, Despatched

3/5/66; 76 Sqn (11/70, 18/4/71), WFU 22/8/73 (76 Sqn Disbanded); 77 Sqn, Despatched on Delivery to 75 Sqn 24/11/76; 75 Sqn (11/76); 77 Sqn (9/82); 75 Sqn (23/1/85). W/O 27/5/85 Coconut Grove Darwin; to NT Aviation Society Museum, Stuart Park Darwin (4/9/86)

| 37 | IIIO(F) | GAF Avalon Received 6/12/65, Flight Shed |
| | IIIO(A) | Received 13/2/66, F/F 1/4/66, Despatched 15/6/66; 75 Sqn; 3 Sqn. W/O 18/3/69 Butterworth (Ditched off Tengah) |

| 38 | IIIO(F) | GAF Avalon Received 15/12/65, Flight Shed |
| | IIIO(A) | Received 24/2/66, F/F 19/4/66, Despatched 27/5/66; 75 Sqn; 76 Sqn (+18/4/71); 75 Sqn (10/79); 3 Sqn (1985, 29/1/85, 4/85); 75 Sqn (3/9/86, 6/87, 7/10/87) |

| 39 | IIIO(F) | GAF Avalon Received 26/1/66, Flight Shed |
| | IIIO(A) | Received 21/3/66, F/F 13/5/66, Despatched 16/6/66; 75 Sqn; 77 Sqn 'Deltas' (4/71, 18/4/71, 4/73, 3/74, 8/8/74—NLG collapse, repaired, 27/10/77, 3/4/81); 75 Sqn (8/83, 5/84, 23/1/85, 3/9/86); 77 Sqn (75 Sqn C/S) (1986, 11/3/87). WFU Williamtown (8/11/87, 75 Sqn C/S) |

| 40 | IIIO(F) | GAF Avalon Received 9/2/66, Flight Shed |
| | IIIO(A) | Received 13/4/66; F/F 13/5/66, Despatched 15/6/66; 2 OCU (+1971); 3 Sqn (Base CO's A/C); 76 Sqn; 75 Sqn; 2 OCU (1/80, 4/2/80); ARDU (loan) (1985); 77 Sqn (25/8/85, 10/85, 10/11/85). W/O 100 km east of Williamtown 2/5/86) |

| 41 | IIIO(F) | GAF Avalon Received 23/2/66, Flight Shed |
| | IIIO(A)? | Received 13/4/66; F/F 7/6/66, Despatched 4/8/66; 77 Sqn (+4/73, 30/5/73). W/O 6/4/76 (9/75?) Nowra after emergency landing and fire; declared CAT 4, dismantled and transported to Wagga Wagga by road; INST A/F Wagga Wagga (7/85, 6/4/86, 21/9/87) |

| 42 | IIIO(F) | GAF Avalon Received 5/3/66, Flight Shed |
| | IIIO(A) | Received 2/5/66, F/F 16/6/66, Despatched 1/8/66; 2 OCU; 76 Sqn (+Mid 1971), WFU 22/8/73 (76 Sqn Disbanded); 2 OCU (1979, 9/82); 75 Sqn (8/84); 77 Sqn (25/8/85, 10/85, 28/8/86, 11/3/87), 'B' Flt (20/8/87) |

| 43 | IIIO(F) | GAF Avalon Received 18/3/66, Flight Shed |
| | IIIO(A) | Received 19/5/66; F/F 31/7/66, Despatched 23/8/66; 76 Sqn (1966); 77 Sqn. W/O 1/9/67 Williamtown (76 Sqn?) |

| 44 | IIIO(F) | GAF Avalon Received 1/4/66, Flight Shed |
| | IIIO(A) | Received 19/5/66, F/F 26/8/66, Despatched 22/9/66; 76 Sqn (+18/4/71); 77 Sqn (+1979, 1980, 8/9/81, 10/81, 4/84, 8/10/84, 8/85, 25/8/85, 10/85, 28/8/86, 8/10/86, 11/3/87, 4/87, 13/4/87) |

| 45 | IIIO(F) | GAF Avalon Received 15/4/66, Flight Shed |
| | IIIO(A) | Received 15/6/66; F/F 16/8/66, Despatched 6/9/66; 2 OCU (+12/4/75); 3 Sqn (1985, 29/1/85, 4/85); 79 Sqn C/S (28/8/86); 75 Sqn(?), ops by 77 Sqn(?); to ARL Port Melbourne 1987, 77 Sqn C/S, to be mounted on pole |

| 46 | IIIO(F) | GAF Avalon Received 2/5/66, Flight Shed |
| | | Received 28/6/66; F/F 29/8/66, Despatched 27/9/66; 76 Sqn. W/O 3/4/67, ditched near Darwin |

| 47 | IIIO(F) | GAF Avalon Received 13/5/66, Flight Shed |

| | IIIO(A) | Received 13/11/66, F/F 20/2/67, Despatched 23/3/67; 2 OCU (+12/4/75, 1977). W/O 7/8/79 Williamtown |

| 48 | IIIO(F) | GAF Avalon Received 26/5/66, Flight Shed |
| | IIIO(A) | Received 26/1/67, F/F 17/4/67, Despatched 5/5/67; 2 OCU (31/3/73); 77 Sqn (8/80, 12/80, 1981—Jubilee C/S, 3/4/81, 10/81, 9/82, 9/83); 3 Sqn (1985, 29/1/85); 79 Sqn (31/3/86); 75 Sqn (3/9/86, 19/6/87) |

| 49 | IIIO(F) | GAF Avalon Received 8/6/66, Flight Shed |
| | IIIO(A) | Received 8/2/67; F/F 2/5/67, Despatched 17/5/67; 2 OCU (+4/72, 12/4/75, 1979, 11/80, 1981, 21/8/83, 16/11/84); 77 Sqn (10/85, 10/11/85, 5/86, 28/8/86, 6/10/86, 8/10/86, 2/11/86), 'B' Flt (20/8/87, 8/11/87); 75 Sqn(?) |

| 50 | IIIO(F)? | GAF Avalon Received 22/6/66, Flight Shed |
| | IIIO(A)? | Received 2/3/67, F/F 12/5/67, Despatched 31/5/67; 2 OCU (26/3/72, 4/74). W/O 2/2/77 Tea Gardens near Williamtown NSW (Buladelah?) |

| 51 | IIIO(A) | GAF Avalon Received 8/7/66, Flight Shed Received 17/9/66; F/F 17/11/66, Despatched 25/1/67; 75 Sqn; 2 OCU (9/82); 75 Sqn (5/84, 23/1/85, 3/9/86, 19/6/87); INST A/F Wagga Wagga Del 23/7/87 (21/9/87) |

| 52 | IIIO(A) | GAF Avalon Received 19/7/66, Flight Shed Received 14/3/67; F/F 28/6/67, Despatched 27/7/67; 3 Sqn. W/O 25/9/67 (25/10/67?) Gloucester Tops NSW |

| 53 | IIIO(A) | GAF Avalon Received 3/8/66, Flight Shed Received 23/3/67, F/F 26/6/67, Despatched 14/8/67; 75 Sqn. No longer with 75 Sqn 1/85; 77 Sqn (8/85, 25/8/85, 10/85, 6/10/86); 75 Sqn (19/6/87, 6/10/87) |

| 54 | IIIO(A) | GAF Avalon Received 17/8/66, Flight Shed Received 5/4/67, F/F 26/6/67, Despatched 7/67; 75 Sqn (10/79); 77 Sqn (10/84, 25/8/85); 79 Sqn (31/3/86) |

| 55 | IIIO(A) | GAF Avalon Received 2/9/66, Flight Shed Received 21/4/67, F/F 5/7/67, Despatched 2/8/67; 75 Sqn (10/79); 77 Sqn (10/83, 10/84, 28/8/86, 8/10/86); Noted Amberley 15/8/87 (For Preservation?) |

| 56 | IIIO(A) | GAF Avalon Received 27/9/66, Flight Shed Received 26/4/67, F/F 20/7/67, Despatched 1/9/67; 77 Sqn; 75 Sqn; Stored Avalon 1972-78; 77 Sqn (1979, 1980, 17/4/80, 1983, 10/84, 2/11/84, 25/8/85, 10/85, 8/10/86); 79 Sqn (1987, 22/1/88); Ferried Butterworth-Darwin 4/5/88 en route to Woomera for storage |

| 57 | IIIO(A) | GAF Avalon Received 12/10/66, Flight Shed Received 3/5/67, F/F 3/8/67, Despatched 4/9/67; 75 Sqn. No longer with 75 Sqn 1/85; 77 Sqn (4/83, 24/5/83, 27/5/85) (2 OCU C/S?) (25/8/85, 1986, 28/8/86) |

| 58 | IIIO(A) | GAF Avalon Received 25/10/66, Flight Shed Received 12/5/67; F/F 17/8/67, Despatched 3/10/67; 75 Sqn; Stored Avalon 1972-78; 77 Sqn. W/O Tanilba Bay Near Williamtown 2/5/80 |

| 59 | IIIO(A) | GAF Avalon Received 9/11/66, Flight Shed Received 22/5/67; F/F 28/9/67, Despatched 9/11/67; 3 Sqn, Del Butterworth 27/9/67(?); 77 Sqn (30/5/73); 3 Sqn Del 7/82 (+8/82, 1985, 29/1/85), last flight 13/2/86 and WFU. |

Stored Butterworth (TT 3875 hours) (3878.2 hours?); to RMAF as Gate Guardian Butterworth, H/O 16/4/88

60   IIIO(A)   GAF Avalon Received 22/11/66, Flight Shed Received 1/6/67; F/F 28/9/67, Despatched 1/11/67; Stored Avalon 1972-78; 77 Sqn (3/4/81, 4/82); 3 Sqn (8/82, 8/83, 29/1/85, 2/85, 24/4/85); 79 Sqn (31/3/86); 77 Sqn (28/8/86); 75 Sqn Tfd 6/87 (19/6/87, 6/10/87)

61   IIIO(A)   GAF Avalon Received 17/1/66, Flight Shed Received 8/6/66, F/F 13/5/66, Despatched 8/6/66; 77 Sqn (1971, 4/73). W/O 24/6/76 into sea off Williamtown

62   IIIO(A)   GAF Avalon Received 30/11/66, Flight Shed Received 26/6/67, F/F 4/10/67, Despatched 18/11/67; 3 Sqn (5/68); 75 Sqn (10/79); 2 OCU; 75 Sqn (10/83, 5/84, 23/1/85); 79 Sqn (1987, 22/1/88)

63   IIIO(A)   GAF Avalon Received 18/2/66, Flight Shed Received 26/4/66, F/F 16/6/66, Despatched 3/8/66; 2 OCU; 75 Sqn. W/O 17/7/72 in ground fire at Butterworth. Fuselage noted at Avalon 25/10/75

64   IIIO(A)   GAF Avalon Received 20/12/66, Flight Shed Received 13/7/67, F/F 4/10/67, Despatched 3/11/67; 75 Sqn. W/O 6/7/76 Butterworth, collided on runway with A3-26

65   IIIO(A)   GAF Avalon Received 17/3/66, Flight Shed Received 8/5/66, F/F 21/7/66, Despatched 19/8/66; 2 OCU; 75 Sqn (+ 1979); 2 OCU (9/82, 16/11/84); 77 Sqn (17/5/85—2 OCU C/S?) (10/85, 1986); to Woomera for storage 3/2/87

66   IIIO(A)   GAF Avalon Received 27/1/67, Flight Shed Received 31/7/67, F/F 9/11/67, Despatched 28/11/67; 2 OCU; 77 Sqn (18/4/71 'Deltas', 18/8/74, 6/75, 5/12/75, 12/80, 3/4/81, 10/84, 8/85, 25/8/85, 10/85, 7/4/86, 28/8/86)

67   IIIO(A)   GAF Avalon Received 14/4/66, Flight Shed Received 30/5/66, F/F 31/7/66, Despatched 6/9/66; 2 OCU; 75 Sqn. W/O 8/6/76 Butterworth

68   IIIO(A)   GAF Avalon Received 16/2/67, Flight Shed Received 17/8/67, F/F 9/11/67, Despatched 24/11/67; 75 Sqn (1971); 2 OCU (9/82); 75 Sqn (5/84)—No longer with 75 Sqn 1/85; 77 Sqn (10/85, 1986); 79 Sqn (1987, 22/1/88)

69   IIIO(A)   GAF Avalon Received 23/5/66, Flight Shed Received 15/7/66, F/F 12/9/66, Despatched 12/10/66; 75 Sqn (+ 1978, 1980); 77 Sqn (8/82, 1983). W/O Tengah 30/3/83 (31/3/83?), collided with Singapore AF A-4, Fin on display outside 75 Sqn Operations Building Darwin (23/1/85). C/S VM-HJD

70   IIIO(A)   GAF Avalon Received 2/2/67, Flight Shed Received 6/9/67, F/F 27/11/67, Despatched 13/12/67; 3 Sqn. W/O 3/10/68 (30/10/68?) Limeburners Creek NSW (struck by own cannon fire)

71   IIIO(A)   GAF Avalon Received 5/7/66, Flight Shed Received 17/8/66, F/F 25/10/66, Despatched 10/11/66; 75 Sqn (10/80, 5/84, 23/1/85, 4/5/85); 77 Sqn (10/85); 75 Sqn (1987); 77 Sqn 'B' Flt (20/8/87, 8/11/87)

72   IIIO(A)   GAF Avalon Received 17/3/67, Flight Shed Received 12/8/67, F/F 27/11/67, Despatched

14/12/67; 77 Sqn (4/70, 4/73, 3/74, 1981—Diamond Jubilee C/S, 3/4/81, 10/8/81, 10/81, 17/3/85, 8/85, 25/8/85, 10/85, 1986, 8/10/86, 11/3/87); RSTT Wagga Wagga, delivered by air 23/5/87, INST A/F (21/9/87)

73   IIIO(A)   GAF Avalon Received 4/8/66, Flight Shed Received 3/10/66, F/F 22/12/66, Despatched 7/2/67; 77 Sqn (1969, 4/73); dep on del to 75 Sqn 24/11/76; 75 Sqn (11/76, 10/79, 11/84, 23/1/85, 19/6/87, 7/10/87)

74   IIIO(A)   GAF Avalon Received 13/4/67, Flight Shed Received 2/10/67, F/F 4/12/67, Despatched 13/12/67; 76 Sqn; 77 Sqn. W/O 27/4/72 Darwin

75   IIIO(A)   GAF Avalon Received 7/9/66, Flight Shed Received 25/10/66, F/F 20/2/67, Despatched 15/10/67; 77 Sqn (18/4/71, 4/73); 75 Sqn (10/79); 77 (+ 4/2/80). W/O 18/2/80 East Sale

76   IIIO(A)   GAF Avalon Received 21/4/67, Flight Shed Received 28/7/67, F/F 7/9/67, Despatched 28/9/67; ARDU (1975, 13/4/75, 1979, 1980, 3/84, 5/84). W/O St Vincent's Gulf SA 3/5/84

77   IIIO(A)   GAF Avalon Received 4/11/66, Flight Shed Received 22/12/66, F/F 20/3/67, Despatched 11/4/67; 3 Sqn (4/2/80, 1981, 3/10/81). W/O 17/5/67, ditched off Newcastle (11/5/67?)

78   IIIO(A)   GAF Avalon Received 12/5/67, Flight Shed Received 12/10/67, F/F 6/12/67, Despatched 5/2/68; 77 Sqn Deltas (4/71) (1975, 12/9/78, 4/2/80, 1981, 31/10/81, 9/82, 5/10/84, 20/11/84, CO's a/c 8/85, 10/85, 10/11/85. 28/8/86 CO's C/S 8/10/86, 11/3/87); Scrapped, fuselage noted in BER compound Williamtown 8/11/87

79   IIIO(A)   GAF Avalon Received 5/12/66, Flight Shed Received 20/2/67, F/F 3/5/67, Despatched 1/6/67; 77 Sqn (+ 28/11/69). W/O 3/4/73 Gloucester, NSW

80   IIIO(A)   GAF Avalon Received 26/5/67, Flight Shed Received 27/10/67, F/F 27/11/67, Despatched 5/2/68; 77 Sqn (4/73, 1975, 3/79, 4/2/80, CO's A/C 9/9/81)

81   IIIO(A)   GAF Avalon Received 30/6/67, Flight Shed Received 15/11/67, F/F 6/2/68, Despatched 22/2/68; 2 OCU; 75 Sqn (8/82); at Williamtown for maintenance 23/1/85

82   IIIO(A)   GAF Avalon Received 20/7/67, Flight Shed Received 20/11/67, F/F 9/2/68, W/O 8/3/68; 2 OCU; 75 Sqn (10/79)—No longer with 75 Sqn 1/85; 2 OCU; 77 Sqn (Loan). W/O 2/8/83 (3/8/83?) into sea off Bega, NSW

83   IIIO(A)   GAF Avalon Received 2/8/67, Flight Shed Received 1/12/67, F/F 23/2/68, Despatched 18/3/68; 3 Sqn (8/82, 29/1/85 CO's A/C); 79 Sqn (31/3/86, 9/86, 8/10/86; 77 Sqn Del 16/3/86 ex storage Woomera (?); to Woomera for storage 3/2/87

84   IIIO(A)   GAF Avalon Received 17/8/67, Flight Shed Received 11/12/67, F/F 7/3/68, Despatched 28/3/68; 3 Sqn (1980); 77 Sqn (21/11/84) ARDU (loan) (3/1/85); 77 Sqn (25/8/85, 10/85, 28/8/86, 8/10/86, 11/3/87); Arr Laverton 21/5/87 (?) for disassembly and road transport to RAAF Museum Pt Cook. Ferried Avalon–Pt Cook by CH-47C 7/8/87

85	IIIO(A)	GAF Avalon Received 5/9/67, Flight Shed Received 20/12/67, F/F 20/3/68, Despatched 23/4/68; 3 Sqn. W/O 4/5/72 Mt Gunong Malaysia
86	IIIO(A)	GAF Avalon Received 21/9/67, Flight Shed Received 25/1/68, F/F 3/4/68, Despatched 21/5/68; 3 Sqn (1982, 29/1/85, 23/4/85); 79 Sqn (31/3/86, 8/10/86); 77 Sqn Del 16/3/86 ex storage Woomera(?); to Woomera for storage 3/2/87(?); scrapped, fuselage noted in BER Compound Williamtown (8/11/87)
87	IIIO(A)	GAF Avalon Received 6/10/67, Flight Shed Received 7/2/68, F/F 16/4/68, Despatched 24/7/68; 3 Sqn (+ 1/73, 1981, 29/1/85, 23/4/85); 77 Sqn (2/11/86); 75 Sqn (6/10/87)
88	IIIO(A)	GAF Avalon Received 2/10/67, Flight Shed Received 19/2/68, F/F 3/6/68, Despatched 24/7/68; 75 Sqn (8/84); 77 Sqn (4/2/85, 25/8/85, 2/86, 8/10/86), 'B' flt (20/8/87, 8/11/87)
89	IIIO(A)	GAF Avalon Received 3/11/67, Flight Shed Received 3/6/68, Despatched 15/7/68; 3 Sqn (+ 1981, 8/82); 75 Sqn (10/83, 23/1/85). W/O into sea 100 km northwest of Darwin 20/6/85)
90	IIIO(A)	GAF Avalon Received 28/11/67, Flight Shed Received 13/3/68, F/F 12/6/68, Despatched 25/6/68; 3 Sqn (+ 1978, 1980); 2 OCU (9/82, 11/83, 16/11/84); 77 Sqn (25/8/85, 10/85); WFU (Last flt 31/7/86) 8/86, converted to spares by 481 Sqn. Fin to HQ 481 Sqn, remains in BER compound Williamtown (1986, 8/11/87)
91	IIIO(A)	GAF Avalon Received 14/12/67, Flight Shed Received 25/3/68, F/F 18/6/68, Despatched 11/7/68; 3 Sqn (10/79); 77 Sqn (16/11/84, 25/8/85, 10/85, 5/86, 6/86, 28/8/86, 8/10/86); scrapped, remains in BER compound Williamtown (1986, 11/3/87)
92	IIIO(A)	GAF Avalon Received 25/1/68, Flight Shed Received 4/4/68, F/F 8/7/68, Despatched 26/7/68; 3 Sqn (+ 1982, 1985, 29/1/85); 77 Sqn (8/85); 79 Sqn (31/3/86, 28/8/86, 9/86); 75 Sqn (?); 77 Sqn (11/3/87); to RSTT Wagga Wagga, del by air 23/5/87. INST A/F 21/9/87
93	IIIO(A)	GAF Avalon Received 16/2/68, Flight Shed Received 19/4/68, F/F 26/7/68, Despatched 16/8/68; 3 Sqn (+3/73); 77 Sqn (10/84, 20/11/84, 4/2/85, 22/2/85, 8/85, 28/8/85, 10/85, 28/8/86), 'B' Flt (20/8/87, 8/11/87)
94	IIIO(A)	GAF Avalon Received 8/3/68, Flight Shed Received 10/5/68, F/F 29/7/68, Despatched 3/9/68; 3 Sqn. W/O 5/12/77 into sea off Butterworth
95	IIIO(A)	GAF Avalon Received 27/3/68, Flight Shed Received 20/5/68, F/F 15/8/68, Despatched 10/9/68; 77 Sqn (10/84, 17/5/85, 8/85, 7/4/86, 5/86, 28/8/86, 26/10/86, 11/3/87). W/O 16/3/87 into sea 20 miles east of Williamtown
96	IIIO(A)	GAF Avalon Received 19/4/68, Flight Shed Received 24/6/68, F/F 4/9/68, Despatched 23/9/68; 3 Sqn (1981, 8/82); 77 Sqn (25/8/85, 10/85, 27/3/86); 75 Sqn (9/87, 7/10/87)
97	IIIO(A)	GAF Avalon Received 10/5/68, Flight Shed Received 15/7/68, F/F 27/9/68, Despatched 24/10/68; 3 Sqn (1/73, 8/82). WFU 5/84 for use as spares; BER compound Williamtown (1986); Nose section to RAAF Fighter Display Centre Williamtown (8/11/87)
98	IIIO(A)	GAF Avalon Received 31/5/68, Flight Shed Received 22/8/68, F/F 15/10/68. Despatched 12/11/68; 3 Sqn. W/O 6/7/72 Jahore
99	IIIO(A)	GAF Avalon Received 21/5/68, Flight Shed Received 24/8/68, F/F 30/10/68, Despatched 22/11/68; 3 Sqn (1981, 8/82); 77 Sqn (8/85, 25/8/85, 10/85, 1986); 79 Sqn (31/3/86, 22/1/88, 16/4/88)
100	IIIO(A)	GAF Avalon Received 10/7/68, Flight Shed Received 10/10/68, F/F 4/11/68, Despatched 3/12/68; 3 Sqn (1980, 8/83); 75 Sqn (10/83, 5/84, 23/1/85, 3/9/86); WFU Darwin and reduced to spares. Fuselage only noted (19/6/87, 7/10/87)
101	IIID	GAF Avalon Received 18/7/66, Flight Shed Received 12/8/66, F/F 6/10/66, Despatched 11/10/66; Del 10/11/66(?); 76 Sqn (4/73); 2 OCU (5/11/76, 9/82); 3 Sqn; 77 Sqn (17/5/85, 8/85, 1986); ARDU (1/7/87)
102	IIID	GAF Avalon Received 14/4/66, Flight Shed Received 16/7/66, F/F 25/10/66, Despatched 23/12/66; 2 OCU (9/5/67, 11/68, 26/3/72, 4/73); 76 Sqn, WFU 22/8/73 (76 Sqn disbanded); 2 OCU (8/78, 4/2/80); 77 Sqn 'Daphne' (31/10/81, 12/81), 'Daphne de Dual' (1984, 10/84, 12/84); 3 Sqn (1985?); 77 Sqn (25/8/85, 10/85, 28/8/86, 8/10/86, 2/11/86); RAAF Fighter Display Centre Williamtown (2 OCU C/S) (8/11/87)
103	IIID	GAF Avalon Received 27/4/66, Flight Shed Received 3/8/66, Despatched 25/1/67; 2 OCU (9/5/67, 4/73); 3 Sqn (10/79, 29/1/85, 28/8/86); 77 Sqn (8/10/86, 11/3/87), 'B' flt (20/8/87, 8/11/87)
104	IIID	GAF Avalon Received 23/5/66, Flight Shed Received 28/8/66, F/F 24/1/67, Despatched 28/4/67; 77 Sqn (+ 17/3/70); 2 OCU (+ 5/11/76, 1980, 11/84); to 77 Sqn 12/84 (+ 10/85, 1986, 8/10/86); 75 Sqn (2/87, 19/6/87, 7/10/87)
105	IIID	GAF Avalon Received 24/5/66, Flight Shed Received 12/9/66, F/F 17/2/67; 2 OCU (8/78, 4/2/80, 9/82). W/O 26/4/84 14 km east of Darwin, remains noted at RAAF Darwin 11/84
106	IIID	GAF Avalon Received 5/7/66, Flight Shed Received 25/9/66, F/F 21/3/67, Despatched 24/4/67; 2 OTU; 2 OCU (9/5/67, 4/73); fuselage noted in hangar, Laverton 16/3/85; School of Air Radio; BER compound Williamtown (9/3/86, 8/11/87)
107	IIID	GAF Avalon Received 5/7/66, Flight Shed Received 12/10/66, F/F 27/4/67, Despatched 22/5/67; 3 Sqn. WFU 10/5/81 and scrapped 6/81 (fuselage corrosion); fuselage noted with DRC Salisbury SA 1985, offered to Penfield ATC-NTU; ARDU (Equipment trials)
108	IIID	GAF Avalon Received 4/8/66, Flight Shed Received 7/11/66, F/F 28/4/67, Despatched 15/5/67; 75 Sqn (4/72); 3 Sqn (8/82); 75 Sqn (+ 23/1/85); 2 AD (9/85 overhaul?); 77 Sqn (10/85); 75 Sqn (3/9/86, 2/87, 7/10/87)
109	IIID	GAF Avalon Received 4/8/66, Flight Shed

		Received 22/11/66, F/F 29/5/67, Despatched 28/6/67; 2 OTU; 2 OCU, W/O 6/10/71 Williamtown
110	IIID	GAF Avalon Received 7/9/66, Flight Shed Received 12/12/66, F/F 22/8/67, Despatched 11/10/67; 2 OCU (4/73, 1/80, 4/2/80, 9/82); 77 Sqn (8/85, 10/85); 79 Sqn (late 1986, 12/87—TT 2675 hrs)
111	IIID	ARDU (13/4/75); 2 OCU (1980, 12/80, 16/11/84); 2 AD (overhaul) (9/85); 77 Sqn (28/8/86, 8/10/86, 11/3/87); 75 Sqn (6/10/87)
112	IIID	2 OCU (+5/11/76, 1979, 11/80); ARDU (8/82, 3/84, 3/1/85, 16/2/85, 18/6/85, 18/2/86, 8/10/86, 21/2/87, 15/11/87, 30/4/88)
113	IIID	2 OCU (+12/4/75, 1980, 4/2/80, 8/9/80, 9/82); 77 Sqn (17/5/85) (2 OCU C/S) (?); 77 Sqn (10/85, 5/86, 28/8/86, 8/10/86, 11/3/87); 75 Sqn (7/10/87)
114	IIID	2 OCU. W/O 10/8/76 into sea 22 km off Williamtown
115	IIID	2 OCU (4/75, 4/2/80, 1982, 11/84); to 77 Sqn 12/84 (+25/8/85, 10/85, 28/8/86, 8/10/86)
116	IIID	F/F 1/12/73; 77 Sqn (4/2/80); 2 OCU (1982, 1984, 11/84); to 77 Sqn 12/84 (+10/85, 28/8/86, 8/10/86, 1/87); scrapped, fuselage noted in BER compound Williamstown (8/11/87)

Notes

1. Serials A3-1 to A3-48 (inclusive) Mirage IIIO(F), A3-49 to A3-100 (inclusive) Mirage IIIO(A). A3-101 to A3-116 (inclusive) Mirage IIID. By 1978 all remaining IIIO(F) aircraft with the exception of A3-2 had been modified to IIIO(A) standard

2. Further to the above; A3-1 to A-35 0 (excluding A3-26)— IIIO(F)

A3-26, 51 to A3-100 IIIO(A)
A3-2 only surviving IIIO(F) (?)

3. Of the total 116 aircraft, A3-1, 2 and 101 were built in France, and 22 more were built in Australia using French components; A3-3, 4, 26, 61, 63, 65, 67, 69, 71, 73, 75, 77, 102, 103, 104, 105, 106, 107, 108, 109, 110

4. Were A3-1 and *City of Hobart* the same aircraft?

5. 79 aircraft remaining on strength in 1982, 77 aircraft on 4/5/84

6. 75 Sqn strength 18 aircraft in 1983, 14 aircraft in 1985 (23/1/85—A3-15, 23, 24*, 27*, 36, 39, 51, 71, 73, 81, 89, 100*, 108*
(*also 3.9.86). 11 aircraft 3/9/86

7. One single-seat aircraft named *Charlotte* 1984

8. 1st aircraft delivered to 2 OCU then 75, 76, 3, 77 Sqns respectively

9. 2 OCU disbanded 1984, reformed 5/85 with F/A-18A, all aircraft to 77 Sqn

10. 1 grey aircraft noted less engine, radome, etc in outdoor storage Avalon 5/1/87

11. 1 aircraft W/O 9/81

12. 1 aircraft W/O 31/10/81

13. 47 IIIO(A), 8 IIID aircraft in service 5/87

14. Last 77 Sqn Mirage Dep Williamtown 22/11/87 for storage Woomera

15. Final four 79 Sqn aircraft (A3-56 plus 3) ferried Butterworth-Darwin 4/5/88 en route to Woomera for storage

16. One ex-79 Sqn aircraft (grey) noted at DoD establishment Orchard hills NSW (A3-20 1 CAMD ?)

List compiled by Nigel Pittaway of Australia

Appendix 7

Indian AF aircraft claimed destroyed by the Mirage IIIEPs of No 5 Sqn, Pakistan AF, during the December 1971 war between the two countries

Date	IAF type	Weapon	Remarks
4 Dec	Canberra	AIM-9B	Night interception over Sakesar, Pakistani pilot was Flt Lt Naem Ata
5 Dec	Hunters (2)	AIM-9Bs	Near Lahore. Pilot Sqn Ldr Farooq Umar
5 Dec	Hunter	AIM-9B	Near Lahore. Pilot Flt Lt Shah
5 Dec	Hunter	AIM-9B	Over Sakesar. Pilot Flt Lt Safdar
6 Dec	Su-7	AIM-9B	Jammu area, over Indian Territory. Pilot Flt Lt Salimuddin
10 Dec	Hunters (2)	30 mm	Destroyed during take-off. Straffing run over the runway at Pathankot airfield
13 Dec	Su-7	AIM-9B	Narowal area, over Indian territory. Pilot Gp Capt Haider
13 Dec	Su-7	30 mm	Narowal area, over Indian territory. Pilot Flt Lt Shah

A Matra R530 missile was launched against an IAF Su-7, but the results were not observed because the Mirage had to break contact. The IAF claimed that six Mirage IIIEPs had also been shot down, although the PAF did not admit to any losses.

Glossary

AAR	Air-to-air refuelling
AoA	Angle of Attack
BAM	*Base Aérea Militar* (Military Air Base)
CAP	Combat Air Patrol
CEV	*Centre d'Expérimentations en Vol*
CEAM	*Centre d'Expérimentations Aériennes Militaires*
CKD	Component Knocked Down
DACT	Dissimilar Air Combat Training
ESM	Electronic Support Measures
FAA	*Fuerza Aérea Argentina* (Argentine Air Force)
FAS	*Forces Aériennes Stratégiques*
FFAR	Folding Fin Aerial Rocket
FMA	*Fábrica Militar de Aviones* (Military Aircraft Factory)
Frag Order	Mission order advanced by phone or telex
GAF	Australian Government Air factories at Avalon
GCI	Ground Controlled Intercept
IDFAF	Israel Defence Force Air Force
JATO	Jet Assisted Take-Off
MER	Multiple Ejector Rack
Mossad	Israeli Intelligence Service
RWR	Radar Warning Receiver
TOT	Time on Target
WFU	Withdrawn from Use
W/O	Written off

Index

AIRCRAFT

A-4 Skyhawk **84, 85**, 88, 92, **140, 179**
Atlas Cheetah **137, 138**
Atlas Impala **137, 138**

CA-25 Winjeel **60**
CASA C-212 Aviocar **107**

de Havilland Venom **41, 104**

ENAER Pantera **127**
English Electric Canberra **174**
English Electric Lightning **52**

F-4 Phantom II **67**, 70, 79, **82–86**, 88, 92, **107, 112, 164**
F-5 Tiger II **41, 93, 102, 121, 127**
F-15 Eagle **70, 92**
F-16 Fighting Falcon 70, 71, 92, **121, 123, 128, 132, 138**
F-18 Hornet **57, 60, 105, 107, 111, 112**
F-84 Thunderstreak **31, 44, 45, 121**
F-86 (CA-27) Sabre **46**, 52, 57, 60, **106, 127, 132, 140, 164**
F-100 Super Sabre **44, 127**
F-104 Starfighter **52, 93, 132**
F-105 Thunderchief **52**
Fairey Delta 2 **16**

Gloster Meteror **164**

Hawker Hunter **41**, 72, 73, 76, 77, 88, **93, 102, 129**

IAI Dagger (Nesher) **34, 140**
IAI Kfir **68–71, 92, 105**
IAI Kfir C7 **35, 127, 128, 138, 140, 163**
IAI Lavi **82**
IAI Nesher **32**, 67–71, 87, 88, **91, 113, 140**
IAI Raam **68–70**
Ilyushin Il-28 'Beagle' **84**

MD.315 Flamant **15**
MD.450 Ouragan **15, 62, 67**
MD.452 Mystére IIC **15**
MD Mystére IVA **15, 42, 62**
MD Super Mystére B2 **15, 45, 62, 77, 92**
MiG-15 *Fagot* **15**
MiG-17 *Fresco* **72–92**
MiG-19 *Farmer* **72–92, 132**
MiG-21 *Fishbed* **62, 72–92**

MiG-25 *Foxbat* **84**
Mil Mi-8 *Hip* **87, 91**
Nord 1500 Griffon **16**
SA.3210 Super Frelon **77, 78**
Saab Draken **52, 93**
SE.212 Durandel 16
SEPECAT Jaguar 41, 44
Shenyang F-6 **132**
Shorts SC.1 **35**
Sikorsky CH-53 **84**
Sikorsky S-58 **77**
SO.4050 Vautour **77**
SO.9050 Trident II **16**
Sukhoi Su-7 *Fitter-A* **77, 79, 82**, 86–88, **91, 128**
Sukhoi Su-15 *Flagon* **84**
Sukhoi Su-20 *Fitter-C* **91, 128**
Tupolev Tu-16 *Badger* **76**, 77–87

ARAB/ISRAELI WARS

Anwar Sadat **87**
Arab losses **92**

Day of Atonement **86**

Early air-to-air combats **72**
Early air-to-ground operations **74**

First Israeli-Soviet encounter **84**
First Mirage kill **72**
First Phantom kill **82**

Identification triangles **92, 128**
IDFAF 'composite' squadrons **67**
IDFAF leading 'ace' **91**
INS *Eylath* **80**

Last big air battle **92**

Mirage victories **79**

Operation 'Boxer' **82**
Operation 'Rimonim' **82**

PLO **80, 86**
President Nasser **74, 80, 82, 84**

Shafrir: first kill **79**
Six Day War **66, 74–79**
Soviet EW radar **84**
Soviet interest **79, 80, 84**

'Three Day War' **84**

UN cease-fire **78, 79, 92**
US mediation **85**
USS *Liberty* attacked **77**

War of Attrition **66, 79, 80**

Yom Kippur War **66, 86, 128, 131, 141**

FALKLANDS CONFLICT

A-4 Skyhawk operations **144, 148, 149, 159, 161, 162, 169**
Air-to-air combat **12, 14, 144**
AM.39 Exocet ASM **147**
AN/TPS-43E mobile radar **144, 167, 169**
Argentine occupation **142**
Argentine surrender **162**
Armament loads **10, 12, 144, 145, 148, 153, 155, 158, 159, 170**
Ascension Island **144**
Attack profiles **12, 146**

British landings **10, 148, 158, 159, 173**
British tactical awareness **147, 162, 169, 170**

C-130 Hercules **14, 147, 149, 151, 169**
Chaff/flares **175**
Comodoro Rivadavia AB **9, 143, 144, 148, 149, 159, 167, 169, 170, 173**

DHC-6 Twin Otter **158**
Dr Mariano Moreno AB **164, 167, 177, 179**
Drop tank/missile confusion **144, 169**

Ejections **13, 149, 151, 155, 158, 163, 166, 169**

FAA losses **152, 158, 163, 177, 179**
FAA range limitations **144, 147, 159, 168–170, 173, 174**
First Dagger operation **144**
First fatal combat **146**
First RN ship sunk **147**
Flying clothing **10**

Generator failures **153, 161**
Gen Menendez **162**
Goose Green **149, 158**
Gun cameras **154**

IAI Dagger **9, 143–150, 153, 154, 158, 159, 161, 163, 167, 170, 179**
Inexperienced FAA pilots **142, 152, 162, 170**

Learjet pathfinder **159**
Lively Island **146**
Lynx HAS2 **162**

Maritime strike training **143**
Matra R.530 AAM **169,** 170
Mirage 5P **158, 163**

Peru **158**
Port Howard **14, 151**
Port Pleasant **159, 161**
Port Stanley **14, 144–149, 151, 161, 167–170**

Rapier SAM **158**
Retarded bombs **155, 158, 159**
Rio Gallegos AB **9, 159, 162, 167, 168, 170, 173, 174, 177**
Rio Grande NAS **9, 143–150, 153, 154, 158, 159, 161, 162, 167, 170, 179**

San Carlos **10, 148–150, 153–155, 158, 159, 161, 173**
San Julian AB **9, 10, 12, 143–150, 155, 159, 162**
SAS/SBS raids **148, 173**
Sea Cat SAM **161**
Sea Dart SAM **155, 175, 177**
Sea Harrier **12, 14, 144–155, 158–162, 167–170, 173, 174**
Sea Wolf SAM **149**
Shafrir AAM **146, 147, 162**
Shore bombardment **145, 148, 158, 161, 174**
Sidewinder AAM **14, 146, 149, 151, 153, 155, 158, 169, 170**
Sortie generation **158, 163, 177**
Spatial disorientation **174, 175**
Super Etendard **147, 148, 162**

Tandil AB **9, 141, 144, 162, 163, 179**
Trelew NAS **174**

Unexploded bombs **149, 150, 161**

Vulcan operations **144, 166, 167, 170**

MIRAGE VARIANTS

Mirage I (MD.550) **16, 17**

Mirage II **17**

Mirage III **15, 17, 38, 62**
Mirage IIIA **18, 19, 62**
Mirage IIIB **21, 22, 42, 46, 51**
Mirage IIIBE **22, 42, 46, 56, 126, 127, 166**
Mirage IIIBJ **63, 67, 68, 70, 71, 179**
Mirage IIIBL **129**
Mirage IIIB-RV **51**
Mirage IIIBS **96**
Mirage IIIBZ **134**
Mirage IIIC **21,** 22, 28, 42, 44–47, 96
Mirage IIICJ **63, 70, 179**
Mirage IIICJ(R) **63**
Mirage IIICZ **134**
Mirage IIID **22, 56, 57**
Mirage IIIDA **140, 164**
Mirage IIIDBR **123, 126**
Mirage IIIDE **106, 112**
Mirage IIIDP **132**
Mirage IIIDS **97**
Mirage IIIDZ **134**
Mirage IIID2Z **134, 138**
Mirage IIIE **20–22, 28, 41, 42, 45–47, 55, 164**
Mirage IIIEA **140, 164, 166–168, 170**
Mirage IIIEBR **123, 126**
Mirage IIIEE **106, 107, 112**
Mirage IIIEL **129**

Mirage IIIEP **132**
Mirage IIIEV **138**
Mirage IIIEZ **134**
Mirage IIIF **41**
Mirage IIIG **41**
Mirage IIIK **41**
Mirage IIIM **41**
Mirage IIING **34**
Mirage IIIO(A) **53**
Mirage IIIO(F) **53**
Mirage IIIO(PR) **57**
Mirage IIIR **31, 41, 42, 47**
Mirage IIIRD **31, 47, 132**
Mirage IIIRS **96, 102**
Mirage IIIRZ **134**
Mirage IIIR2Z **134**
Mirage IIIS **93, 102**
Mirage IIIS/RS **20**
Mirage IIIT **35**
Mirage IIIV **37**
Mirage IIIW **41**

Mirage IVA/P **51**

Mirage 5AD **121**
Mirage 5BA **121, 122**
Mirage 5BD **121, 122**
Mirage 5BR **121, 122**
Mirage 5COA **127**
Mirage 5COD **127**
Mirage 5COR **127**
Mirage 5D **129**
Mirage 5DAD **121**
Mirage 5DD **129**
Mirage 5DE **129**
Mirage 5DG **128**
Mirage 5DM **139**
Mirage 5DP **132**
Mirage 5DP1 **132**
Mirage 5DP3 **132**
Mirage 5DPA2 **132**
Mirage 5DR **129**
Mirage 5DV **138**
Mirage 5E2 **128**
Mirage 5EAD **121**
Mirage 5F **32, 34, 44, 47, 126**
Mirage 5G **128**
Mirage 5G-II **129**
Mirage 5J **32, 41, 44, 47, 67, 126**
Mirage 5M **139**
Mirage 5P **132, 158, 163**
Mirage 5P3 **132**
Mirage 5P4 **132**
Mirage 5PA **132**
Mirage 5PA3 **132**
Mirage 5RAD **121**
Mirage 5RG **128**
Mirage 5SDD **128**
Mirage 5SDE **128**
Mirage 5SDR **128**
Mirage 5SSE **128**
Mirage 5V **138**

Mirage 5O **34, 35**
Mirage 5OC **126**
Mirage 5ODC **126**

Mirage 5OFC **34, 47, 126**
Mirage 5OG-II **129**
Mirage 5OK **35**
Mirage 5OM **35**

Mirage 2000 **34, 42, 44–46, 121, 128**

Mirage 4000 **35**

Mirage F.1 **34, 35, 45, 46, 51, 131, 134**
Mirage F.1-CR **32, 47, 107, 111**

Mirage Milan **41**

MILITARY UNITS

Abu Dhabi
I Shaheen Sqn, UAEAF **121**
II Shaheen Sqn, UAEAF **121**

Argentina
1 Escuadrón **142, 144**
2 Escuadrón **142**
V Brigada Aérea, FAA **179**
VI Brigada Aérea, FAA **141, 179**
VIII Brigada Aérea, FAA **164, 179**
Aérea Material Rio IV, FAA **141, 159, 177, 179**
Comando Aérea de Defensa, **166**
Escuadrón Aeromovil I, **9, 143, 145, 147, 162**
Escuadrón Aeromovil II, **9, 143, 159, 162**
Escuadrón Caza Interceptor, **167**
Escuadrón Dagger, **140**
Escuadrón Mirage **164**
Escuela de Aviación Militar, FAA **141**
Fuerza Aérea del Sur **144, 145, 148, 158**
Grupo 1 Aerofotografico **159**
Grupo 1 de Transporte **147**
Grupo 2 de Bombardeo **174**
Grupo 4 de Caza **140, 179**
Grupo 5 de Caza **148, 154, 161, 179**
Grupo 6 de Caza **9, 112, 140–144, 147–149, 152–159, 162, 163, 166**
Grupo 6 de Transporte **158**
Grupo 8 Base **164**
Grupo 8 de Caza **141, 159, 164, 166, 167–170, 173, 174, 177, 179**
Grupo Technico 8 **164, 166**

Australia
ARDU **60**
No 2 OCU **57**
No 3 Sqn **60**
No 75 Sqn **60**
No 76 Sqn **60**
No 77 Sqn **57**
No 79 Sqn **60**

Belgium
1ére Esc/Smd **121, 122, 123**
2e Esc/Smd **122, 123**
2e Wing Tactique **122, 123**
3e Wing Tactique **122, 123**
8e Esc/Smd **122, 123**
42e Esc/Smd **122, 123**

Brazil
1° Ala de Defensa Aérea **123**
1° Escuadro **123**
1° Grupo Defesa Aérea **123, 126**
2° Escuadro **123**

Chile
Grupo de Aviación No 4 **126**

Colombia
1° Grupo de Combate **127**

France
CAFDA **42, 44, 45, 46, 51**
EC 1/2 'Cicognes' **21, 42**
ECT 2/2 'Côte d'Or' **42, 46, 47, 54, 106, 130, 139, 164**
EC 3/2 'Alsace' **42**
EC 1/3 'Navarre' **44**
EC 2/3 'Champagne' **44**
EC 3/3 'Ardennes' **44, 47**
EC 1/4 'Dauphine' **44**
EC 2/4 'La Fayette' **45**
EC 1/5 'Vendée' **45**
EC 2/5 'Ile de France' **45**
EC 1/10 'Valois' **45**
EC 2/10 'Seine' **45**
EC 3/10 'Vexin' **46**
EC 1/13 'Artois' **42, 46, 54, 57, 126**
EC 2/13 'Alpes' **46, 126**
EC 3/13 'Auvergne' **46, 126**
EC 1/30 **45**
EC 24/118 **47, 51**
EC 33/330 'Côte d'Argent' **51**
EE 2/328 **51**
ER 1/33 'Belfort' **42, 47**
ER 2/33 'Savoie' **42, 47**
ER 3/33 'Moselle' **31, 32, 47**
FATac **42, 44–47, 51**

Israel
'E' Sqn **67, 72–92**
'H' Sqn **87**
'RD' Sqn **63, 67, 71–92**
No 101 Sqn **63, 67, 71–92**
No 119 Sqn **63, 67, 70, 72–92**

Pakistan
No 22 OCU **132**
No 5 Sqn **132**
No 8 Sqn **132**
No 9 Sqn **132**
No 20 Sqn **132**
No 33 Sqn **132**

Peru
Escuadrón 12 **132**
Escuadrón 13 **132**
Grupo 13 de Caza **132, 141**

South Africa
No 85 Advanced Flying School **137, 143**
No 85 Air Combat School **137**
No 2 Sqn **134**
No 3 Sqn **134**
No 5 Sqn **138**

Spain
Ala de Caza No 11 **106, 108, 112**
Ala de Caza No 12 **108, 112**
Ala de Caza No 14 **111**
Ala de Caza No 15 **107, 110, 112**
101 Escuadrón **106**
103 Escuadrón **106**
111 Escuadrón **106**
112 Escuadrón **106, 110**
MACOM **107**

Switzerland
Fliegerstaffeln 10 **104**
Fliegerstaffeln 16 **97, 100**
Fliegerstaffeln 17 **97, 100**

United Kingdom
HMS *Alacrity* **147**
HMS *Antrim* **149, 152, 158, 162**
HMS *Ardent* **149, 150, 152, 158, 162**
HMS *Argonaut* **149**
HMS *Arrow* **147**
HMS *Brilliant* **149, 150**
HMS *Broadsword* **149, 155**
HMS *Cardiff* **162**
HMS *Coventry* **155**
HMS *Exeter* **177**
HMS *Glamorgan* **147**
HMS *Plymouth* **161, 162**
HMS *Sheffield* **147**
No 800 Sqn, RN **146, 149, 153, 155, 158**
No 801 Sqn, RN **144, 151, 169**
No 815 Sqn, RN **162**
RFA *Sir Galahad* **159, 161**
RFA *Sir Tristram* **159, 161**

Venezuela
Escuadrón No 33 **138**
Escuadrón No 34 **138**
Escuadrón No 36 **138**
Grupo Aéreo de Caza 11 **138**
Grupo Aéreo de Caza 12 **138**
Grupo Aéreo de Caza 16 **138**

Zaire
211 Escadrille **139**
2 Groupement Aérienne Tactique **139**
21 Wing de Chasse et d'Assaut **139**

POWERPLANTS

Armstrong-Siddeley Viper (MD.30) **16**
Bristol-Siddeley Orpheus 3 **37**
General Electric J79 **68–71, 138**
Hispano Verdon 350 **15**
Pratt & Whitney TF-30 (SNECMA TF-104B) **35, 39**
Rolls-Royce Avon RB.146 **52**
Rolls-Royce Nene **15**
Rolls-Royce RB.108 **35**
Rolls-Royce RB.162 **39**
Rolls-Royce Spey **68**
SEPR.66 rocket **16**
SEPR.841 rocket **18, 19, 21**
SEPR.844 rocket **30**
SNECMA Atar 09B **18, 19, 21, 28, 63, 67, 70**

SNECMA Atar 09C **20, 22, 28, 57, 67, 70, 96, 179**
SNECMA Atar 09K-50 **20, 34, 126–128, 132, 134, 138**
SNECMA Atar 101D **15**
SNECMA Atar 101G **15, 17**
Turbomeca Gabizo **17**

SYSTEMS/WEAPONS

AA-2 'Atoll' AAM **77, 82, 83, 85**
ADHEMAR system **27**
Aerospatiale AS.20 ASM **21**
Aerospatiale AS.30 ASM **21, 93**
Agave radar **34, 35, 132**
AGM-54 Shrike ASM **112**
AGM-65 Maverick ASM **93, 112**
AIM-9 Sidewinder **21, 30, 66, 70, 84, 89, 91, 92, 93, 96, 107, 112, 138**
AIM-26 Falcon AAM **93, 97**
AM.39 Exocet ASM **132**
AN/APQ-159 radar **112**
AN.52 'Special Store' **44**
ASMP nuclear missile **45**
AS-5 *Kelt* ASM **87**
AS.37 Martel anti-radar ASM **44**
Auxiliary rocket **27, 30, 63**
Avionics **27**

Bofors L/70 AA guns **77**

Cyclope IR tracker **31, 32**
Cyrano Ibis radar **19, 21, 65, 80, 174**
Cyrano II radars **23, 30, 55, 72, 84, 93, 126, 132**
Cyrano IVM radar **34, 35**

Defa 552 30mm cannon **21, 27, 63, 66, 72, 92, 96, 108**
Doppler nav system **93, 164**

Elbit armament panel **138**
Elbit WDNS82 **138**
Elta EL/M2001B radar **67, 138**
External stores **30, 32, 138**

FLIR pods **112**
Fly-by-wire system **35**
FROG SSM **88**
Fuel system **27, 28, 30, 32, 69, 105, 112, 168**

Hawk SAM **82**
Hispano 404 20mm cannon **15**
HUD **128, 132, 163**
Hughes TARAN radar **93, 96, 97, 100, 102**

Instrument panel **27**

JATO **93, 102**
JL-100 weapons pod **30**
Kukri AAM **137**

Landing gear **28, 69, 96, 102, 126, 138**
Laser rangefinder **128, 132**
Litton LW-33 INS **132**
LUA-32 rocket pods **30, 110, 111**

Martin-Baker seats **23, 57, 67, 105, 107**
Matra R.511 AAM **21**

Matra R.530 AAM **21, 30, 44, 63, 66, 73, 92, 129**
Multi-function displays **112**

Paveway laser-guided bomb **60**
Piranha AAM **125**
Python III AAM **127**

R.550 Magic AAM **30, 44, 46, 57, 132, 137, 167, 170**
Rafael Mahut **67**
Rapport ECM system **121, 122**
Reconnaissance cameras **31, 56, 57, 63, 96, 132**
Reconnaissance pack **28**
Refuelling probe **132, 163, 179**
RPK-17 reinforced tanks **30**
Runway cratering bombs **75**
RWR **23, 126, 142, 163**

SA-2 *Guideline* SAM **76, 77, 84**
SA-3 *Goa* SAM **84**
SA-7 *Grail* SAM **131**
Sagem ULISS 81 INS **128**
Shafrir 1 AAM **66, 72, 79**
Shafrir 2 AAM **66, 70, 82, 85, 87, 88, 89, 92, 127, 142**
SINTA system **163**
SLR-1 side-looking radar **32**
Stinger SAM **131**
Styx SSM **80**

Thomson-CSF gunsight **23, 57**

GENERAL INDEX

Abu Dhabi **121**
Accidents **19, 20, 37, 39, 64, 70, 96, 123, 129, 138, 166, 177**
AMD/BA company evolution **15**
Angola **134, 137**
Area Ruling **17**
Argentina **34, 68, 70, 112, 126, 132, 140**
Arms embargo **63, 67, 68, 132, 137, 140, 164**
Atlas Aircraft Corporation **137**
Australia **52**
Australian LOTE programme **57**
Avions Fairey **121**

'Balzac' **37**
Beagle Channel crisis **126, 140, 148, 162**
Beit Shemesh **67, 68**
Belgium **121**
Boeing **41**
Brazil **57, 112, 123**
Bush War **134**

Canards **35, 41, 70, 105, 112, 126, 128, 138**
CASA **112**
CEAM **20, 47, 54**
Ceselsa **112**
CEV **20, 54**
Chad **131, 139**
Chile **34, 47, 126, 140, 148, 162**
Colombia **127**
Commonwealth Aircraft Corporation **54**
Cost escalations **96**

DACTA (FAB) radar chain **125**
DACT training **102, 121**

Danny Shappira **19, 62, 63, 67, 68**
'Deci' combat range **102, 111**
Djibouti **46**

Egypt **128, 52–72**
Embraer **125**
ENAER **126**
EPNER **19**

Fairey Aviation **16, 17**
Falklands War **9–14, 112, 140–180**
Federal Aircraft Works **41, 93, 96, 97, 102, 104**
FLORIDA radar system **93, 100**
Flying characteristics **30**
Flying controls **28**
FMA **164**

Gabon **128**
Government Aircraft Factories **52**

Henri Deplante **16**

IDFAF Museum **71**
Inlet design **30, 34**
ISMA programme **102**
Israel **19, 32, 47, 62, 126, 179**
Israel Aircraft Industries **67, 68, 112, 126, 137, 163**

Jacqueline Auriol **21**

Kamra Aeronautical Centre **132**
Kavern mountain shelters **96, 100, 102**
Korean War **15, 60**

Lebanon **129**
Libya **128, 129**

Mirage upgrades **57, 70, 104, 112, 123, 126, 128, 132, 137, 138, 142, 163**
Mossad **67**
Mozambique **134**

Musée de l'Air **19**

NADGE radar system **100**
Namibia **134**
NBC contamination **102**
Nuclear strike role **44**

Operational training **42**

Pakistan **132**
Peru **132**

QRA **100, 107, 121**

RAAF Fighter Display Centre **57**
Reconnaissance aircraft **31**
Roland Glavany **16, 18, 19**
Royal Air Force **41**

SABCA **121, 123**
Saudia Arabia **128**
SEPR **16**
Shock cones **18, 30**
South Africa **34, 134**
Steep approaches **102**
SWAPO **134**
Swiss AF Museum **96**
Switzerland **19, 20, 41, 67, 93**

UNITA **134, 137**
United Arab Emirates **121**
US 6th Fleet **77, 108, 131**

Venezuela **57, 138**
VTOL **37**

'Wild Weasel' role **44**
Wing **28, 30, 138**
Wing fences **18**

Zaire **139**